Pantelis A. Mavrogiorgis

THE VILLAGE
AGIOS GEORGIOS SIKOUSIS

Part 1: History

Translated by Father Nicholas Palis
Edited by Hope Delane Demertzis &
Nikolaos K. Papagiannakis
Editorial Consultant Efstratios Demertzis

Cover Photo:
"Agios Georgios Sikousis from Tsoumbari"
Old photograph by Perikles Papahatzidakis

From the archives of the Benaki Museum

In memory of my father

Anastasios Mavrogiorgis

Village Educator

Pantelis A. Mavrogiorgis
The Village Agios Georgios Sikousis
ISBN: 978-1-7324142-0-4

Translated from the Greek by Father Nicholas Palis
Edited by Hope Delane Demertzis & Nikolaos K. Papagiannakis
Editorial Consultant Efstratios Demertzis

Layout and Design by John S. Bougiamas & 360 Consultants

Greek Edition © 1990 by Pantelis A. Mavrogiorgis
Published with a generous grant from the Agios Georgios Sikousis Society

English Edition © 2018 by Sikousis Books an imprint of Saint George Sikousis
Syllogos, Ltd.

The Saint George Sikousis Syllogos
would like to acknowledge
Panagiotis Billis,
"Building Your Best"
and Kalliope Barlis
for their generosity
funding the translation
from the original Greek.

FOREWORD

It is a great honor I was asked to write the foreword to the English language edition, of the book *"The Village Agios Georgios Sikousis"* by Pantelis A. Mavrogiorgis.

This edition is the work of a great many people, however none of this would have happened, and you would not be holding this book in your hands, if not for the hard work and vision of the Board of Directors of the Saint George Sikousis Syllogos and its predecessor organization, the Agios Georgios Sikousis Society.

Our organization was the original patron and driving force for the publication of this book in the original Greek in 1990. It is only fitting that the Syllogo would drive the translation and publication of the English version as well. From the hard work of Argyris Monis in securing permission for this translation, to the early translation work, funded by Panagiotis Billis, to the final weeks of translation, editing, design and layout, a team that includes Nikolaos K. Papagiannakis and Kalliope Barlis worked tirelessly to meet our deadline and accurately complete a book we hope you will find both interesting and enlightening.

This year, we are celebrating the 500th anniversary of the founding of our village so the significance of this translation being published is all that more important. The Syllogo made a concerted effort to make certain the work was completed on time for the festivities attendant to such an important anniversary.

Sadly, the author passed away a few years ago and will not see this next iteration of his seminal work. In the near future, we hope to provide an update to his important work in addition to translating the other two parts of his heartfelt trilogy to his and our birthplace, Agios Georgios Sikousis. I am certain his family appreciates that a new generation of readers is discovering Mr. Mavrogiorgis' work giving those who trace their heritage to Agios Georgios Sikousis valuable pieces of their ancestral history. We are thankful to them for authorizing this translation.

A conscious decision was made for the translation to be faithful to the original text, therefore the book's content ends in 1990, the year the original Greek version was published. Rest assured the advancement and development of the village has proceeded apace. It is our hope a future researcher, will pick

Pantelis A. Mavrogiorgis

up where Mr. Mavrogiorgis left off and bring the history of the village into the third millennium and its second quincentenary of its existence.

On a personal note, as the father of two children who are only half Agiorgousoi – is anyone really only half an Agiorgousis? – the importance of having this translation available to them is far better than any lesson I would ever be able to provide them. This book will allow them and all of the Agios Georgios Sikousis diaspora to be able to say: "Do you want to know about where we came from? Read this book!"

So, Theodore and Phoebe, this book is for you - as well as to my niece Argianna and nephew Luca who are also half Agiorgousoi.

John S. Bougiamas
Oyster Bay, New York
June 2018

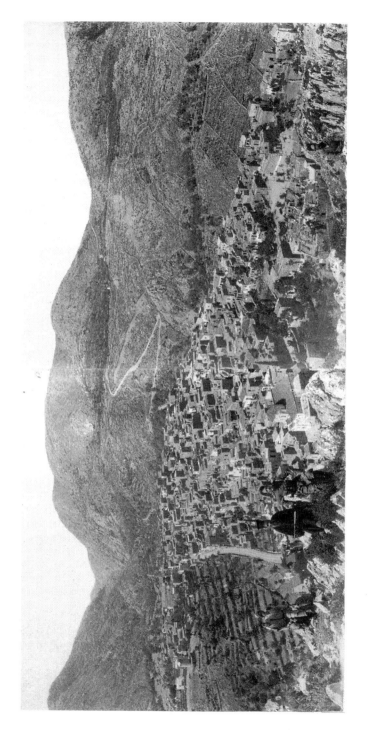

General view of the village from Kalivakia, 1937
(Photographer: A. Sami Bei, primary photographer of Sultan Hamit)
Giannis Mylonas, Giannis Kourgelis, father Stylianos Salagaras can be seen at the bottom

Pantelis A. Mavrogiorgis

PART ONE

HISTORY

PREFACE

This book is a loving tribute to *Agios Georgios Sikousis*, the village in which I was born and raised.

The purpose of the book is not to present academic research because the subject is neither conductive for pure scientific research nor the author has the prerequisitives for such a task.

We strive to provide the reader with some knowledge of the history of the village and the hardships experienced by its past residents. The target audience are fellow villagers and the next generation of Agiorgousoi. While this book makes every effort to cover most aspects of the history of life in the village, the writer requests your understanding whenever any errors or omissions are discovered.

The book is comprised of three parts relevant to life in *Agios Georgios Sikousis*. Part One presents its history. Part Two its folklore, and Part Three its language. Part One offers enough historical detail to whet the appetite of a future researcher. It delves into the larger society through a discussion of the island of Chios, on which the village is located. In order to make the historical content more appealing, I have included segments of folklore there, rather than inserting them into the second part of the book.

In the book itself, my use of the Greek language is deliberately simple and often sprinkled with expressions exclusive to our village, as I believe that it lends special warmth to the text. Also, there are footnotes throughout which provide bibliographic and other types of information.

I would also like to express my sincere appreciation to my fellow compatriots in America. I specifically wish to thank the Agios Georgios Sikousis Society of New York, the organization that eagerly and most generously undertook the publication expenses for this book.

Pantelis A. Mavrogiorgis

CHAPTER 1
Setting Out

From *Vounaki* near the town square we set out by car, driving south toward the *Mastichochoria* (Mastic Villages) on our way to the village of Agios Georgios Sikousis. We pass *Varvasi*, the neighborhood inhabited by the Greeks who were uprooted during the misfortune of 1922 from *Ionia*, which is directly across from Chios. Once we pass the Church of Christ, a right turn takes us into the area of *Lollodendra*, another neighborhood with fields and gardens at its borders. In olden times, there were very tall trees along this road which would bend during powerful winds, giving the impression that they were crazy (*lollo* in Greek).

The ascending road takes us to *Grou*, which has two chapels: *Profitis Ilias* and *Agios Nikolas*. I recall this area as one of great poverty and misery, dry in nature and sporting only a few trees – conifer and almond. Today, however, it is completely transformed with greenery, due to the abundant waters that were the result of drilling. The homes are beautiful and comfortable, and its residents have a good life. As we continue westward along the asphalt road, we notice that the villages of *Vasileionoiko* and *Chalkeios* appear prosperous. There are century-old olive trees, huge trees that produce resin, and sprawling almond trees.

The last village along the *Kambochoria* (plain villages) is *Zyfias*, also known as *Tzoufias*. This area features a wealth of produce, with hearty wheat, abundant greens, and beans for roasting. This village is set in the foothills, so our car labors heavily to ascend the steep and curvy roads of the ageless mountains. Midway through the ascent, the slope is cool and shaded, and myrtle trees and water appear. In the past, there had been an imposing edifice here – constructed of cubed, reddish *Thymianousikia* rock – with three arched openings leading to its interior. To this day, there is still an oddly shaped dome-covered canal, under which water issues from a channel fed by springs deep inside the mountain.

As we climb past *Plagia* (slope), we enter the Argiorgousika fields. We pass *Patela*, *Tou Mavrou*, and the *Stenotopia*; and continuing our ascent, *Vothonas* is on our left – from which all the "*Kato meri*" (lower areas) of the village are visible. As we turn by *Tsoumbari*, we see a village that gives the impression of a continuous dry stone, as the homes seem to be piled one on top of the other. The vision elicited by the open doors and windows of these

---

Sculpted lintel of the church of Agios Georgios

Pantelis A. Mavrogiorgis

homes, which trick the imagination into believing that only winged people could possibly dwell within such abodes.

Shortly after, we arrive at the *Plateia of Agios Panteleimonas*. Around us are cafes and good-hearted inhabitants, who greet us with curiosity, as if they want to know who we are, since we have come from *Chora* - the capital of Chios.

CHAPTER 2
First Acquaintance

The village is at the southern end of the central mountainous complex of Chios and is at a 400-meter elevation. It sprawls through the mountain passes of *Petsodos* and *Isia*. From a distance, it appears to hang upon the "eyebrows" of the mountains themselves. At its height, the village faces the east, a captivating and much-changed view that embraces the *Kambos* (plain), along with the *Kambochora* – its surrounding area, including the elevations of *Korakaris* and *Agios Menas*. From there, the eye can follow it to the waters of the Aegean, the monotony broken only by two small islands – on "*Paspargos*" there is the blinking beacon of the lighthouse; and the island of "*Gouni*" is also visible. Further east, I sigh as I look toward ancient *Ionia*. There is *Mimantas*, a tall mountain known today in Turkish as *Karapourno; Argmenno*, or white ground of Asia Minor (Turkey); the Greek city of *Krini*, now known as *Tsesme*; *Alatsata*; *Kato Panagia* and other smaller boroughs can also be seen.

From this location, the night view elicits the magic of a fairy tale. Moonlight and scattered electric lights, marking the life of the villagers, weave a pattern on the black fabric of night. From *Chora* (Chios City), which is to the east, our village is approximately twelve kilometers. In the old days, it took us about two-and-a-half hours to traverse the distance on foot. The village of *Lithi*, to the northwest, is about the same distance. To the south is *Tholopotami*, which was a one-hour walk for us; as was *Vessa*, to the west of our village.

The area of *Agios Georgios* that lends itself to grazing and cultivation is bordered by *Plagia*, *Krina*, and *Sklavia* to the east; *Notsokipos* and *Lykouri* to the southwest; and *Koumarous*, *Droposi*, and *Profitis Ilias* to the north. Today, the village has a population of about 800; whereas before the war (circa 1940), there were more than 2,000 souls who resided there. Incidentally, in 1885 Agios Georgios had 2,148 inhabitants: farmers, workers, *kaminarides* (lime or charcoal burners), stone-cutters, builders, and so forth. However, today's village population includes merchants, scholars, maritime seamen, and many immigrants. The community is administered by a president, along with a community council. There is an elementary school with two teachers; while before the war there were five teachers and over 300 students. And out of the three churches that exist in the village, only one is in operation today. There is also an electrical distribution system in place, various cooperatives and associations exist, and it is the seat of a police station, as well. These topics will be covered more extensively elsewhere in the book.

CHAPTER 3
The Name of our Village

The village name is derived from the ancient monastery that was located there and was created in honor of Agios Georgios Tropaioforos. It is well known that in ancient times, various places took their names from the names of gods or heroes who were worshipped at that time. For example, in Chios, there is an area named *Fana*, and the name was inspired by the temple of *Fanaios Apollonas*; and there is *Giosonas*, which is named after the hero *Iason*; and the *Poseidion* Mountain is named for the temple of the god *Poseidon*.

This style of naming places continued through the Byzantine years, and from that time forward the names of various Christian saints were given to areas with which those saints were religiously connected. Among the most striking examples are *Agios Nikolaos*, the capital of the prefecture of *Lasithi* in Crete; *Agioi Saranta*, the Greek city in Albania; and Sofia, the capital of Bulgaria, whose name comes from *Agia Sofia*.

Now I will explain the word **Sikousis**, which both defines and differentiates **Agios Georgios**, the first portion of the name of our village. Antisthenes, the Cynic, a philosopher of antiquity said,

"Research and education begin with the examination of names."

His objective was to make others aware that the basis of education is the understanding of the origin of those names. This is truly the case where the derivation of *Sikousis* is concerned. A person who lives in *Sykia* or in *Sykies*, is called a *Sykousis* – just as a resident of *Tholopotami* is known as a *Tholopotamousis*, or a person who lives in *Dafnonas* is a *Dafnousis*, and someone living in *Zyfias* is a *Zyfianousis*. With this reasoning in mind, the name of *Agios Georgios Sikousis* must refer to a saint whose church is in *Sykies*, as though he himself were a resident of that place.

Therefore, the suspicion exists that centuries earlier, prior to the founding of our village, there was probably a small village with the name *Sykai* or *Sykous*, yet only the national name **Sikousis** was passed down to us. Even today, there are villages with the name *Syke* in existence, as in *Fthiotida*, *Dorida*, *Sarantaporo*, *Corinthia*, and elsewhere.

[**Editor's Note:** In English, the transliterated form of the village's name is "Sykousis." In this book we use the more commonly used form where the "y" is replaced with an "i" - "Sikousis."]

There is a theory known as "the science of signatures," which supports the possibility of the existence of an initial neighborhood where our village lies. In the Museum of Chios, a carved inscription of King Attalos is preserved. It dates to the 3rd century B.C. and was found in *Aplotaria*, a well-known marketplace road, in the city of Chios. I will quote a section of this inscription, which is extremely important in terms of name origin and historical information regarding Chios and, thus, useful for the purposes of our research.

> *"Always taxes, always taxes, for money, so King Attalos*
> *could finance the construction of the walls.*
>
> *Theanous of Damasistratou is the guardian of the child – for*
> *which Thrasykleon, the Sykaefs (the Sykaean) will gather money."*

The memorable high school principal and historian of Chios, Georgios Zolotas, who studied and published the inscription, writes that, "The word *Sykaefs* denotes, in any case, the citizen or inhabitant of the prefecture or town in Chios called *Sykai*."

Around 1960, workers were digging up the streets in the village to install a sewer system when they made a priceless archaeological discovery in the road between the church of Agios Georgios and the church of *Agios Nikolaos*. In the language of archaeological science, this item is known as *"Naoschimo Eidolio,"* a small, marble, temple-shaped idol in the carved form of a goddess, facing forward, and seated on a throne. She is surrounded with a chiseled, orthogonal frame having a triangular overlay on the upper portion, thus creating an impression of a small temple in which the idol of the goddess is preserved.

At that time, Antonios Stefanou, the high school principal and the trustee and overseer of antiquities in Chios, placed this precious discovery in the Archeological Museum of Chios, and ventured to say that it was the rendering of the goddess Artemis or Cybele and was probably created as an offering by a local believer of the ancient pagan religion. Stefanou writes that,

> *"The discovery is very precious, not only in and of itself, but*
> *because it grants proof of a very ancient life in the area of*
> *Sikousis."*

It is only possible to accept Stefanou's conclusion if we are certain that an ancient shrine of Artemis or Cybele had existed within the village, dedicated by an idol-worshipping believer. Then it makes it possible that some individual, who later discovered this shrine, decided to confiscate it and use it – in his ignorance – as an adornment for his home. It is also a well-known fact that within the walls of buildings, and in other places as well, architectural segments of ancient temples and various inscribed artifacts are often found. In spite of that, when analyzing the word *"Sikousis"* linguistically, the national name *Sykaefs* – carved in the inscription of Attalos – and the temple-shaped idol, which was discovered buried in the grounds of the village, create an almost certain possibility that an ancient village, known as *Sykai* or *Sykous*, once existed there. Amantos' book, *Arthra kai Logoi*, mentions that the name Sikousis may support the idea that an ancient village named *Sykai* existed in that location.

CHAPTER 4
The National Names of the Inhabitants

"National Names" refer to terms which indicate the location from which an inhabitant hails. In today's society, a male from our village is known as an *Agiorgousis* and a female as an *Agiorgousaina* – as these names are derived from the village of Agios Georgios. In the Modern Greek language, though, it is customary to omit a syllable when a word is particularly lengthy. For example, rather than calling a man by the full name of someone from the village of Agios Georgios, as in the seven syllable *Agiogiorgousis*, it is thus abbreviated to the five-syllable *Agiorgousis*. Note that, in written text, we discover other national names that are no longer used today, like *Sykous, Sykountios, Sykousis,* and *Sykeos*. Here is a more detailed explanation of those names.

1. Sykous. The name *Sykous* refers to an area filled with fig trees; just as *Spartous* is an area covered with spartium. *Dafnous* makes reference to laurel, and *Elaious* describes olive trees. While these are names of actual locations, they are also national names, like *Sykountos*, in the genitive or possessive case. In A. Karava's book, *Topographia tis Nisou Chiou*, published in 1866, the author refers to the population of the villages on page 55, when he writes,

> "Agios Georgios **Sikousis** or **Sykous**: families 264."

However, in notary documents, the phrase ". . . of Agios Georgios **Sykountos**" (instead of *Sikousis*) is written as follows:

> "Today, on the sixth of the month of May of 1879, were presented before me Panagiotis Pouleros, Notary of the Village of **Agios Georgios Sykountos**; Irene, wife of the departed George Patounas . . . "

Another example comes from a will created on January 1, 1880, which reads:

> "Be wakeful, for you do not know the day nor the hour during which the Son of Man is coming. With this gospel passage in mind, Mr. Michail Vafeas, inhabitant of **Agios Georgios Sykountos**, being in his right mind and fearing the suddenness of death, decided . . . "

2. Sykountios. In the periodical "Chiaka Chronika" v. 2 on page 87 the Archmandrite Kyrillos Trechakis, Abbot of Nea Moni writes the following:

---

*"The little field, 'Platanos,' is known today as the land of Agion Martyron Platonos and Romanos , and is located to the south of the Monastery. It is the Idroposion (Droposi) owned by the **Sykountians**. To the east is the mountain Kochlias (Saliakomyti?), which forms the border of the present Monastery and of **Sykountos**.*
"

The word comes from Sykous - Sykountios - Sykousis.

3. Sykousis. This name was already covered in great detail in Chapter 3, "The Name of our Village."

4. Sykéos or **Sýkeos** Since the name ending –eos causes some confusion, I decided to include it among the National Names, although with some hesitation. According to Rodokanakis in his book "Joustinianai - Chios" on page 23:

*"There was along all the shore (during the time of the Genoese) very many round little towers and large square towers, of which the most fortified were of Agiou Galaktou Kardamylon ... Karyon, of **Agios Georgios Sykeou** of Penthodou (Petsodou).*"

In the chrysobull of Emperor Michail Palaeologos in 1259, which enumerated the estates and inheritances belonging to Nea Moni Monastery, among other things we read,

*"Inheritance of **Sykeou**,"*

a term identical to Agios Georgios Sikousis.

5. Sykaefs. This national name is found within the inscription of King Attalos, as already noted. In addition to the national names mentioned previously, we found that Sykasios and Sykeotis were not attributed to our village or to its inhabitants. In actuality, Sykasios was associated with the god Zeus, who was worshipped in Athens under that surname. It referred to Zeus cleansing or purifying,

"because figs were used in purifications."

According to high school principal Georgios Madias in an article published in the newspaper *Proodos* on June 13, 1944 titled "I Polichni Ag. Giorgis o Sikousis" among others, he writes:

"At other times Zeus the Sykasios protected these places (of our village) as well as all the mountainous areas of Zeus the Pelinnaios ... But here on Chios, in those beautiful years, Zeus was so humbled, since he was also surnamed Sykasios, the Protector

---

*of Figs. Figs must have been, of course, very beloved both then and now, for the Great Martyr Agios Georgios to also be called Sykasios – **Sykousis**."*

Despite my great respect for the memory of my high school principal, Georgios Madias, I believe that his article is merely derived from the spirit of his great love for antiquity.

6. Sykeotis. This was the name of the church of Agios Georgios in Constantinople, from which the surrounding field received its name. According to Anna Komnine:

*"The Comninians entered courageously, gazing over the field of The Great Martyr Georgios, the so-called **Sykeotou** . . . ."*

7. **Sykeatis.** From the thesaurus of Er. Stefanou comes the following:

*"**Sykeatis** Dionysos gui (who) in **Sykea** urbe (city) colebatur (was worshipped)."*

CHAPTER 5
The History of the Monastery

A. The Ancient Codex (Code) of the Village

We use the word "codex" (*kodikas*) for a book with woven manuscript pages, which usually contains material regarding legal actions such as purchases, sales, dowry agreements, wills, and community decisions. In the old days, the codexes or ledgers were kept by the notaries of the villages, as they were responsible for writing such agreements. *Kodikas* is also a word used by villagers to refer to people who are knowledgeable about their neighbors' personal histories regarding various issues and family trees – or "the root and the spawn" of each person.

The oldest codex of the village, chronologically the most ancient one, contains eighty-five pages of thick paper, made from rags, with parallel and vertical watermarks. It is long and narrow, 32 centimeters in length and 15 in width. The very first page contains the 1518 will of the priest-monk Sofronios Sepsis, who was the last abbot of the Monastery from which the village of Agios Georgios Sikousis was created.

The rewritten estate data of the monastery follow. On page 21, "the notary letters begin where the matters of the Monastery of The Holy Great Martyr Georgios are contained: rentals, sales, grants, and others. However, this book is not the same age as the will of 1518, but is a copy from the year 1806, which is mentioned both on pages 1 and 122. On the first page and at the top of the will, the following is written:

> *"This is an exact copy of the ledgers of the holy, glorious, great martyr Georgios, also known as **Sikousis**, on the island of Chios."*

The Metropolitan of Chios, Dionysios, signed the document, attesting to the validity of the contents.

On page 122, it says:

> *"On January 17, 1806, the present ledger of the Holy, glorious, great martyr Giorgios Tropaioforos kai Thavmatourgos (George the Triumphant and Miracle Worker), who was also surnamed **Sikousis**, was copied by me, Joachim Stamoulou, the humblest*

among deacons."

For further verification, Dionysios, Metropolitan of Chios, signs it again that same year.

Subsequently, whatever else was then written after page 122 was added in 1818; and it was verified by the ever-memorable Metropolitan of Chios, Platon Fragiadis, who then signed it. During the national uprising of 1821, Metropolitan Platon was hung by the Turks – along with other Chian elders.

This codex is considered precious for the history, topography, and dialect of Chios. During the Turkish Occupation, it was located at the *Mnemoneio* of our village. Following the liberation in 1912, it was placed in the Storage Room of Testaments in *Kalamoti* along with other community ledgers; from there, it was placed in the Public Library of Chios *"Adamantios Korais."* Today, it may be found in the Historical Archives of Chios.

B. The Will of Sofronios Sepsis

The will is presented here in its entirety. The numbers referenced in parentheses are explained in the section which follows.

"In the name of our Lord, Amen. Today, Ieromonachos (priest-monk) Sofronios Sepsis, from the village of Pyrgi, finding [the Monastery of] Agios Georgios Sikousis neglected and in ruins, took over the responsibility of caretaker and renewed it (1) for the benefit of his soul and the arrangement of the affairs of the Monastery itself, which is located near the Plagia [Slope] (2) and in the old homes of Profitis Ilias (3) and at the Koumaries (4) and Lakkia (5) and up to Graias Mandra (6). Sofronios did this to have God as a helper and the intercessions of the Saint [Agios Georgios]; and he built homes at the Monastery and restored whatever was destroyed, like a perfect master of the house. He also employed worthy people as farmers to work the fields entrusted to them: Michalis from Pityos, Ioannis Kasfikis from Avgonyma, Giorgios Katzaroudis from the port of Lithi, Giorgios Katzanidis from Ververaton, Giorgios son of Michalis Charkis from Pyrgi, and Theotokis Kastanadis and Monios Melachroinos. These above-mentioned individuals, who may choose to become residents of the village, are tasked with selecting whomever they wish to operate the affairs of the Monastery. The men whose names appear in this document are hereby given the authority to oversee the workers they choose and remove any of them who are negligent

or engage in thievery. These men also have permission to select a trustworthy Steward (7), whose job it will be to gather all incoming revenue of the Saint and appoint a priest to perform the sacred services of the Church, morning, noon, and in the evening. During the feast day, this group will also invite chanters – as many as needed; and anyone who happens to be at the celebration of the Saint should be offered hospitality at the expense of the Saint (8). Also, the relatives of papa Sofronios should be invited to the celebration as founders.

And I write, the Church income should be collected and kept in one location: money may be spent for the lantern burning (9), the Authority (10) should be given eight gold coins (11), and the remainder should be saved for renovations. But whoever spends this money in vain will face God and the Saint on Judgment Day. Thus, those mentioned above pledge to follow the rules set forth in writing in order to manage these tasks as caretakers, and annually pledge to appoint priests and Gerontes (Elders) (12); while the remaining people must submit to the responsible Elders and give an account on behalf of the Monastery, regarding the income of the Church and the expenses for the maintenance of its property, known as anastimata (incomplete items) (13). Kyrios Sofronios states that if at any time unmaintained things appear (14), or if anything is wasted regarding the Monastery property, let God become their judge, physically and spiritually.

Kyrios Sofronios invites the most honorable noblemen to become Board Members of the Monastery: Miser Frangiskon (15), Miser Simou Gioustinia (16), and Miser Peri Gioustinia, and Miser Giouzepe Gioustinia. Their responsibilities are to be overseers, examining every matter concerning the Monastery, and removing anyone who appears to be a negligent individual or a thief. Those people who are removed thusly should be given whatever justice demands.

If a Board Member or Steward is seen as a thief or as working solely for personal profit and not for the benefit of the Monastery, remove him. Then the residents of the village have permission to appoint another Board Member, give an annual accounting to the sitting Board Members, and – when necessary – appoint another Steward.

For this reason, the present will has been created in my home, Sofronios the Monk, with love, certainty, and truth.

Written in the year 1518 in the month of November, 4ᵗʰ day, 3ʳᵈ hour.

WITNESSES:

Monk Kyr Theodoulos
Theologos Kourtikis
Georgios Sepsis
Kostas Papadopoulos
Leon Kardamilitis and partners
Written by notary Theodoros Damalas"

C. Comments on the Will

(1) Anestise (Resurrected): Refers to the remodeling, building, or repairing of homes that were destroyed or in ruins, and the caretaking of the Monastery property by someone treating all of it as though it were his own.

(2) Plagia (Mountain side): It is located in the countryside between the villages of *Zyfias* and *Agios Georgios.*

(3) The old homes of Profitis Ilias (Prophet Elias): Another location from which Sofronios Sepsis determined the boundaries of the Monastery. We do not know exactly what these old homes were nor where the area of *Profiti Ilia* was located. Personally, I wonder if it might be where the chapel of *Profiti Ilia* stands today, which is above the village of *Dafnonas* at a height of 680 meters. Were the old homes actually ruins of a neighborhood inhabited by shepherds or the monastic cells of anchorites (religious recluses)? Probably the latter is true, if we take into consideration that *Profitis Ilias* – southeast of *Gerontikon* – was a chapel of Nea Moni, like *Agios Platon.*

(4) Koumaries: This was an area northwest of the village, and today it is known as *Koummaroi.* (The name is derived from the plant known as *kommaros – koummaria* [Arbutus])

(5) Lakkia: A countryside location northwest of the village. It is currently called *Lakkoi* or the *Lakki* and belongs to the village of *Lithi.*

(6) Graias Mandra: Another area in the countryside, it lies beneath the mountain of *Profitis Ilias,* according to the topographical map of Nea Moni. Today this area is known as *"Morou Mandra."*

(7) Steward: This is the person who handled the income and expenses of the monastery.

(8) From the expenses of the Saint: This refers to the Church's expenses.

(9) Lantern burning: The quantity of oil necessary to light the vigil lamps of the Church for one year. It should be noted that, to this day, the vigil lamps of the churches of the village are burning day and night.

(10) Authority: The Administration of the Genoese, who were then the rulers

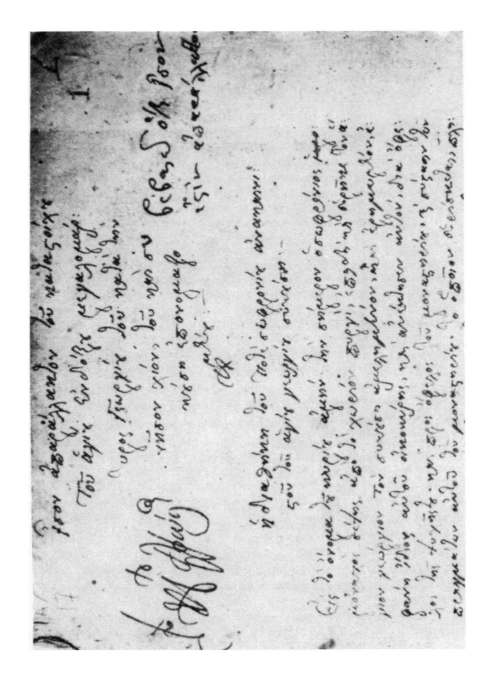

A sample of the will of Sofronios Sepsis

of the island. (The sum of 12 gold coins would be given as a payment of taxes to the state.)

(11) *Yperpyra* or *Perpyra* (gold coins): These were the gold coins of the Byzantines, and their value differed at certain times. (*Yper* is a prefix of *pyrros*, which means "blond.")

(12) Gerontes (Elders): This does not refer to the abbot of the Monastery, who is still called *Igoumenos* to this day, but to those who presided over the new village's municipality.

(13) Anastimata: Maintenance of the fields and trees.

(14) Anoikodomita Pragmata (Incomplete Items): This expression refers mainly to unreconciled and/or suspicious financial matters that prevented construction.

(15) Miser or Misses: Mainly from the Genoese *Messer,* the Italian *Mon Signiore*, the French *Monsieur*, and the English *Mister*.

(16) Gioustinia: This is a surname that the Genoese of the Maona had (Justinianai), which passed on to Frankish Chian families.

D. The Ieromonachos Sofronios Sepsis

The only information we have about Sofronios Sepsis comes from his will, from which we can draw conclusions about his personality, and also declare that he was the very first resident of our village. He settled into the now-abandoned Monastery of Agios Georgios before 1518, probably coming from the Monastery of Nea Moni. I surmise this because *Ieromonachos* Sepsis was acquainted with the surrounding villages of *Avgonyma, Lithi,* and *Ververato* and invited farmers to work in the fields of the Monastery of **Sikousis** and settle in the village.

Sofronios seemed to be a progressive and active man, which I conclude from the fact that once he arrived at the neglected Monastery, which had been abandoned by the monks, "he resurrected it," built homes and repaired destroyed buildings, as though he were the homeowner. Because of his activities on behalf of the Monastery, he became, by right, its owner. For that reason, his relatives from *Pyrgi* are considered the founders of the Monastery. He was a sharp man, a positive thinker with good organizational abilities, who showed much forethought.

From his will, we gather that he was able to foresee the need to define the borders of the Monastery, taking into consideration both the farmlands and the mountainous regions. He knew that it would be difficult for monastic life at Agios Georgios to be revived, since Nea Moni attracted the majority of monks so – rather than inviting monks – he simply sought out farmers from the surrounding villages and enticed them to work "the things" of the Monastery.

From the outset, we perceive that these farmers are neither feudal

Pantelis A. Mavrogiorgis

farmers nor serfs. They are free people with the right to invite other farmers to join them and share equal rights, while becoming **"community in the village,"** a concept mentioned for the very first time in Sofronios' will. Thus these settlers actually begin the transformation of Agios Georgios from a monastery to a village. Sofronios also organizes the Church and defines the role of *Oikonomos* (Steward) as an administrator responsible for the financial elements of the Monastery, and *Epitropous* (Board Members) as overseers. He also specifies the liturgical role of the church.

Sofronios' will not only contains a Constitutional Charter regarding the manner in which the church functions, he has also created a similar document governing a well-regulated society within the newly formed village. He gives the right to the colonists to select Board Members, and authorizes a Steward to choose priests and Elders. It seems that the Elders constitute the executive power of the village, because the will specifies that:

> *"Those found in this place must submit to the Elders."*

This first social group of the village is governed by the aforementioned will and moral rules. The *Oikonomos*, as administrator of the estate of the former Monastery, is accountable before the Board Members and the colonists of the village. Those who undertake jobs must be hardworking, trustworthy, and have good ethics (known as people with *kathara cheria* – clean hands). In this community, there was no room for thievery and selfishness. Thieves and the negligent are sent away immediately, whether they are farmers of fields or those with other responsibilities, and are replaced by village inhabitants.

It is noteworthy that those whom Sofronios appoints as trustees of the Monastery and as executors of the will are all the most powerful people of the time, the Genoese Justinianes. This may indicate that Sofronios was well known in many social circles, or that the Justinianes possibly maintained some unwritten right of ownership in the affairs of the Monastery. I speculate that this priest-monk probably had some formal education. Although his will was formulated in his home, it does not seem as though he wrote it himself. At the end of the will, and after the signature of the witnesses, we notice that it came from notary Theodoros Damalas.

E. The Sepsis Family

The Sepsis family must have been among the "good families" of Chios. According to George Zolotas:

> *"From the middle of the 16th Century, there were eminent Chians who settled in Smyrni for trade reasons, among whom were the*

---

*Rodokanakis, Rallis, **Sepsis**, and Koraes families."*

Zolotas also writes that the Sepsis family had a home in *Aplotaria* and a farm estate near the *Sinaïtiko*, a farm field which belonged to the monastery of *Agia Aikaterini* of Sinai, where Zolotas himself discovered an inscription in marble within the walls of a well in the yard, which reads,

"DOMINICUS SEPSI 1550."

Other Sepsis family members mentioned by Zolotas include Benedict, Francisco, Zanni, and Zorzi, who were all Catholics.

In his book *"Tourkograikika"* Krousios speaks of a letter dated July 18, 1580, which John Koresis sent to the Patriarchate, recommending that Hippolytus, Bishop of Chios, be replaced.   That letter mentions a priest, Sakellarios Ioannis Sepsis, who was appointed exarch to the churches of *Pyrgi* and *Volissos* – characterized as Exarchate of the Patriarchate – after the conquest of Chios by the Turks.

Another inscription,   found in *Panagia Krina*, refers to the priest, Stamatios Sepsis.

> *"The present boast was painted at the expense of the priest Stamatios* Sepsis, *who was once Demetrios* Sepsis *from the town of Vavilon and was then a member of the Board."*

In a will dated 1706 from the village of *Pyrgi*, the name Vgerous, wife of the main priest of *Pyrgi*, Protopapa Nikolaos Sepsis is recorded. And one of the witnesses who signed the will of Sofronios Sepsis was George Sepsis. These facts seem to provide evidence that the Sepsis family was well known in Chios, although some members were Orthodox and some were Catholic, and that there were distinguished clergymen among them. However, it is difficult to determine Sofronios Sepsis' actual relationship with these individuals, with whom he shared a family name.

F. Issues Related to the Founding of the Monastery

Any researcher who decides to document the history of the Monastery will be faced with numerous difficulties and unanswered questions, because the information drawn from various sources is indirect and unproven, comprised of conjectures and hypotheses which complicate, more than serve to enlighten, as one pursues this historical journey. The initial problem that presents itself is the following: When and by whom was the Monastery of Agios Georgios Sikousis actually founded? Is it older than the Nea Moni Monastery which was built in the 11th Century and funded by Konstantinos Monomachos, Emperor of Byzantium, who ruled from 1024 until 1045?

> *"The Monastery of Agios Georgios Sykountos or Sikousis, according to tradition, is more ancient than Nea Moni. Accordingly, the osioi treis Pateres (Three Venerable Fathers) – Nikitas, Ioannis, and Iosif – were initially monks in this Monastery [Sikousis] and, after leaving there, they served as ascetics in the cave of the Provateion Mountain, where the Monastery of the Holy Fathers is found today and, thus, it is named after them. The Monastery of Agios Georgios was in the western part of the island, where the village of the same name exists today.*
>
> *But precisely when this was founded and by whom is unknown. In any case, however, it was abandoned and had disintegrated over the years prior to the founding of Nea Moni, as mentioned above. Afterwards, the priest-monk Sofronios Sepsis rebuilt the church and the lands of the Monastery, as we learn from his will of the year 1518. "*

The erudite Archimandrite Ioannis Andreadis clearly mentions that Agios Georgios was an older Monastery than Nea Moni. He bases his viewpoint only on the oral "tradition," where there are no definitive sources to support historical truth.

Osios Nikiforos (Saint Nikiforos) of Chios and Gregory Foteinos were both Brothers of Nea Moni; and Foteinos, Bishop of Myriofytou and Peristaseos, also served as abbot during two periods. They are the authors of the book *Neamonisia*, in which they write:

> *"The Holy Fathers existed during the reign the Emperors of Byzantium Michail Paflagonos, Michail Kalafatis, and Konstantinos Monomachos. They were ascetics in Provateion, one of the mountains of the island, but it is unknown what part of Chios they originally came from."*

They fail to mention whether or not the Holy Fathers ever resided in the Monastery of Sikousis. We should consider *Neamonisia* a more authoritative source regarding the history of the monasteries of Nea Moni and Sikousis.

At this point, I would like to briefly introduce the General of Byzantium, Vardas Fokas, and the Emperor Michail Kalafatis, both exiled to Chios. When Ioannis Tsimiskes ascended the throne of Byzantium in 969, General Fokas was proclaimed King of Cappadocia, which caused Tsimiskes to exile Fokas to Chios. The historian, *Leon o Diakonos* (Leon the Deacon), who lived during those years, wrote:

> *"The emperor declared that Vardon Fokas, who is tonsured as a clergyman on the one hand, be limited – along with his wife and children – to the island of Chios."*

Emperor Michail (the Fifth) Kalafatis (1041-1042) was also exiled to Chios by Konstantinos Monomachos, due to legal issues with his predecessor Zoe, whom he had exiled to *Pringipo*. According to Konstantinos Sgouros in his *I Istoria tis Chiou* published in Athens in 1930:

> *"If the noble and brave monk, Vardas Fokas, was exiled to Chios in 971 by Ioannis Tsimiskes, I don't know whether he spent the seven years of his exile in Nea Moni – or however else it was called previously – or elsewhere on the island – for example, in Agios Georgios Sikousis, which the Neamonitai (Nea Moni monks) consider, according to oral tradition, the father of their own monastery."*

Sgouros further states that:

> *"The Fathers of Nea Moni consider the Monastery of Agios Georgios Sikousis to be the parent of Nea Moni even today, as the erudite Archimandrite kyr Kyrillos Trechakis – who served as abbot more than once – informed me. If this is true, it advocates in favor of the probability that Fokas lived in the original Monastery after he was tonsured, since it was a safe place, difficult to approach, prior to the time when Monomachos had Nea Moni built."*

We observe, in both of these excerpts, that according to information that Sgouros received through "oral tradition," the Monastery of *Sikousis* is older than that of Nea Moni and provided a foundation for the later construction of the Monastery of Nea Moni.

In examining the beliefs of the historians and archaeologists, we first look to the work of Konstantinos Amantos, academician and Professor of Byzantine History at the University of Athens. He speaks of the two exiles, Fokas and Kalafatis.

> *"Emperor Ioannis Tsimiskes exiled Vardas Fokas, a general whom he viewed as a dangerous opponent, to the island of Chios. Fokas returned to Constantinople during the reign of Basil, the Bulgarian Killer. Later on, the Emperor Konstantinos Monomachos also exiled Michail Kalafatis, who had reigned before him. Kalafatis was well taken care of by the great landowners of what is*

Dafnonas today: (the families of) *Vestarchon, Kanavoutson, and Strategon, and others. Undoubtedly he was asked to help or in some way indicate how the Emperor could be convinced to create an outstanding monastery."*

On page 258 of the 2nd volume of his monumental work *Istoria tis Chiou* Georgios Zolotas declares:

> *"This noteworthy church* (Nea Moni), *a true perfect example of the development of art, may be used **as a prototype for other churches** and, of course, for the churches of Chios, Krinas, Agion Apostolon of Pyrgi, and Agios Georgios Sikousis."*

Giorgios Soteriou, Professor of Christian Archaeology, visited Chios in 1916 and examined its Christian monuments. He published the following in the *Archeologiko Deltio, Parartima* ("Archaelogical Bulletin," Appendix):

> *"During my travels in Chios, I found three churches, copies of the catholicon [main church] of Nea Moni. The most ancient of these is probably Panagia Krina, by the village Sklavia. Along with this, there are another two churches: Agios Georgios Sikousis, serving as the main church of the village of the same name, completely transformed by later additions; and Agioi Apostoloi, a church in the village of Pyrgi, which is excellently preserved to this day."*

From the scholarly data above, we conclude that Agios Georgios Sikousis is a later creation than Nea Moni, as C. Bouras, a current Professor of Christian Archaelology believes. Bouras considers the Monastery of Sikousis to be a 12th Century structure. Now that we have determined that the Monastery of Sikousis is younger than Nea Moni, the question is: By whom and under what conditions was the Monastery of Sikousis founded? Zolotas attempts to answer this question:

> *"The beautiful small churches of Chios, built according to the model of the Neomonitisis Panagias* (Nea Moni) – *such as Krina, Sikelia, Agioi Apostoloi, and Sikousis, were founded as private churches of great noble families of Chios, and seem to have come about in opposition to the despotism of Nea Moni.*
>
> *These noble families came from Constantinople and settled in Chios during the years of the Dynasty of the Comninians (1057-1185)."*

If Zolotas' opinion is accurate, we can then assume possibility exists that Agios Georgios Sikousis actually began as a private church and later developed into a monastery.

CHAPTER 6
The Estates of the Monastery

A. The Monasteries' Methods of Acquiring and Managing Estates

The monasteries and churches had uncultivated forests, fields, farmhouses, and homesteads under their jurisdiction. These acquisitions occurred through the exercise of rights within the natural surrounding areas of the monastery and by the cultivation of barren lands, especially where spring water existed. Such tracts of land, or estates, known as *metochia*, remain in existence today and have small churches on land that has been planted with trees and nourished by spring water. Generally, several monks, living in small houses on that land, cultivate and maintain these grounds. An example of that is the *metochi "Platanou"* with the chapel of *Agios Platanos*, which originally belonged to Nea Moni and is currently owned by the hermitage of *Agion Pateron* (Holy Fathers).

Outside of the above method of acquiring and maintaining land, there exists a custom, which began in the Byzantine Era, in which individuals deed land to churches and monasteries, and the names of these donors are recorded in the ledgers of the monastery, in commemoration, for the salvation of their souls. Those who sought the intercession of a saint during difficult times also gave gifts of this sort. Here is an example of a document recording one such donation:

> "1728 *April 26. Today Kyakou, wife of the deceased Vasilis Stratakiou, voluntarily dedicates to the church of Agios Georgios Sikousis one fathom of land, in Katous, with trees, just opposite Fasapou's threshing floor. That fathom, together with whatever uncultivated land that exists, including the carob tree, is all dedicated to the Saint. This is to be divided into thirds, as payment, for her and her husband, Vasilis, to be commemorated. For the priests who will be performing the commemorations, there will be an additional split into three for those priests to receive 28 piasters from the field. This document attests that the above occurred.*
>
> *Antonis Pontikakis*
> *Neamonitis Perdeas (Witnesses)"*

The monasteries also obtained estates from every monk who took refuge therein, in order to practice asceticism. As long as these monks lived, they cultivated these lands, deeding them all to their respective monasteries upon their deaths. In the event that a monk had a relative who planned to also enter monastic life, that monk maintained the right to leave one-third of his estate to that relative. With the legal right to benefit from another's property and enjoy its advantages, the monastery would use that income and income from other sources for its liturgical necessities, to make repairs to the church, to meet the expenses of other estates under its dominion, to feed its monks, and to pay the taxes levied by the occupying Genoese – and later, by the Turks.

When the monks did not live communally within the walls of the monastery, they would be given bread, wine, olives or cheese on a daily basis. On Sundays and during great feast days, they would then be invited to sit at a common table in the refectory of the monastery. Many monks chose to permanently remain in fields that they either owned or rented from a monastery.

Lay farmers, known as *anestates*, usually donated one-third of their annual produce to the monasteries. Such fields were referred to as *apotrita*, not only because of the produce donated but also because that lay farmer had ownership of one-third of the field itself. This allowed that farmer to remain on his land throughout his life span and to pass the land to his children upon his death. However, this system often caused lay people to encroach on the rights of the monasteries.

Apotrita – considered a monastic right – sometimes, but not always, referred to money. A monastery might rent land to be farmed, with the agreement that the farmer would only get to keep three-fifths of the produce or, in other cases, one-half of it. But there were cases where rent was paid not in produce, but in cash: *doukata, perpyra, aspra, and grosia.* However, when a barren field was used by a farmer, the monastery had fewer expectations. Here is an example taken from page 30 of an old codex of our village:

> *"Today, the Abbot of Sikousis – with the noble ruler Misser Simoun Gioustinias and Board Members of the Saint – as ruler and governor of the Board Members of the Monastery, gives the premises south of the mill, held by Stavrinos Vasilakis, son of Ioannis, the departed papa Nikolaos, to work as a good farmer and anastatis, and to share its fruits thusly: one-third to the Monastery and two-thirds to the farmer. He also gives, in the name of the Saint, six pites of oil to his church. This gift was made and sworn to its truth by the witnesses below in the year* **1636, July 12**[th]**.**
>
> *Simous Gioustinias, I certify*

> *Giorgos Lithomenousis, I certify*
> *Michalis, son of Nikolaos, I certify*
> *Nikolaos, son of papa Ioannis Valagros*
> *Andreas Gioustinias"*

To avoid confusion, I wish to clarify that the church and the estates of the old monastery continued to be known as Monastery even after 1518, and the priests were called "abbots."

B. Estate Data and the Monastery of Sikousis

Since no sources exist to verify the founding, development, and the course of life of the Monastery, this section will be limited to information taken from old codexes. From these, we are able to discern the size and type of the estate, who secured it and under what circumstances, sales and purchases involved, and the disagreements that it fostered with laymen. We can also learn something about the abbots and Board Members of the Monastery after the year 1518.

Originally, the 1256 *chrysobull* of the Emperor Michail Palaiologos declared that

> *"Sykeos (Sikousis) is a dependency of Nea Moni, with all of the arable land, pastures, and holdings."*

The entire area of the pastures – the mountains and grazing fields – still belonging to the community today and include *Kartera, Isia* or *Melissa, Pagovounos, Petsodos, Piso Nera, Profitis Ilias, Distomo, Ereikani, Kakia Rachi, Voukrano, Kamatso*, and others, as well. The arable land, which is cultivatable, the homes and the homelands, all documented in the codex, are so numerous that they run from pages 3 to 21. That shows us that the Monastery had houses within the *Chora* and, specifically, in the area of *Vlattarias*, which is located south of the community garden. The Monastery also had orchards in the area of *Atsikis*, a continuation of *Aplotarias*, and orchards, fields, and estates in almost all the areas of *Kambos*, such as *Talaros* at *Sori* (*Panagia Syriotissa*) in *Kardamada,* and others. Zolotas writes that almost the entire *Kambos* and the *kambochoria* belong to the *Metochio* (dependency) of Sikousis. Furthermore, the Monastery had farm estates in *Thymiana, Tholopotami, Didyma, Kalamoti, Dafnona, Ververato, Zyfia*, and elsewhere.

While it would be much too difficult and outside of our objectives to present an entire copy of the register from the Codex, to satisfy even the most curious among our readers, we have copied some data, as displayed below.

> *"At Ploumari (in Lithi), Agios Georgios Sikousis has a home with a*

yard near the path of this monastery.

At Kalamoti, it has a dependency, Agios Georgios apidiotis.

At Lithi Limena, in Ploumari, a dependency with a church of the Taxiarchi (Archangel), it has one home near the church.

At Tholopotami, a field of five modia, 2 olive trees, 1 almond tree.

At Tholopotami, it has vineyards, 2 pinakia. Andreas cultivated it to share it with Agios Georgios, near the Monastery and the edge of Mountouloufou.

At Didyma (in Chalandra), a field of 5 modia.

At Voukarian (in Nenita), a field with 5 modia, a carob tree near Nikitas Orphanos and Ioannis Skyras.

At Vlattarian, one home built by Doukas Petrokkokinos.

This place has a dependency with 4 homes, 1 mulberry tree, and is near Xenos Skylitsi and Michail Kavonos.

At Atsiki, an orchard of tsiropinaki, 3 pinakia, 5 ancient mulberry trees.

At Sterna (in Talarou), an orchard with 1 modius, 2 pinakia, 23 mulberry trees, 7 fig trees, all planted by papa Ioannis Moukas.

At Agios Georgios, a field with 3 modia, near Isidoros Monis.

This is being held by Ioannis Kritis and Nik. Akritas.

At Stavros (the Cross), a field with 6 modia near the property of papa Nikiforos.

At Makri, arable fields and 50 wild modia near Krina and Eso Kipou.

At Troposi (Droposi), 2 homes built by Sideris Tsangopodis with a yard near this Saint, with beans all around.

At Droposi, an orchard, with 7 modia, 12 mulberry trees, 3 walnut trees, 12 fig trees. Behind that orchard is a field of 2 modia, 7 apple trees, 6 pear trees, mulberry trees, 6 stumps (koutsoures), 1 almond tree."

While it was in operation, the Monastery had financial autonomy and provided for the living expenses of the monks. It is possible that it had its own olive press, wine presses, and one or more windmills, as indicated by a rental document from the year 1635. The ruins of the windmill are still preserved in *Kalyvakia*, in the *Petsodos* Mountain.

"In the name of our Lord, Amen. Today I, the Abbot of Agios Georgios Sikousis, with the support of the noble Board Members of that church, will rent the mill for one year to Stavrinos for 1,000 aspra, and with the stipulation that he will grind as much wheat as the Monastery needs. The mill was created with strong pterotes from ten good beech trees, and has four new armena, as

*the others have worn out. Therefore, Stavrinos must leave this
mill in the same condition as he found it, as specified above. If
something gets destroyed, Stavrinos must repair it at his own
expense. This document is created as an indication of truth.*

1635, April 23rd
Mastrogiorgis Kountouris, Witness
Georgios Kalargyros
Georgios, son of Kyriakou Makris"

(Aspro: Byzantine and later turkish coin of a smaller value of "argyro" (silver).
Pterotes: the antennas where the sails of the windmills were tied.
Armena: the sails of the windmill.)

It is a well-known fact that many monasteries, aside from their land
estates, also have other items of value: gold and silver ecclesiastical vessels,
priestly vestments made with exceptional skill, ancient manuscripts, rare books,
and other precious items. In 1673, Vansleben and in 1729 Abbas Fourmont
visited Nea Moni, to purchase manuscripts and books. We find it odd that there
is no information to indicate that the Agios Georgios Monastery had those items.
In fact, a later document indicates that Sikousis had only the vessels necessary
for its liturgical needs, leading to the speculation that it must have been a rather
poor monastery. Here is what a document, dated October 10, 1653, says:

*"I, Papa Ioannis Valagos, Abbot of Agios Georgios – who succeeded
the Abbot kyr Ioannis Thomazis -- received the following books
of the church: one Paraklitiki, one Psaltirion, one Epistle, five
printed and one handwritten Menaia, and one Pentekostarion.
The sacred vessels I received were: a silver tray and chalice gilded
with silver, one bronze censor, five large candle lanterns, two
woven aprons – one made of poor fabric; two iron candelabras,
four basins in the floor, two plane tree covers at the tower, six
basins, two tables, two benches, and one register."*

C. Land Differences

Over the years, the ownership of the lands comprising the estate of the
Monastery began going to various laymen. Initially, the Genoese, who ruled
Chios from 1346, began usurping the best estates on the island. The Genoese
Justinians took possession of Kambos and its lands, the dependencies of
Sikousis and *Sklavion, Krinas, Plagia*, and others. On November 10, 1511, the
noblemen of Chios prepared a document to present to the governor and the
Central Administration of Genoa, detailing the detrimental and unjust events
occurring at Nea Moni and other monasteries and requesting intervention.

Pantelis A. Mavrogiorgis

Another reason for why monastic estates were being taken over by others was because people were hired under the rules of *Apotriton*. Therefore, these tenant farmers tended their lands during their entire lives, often refused to give one-third of the produce to the respective monastery, passed the lands down to their offspring as an inheritance, and refused to recognize the Monastery's ownership. There is information within a codex of the village, which says that on April 8, 1646, the monastery's Abbot Georgios Avasgos and Board Members Peris Gioustounias and Simous Gioustounias went to *Lithi* to solve the differences they had with Georgios Kambanaris and Vasileios and Georgios Papagas, who were holding an estate of the Monastery in *Ploumari*. They admitted that the garden was a plot of land belonging to Sikousis, and that they were the *imisiarides* (the people who would cultivate the plot and give half of the proceeds to the Monastery). This resulted in a new agreement being drawn up.

On page 42 of the old codex, we discovered another related matter referring to an estate in *Kalamoti* in the year 1627:

> *"In the presence of our humble and precious clergyman, the Abbot of Agios Georgios Sikousis, and the Members of the Board of the Monastery, we present the following. Misser Peris Gioustounias, son of the late Misser Giourimou, and Misser Peris Gioustounias, son of the late Misser Parise, had a difference of opinion with Nikolas Syrimas from Kalamoti over a plot of land, which Syrimas of the Agios Georgios Monastery holds as an anestatis. It is located by the baths in the field of Kalamoti, as is shown in the Notary Registry, and it once belonged to Kokkos, son of the late Frantzis. Both parties are currently fighting over this plot of land. When we also were in the village of Kalamoti, we examined that registry as well and found that this plot of land was under the authority of the abbot who was then in charge of the Monastery. We read this registry to Nikolaos Syrimas, who quickly gave one-third of the proceeds to the divine church of Agios Georgios. For this reason, the current abbot of this church, papa kyr Ioannis, and the Board Members before us hereby grant permission to Nikolaos Syrimas to be an anestatis for the remainder of his life. Therefore, he and his heirs must give one-third of this plot of land to the Abbot of the Monastery of Agios Georgios Sikousis. He does not have permission, nor do his heirs, to sell or lend this land to anyone else.*

> *Therefore, the present letter of agreement was written into our own registry in the year 1627, in the month of June."*

The above agreement was created by the Public Notary Manuil, priest and Sakellarios of Chios. Therefore it is quite good compared to other notary documents.

As the years passed, due to various historical events, refusal to respect the rights of the Monastery greatly increased. It reached a point where the Metropolitan of Chios, in a document he wrote on November 18, 1763 – which is contained in the village codex, number 1043 – he threatens anyone who will not pay what is due to the Saint with excommunication.

> "Whoever of the anastatas doesn't give what is right to the Saint through the abbot, or the individual appointed by the abbot, let him be cursed by the Saint. Such a person will also be excommunicated and not forgiven after he is dead and bloated."

It was necessary to invoke these penalties a number of times regarding the estate of the Monastery and within the villages of *Lithi, Zyfias*, and *Kalamoti*. The result was that the Monastery ended up divesting itself of its possessions in those areas during 1843.

After the Revolution of 1821, the massacres and destruction that occurred in Chios resulted in many Chians immigrating to different parts of Greece, like *Syros, Evoia,* and *Peiraias*. The then Metropolitan of Chios Sofronios, created a twelve-member Board drawn from inhabitants of the village on April 20, 1848, and he tasked them with orders to investigate and precisely ascertain which of the "homesteads and houses" were being deliberately withheld after the destruction. The Metropolitan also granted the Board Members the right to reconcile with any of the inhabitants. However, if no such reconciliation took place, then his directive was

> "for the homesteads and houses to be sold by the Board in a public sale."

Thus, the Monastery – and later on, the church of Agios Georgios – lost its entire estate and was left only with the plot in *Notso Kipos*, which was purchased in 1843. In another chapter, we will present a copy of the purchase agreement.

D. Differences with Nea Moni

Agios Georgios, as a monastery, was a *metochi* (dependency) of Nea Moni. With the decline of the Sikousis Monastery and the corresponding development of the village with the same name, border differences arose between Nea Moni and Sikousis, which can be found in a document dated 1640. This was written in the codex of the village and copied by Grigoris Foteinos for use in his book.

Pantelis A. Mavrogiorgis

"In the name of the Lord, Amen. The Abbot and the Fathers of the divine and sacred Nea Moni, have a difference with the most noble rulers and administrators of Sikousis, concerning a location in between these two divine monasteries. With both parties physically at this location, the abbot referred to the royal chrysobull of the Monastery, which proves that the domination and authority of the Monastery is up to Komaron. The rulers have also proved, from the registry of the authority, that the dominion of the Saint goes up to Agria Melissa. The other parties were not able to prove the truth and were excommunicated by His All Holiness, our Bishop Neofytos, ruler and master. Mastrogiorgis Kountouris and Stefanos, son of Michalis of Angelinas, testified that the properties of Nea Moni extend to Agria Melissa and Volaka. From there and down to Koumaroi, the lands belong to Agios Georgios.

And thus they witnessed in fear of God.

Therefore, both parties – having called the aforementioned witnesses, are now comfortable and no longer in distress over boundary disputes. Nevertheless, if the Fathers of Nea Moni find the ancient letter regarding this matter, and it proves that the boundaries of the above property go up to the Thiridon, as they say it does, then the present document shall be considered invalid, and the witnesses will have no further power over this. Unless such verification can be shown, however, let the present document stand.

Written in the year 1640, in the month of February, 24th day
Abbot Meletios, Ieromonachos, and those with me:
Vitsentzos Gioustinianes, board member, I certify
Antonios Gioustinianes, I certify
Petros Grimaltis, I certify"

E. Doubts That the Monastery Functioned Again After 1518

From the documents contained in the old codex of the village, some of which we have presented on previous pages, it is possible to speculate that the Monastery functioned during a second period of time, with the simultaneous development of the village. What gives rise to this impression is the fact that Agios Georgios continues to be characterized as a monastery, and the priests are still referred to as abbots (*igoumenoi* or *kathigoumenoi*).

The late Alexandros Galanos, teacher and researcher of the historic affairs of the village, in his lecture to the Agiorgousoi – which was published in 1958, after he read the document of 1640 which related to the border disputes of Nea Moni and Sikousis, said:

> *"As you heard in the document I just read, which was published in 1640, one-hundred and twenty-two years after the founding of our village, there is talk of the differences between two parties concerning these **divine monasteries of Nea Moni and Agios Georgios.** This forces us to accept, that even after 1518, when the village was established, a new monastery was created with monks, since abbots are mentioned in the old codex up to 1751."*

In examining certain parts of this document, we ascertain that the two parties in the dispute are not equally represented. Nea Moni is represented by the Abbot and the Fathers who accompanied him; while Agios Georgios is represented by "the most noble rulers and administrators" – in other words, the Board Members. And, subsequently, the document says that "the domination and the authority of the Monastery is up to *Komaron*," whereas for Sikousis it mentions "the domination of the Saint," not of the Monastery. Therefore, this document seems to verify that the Monastery is not in operation once again.

Alexandros Galanos presents another viewpoint regarding the agreement over the mill. In that particular document, it states that the mill is secured for "a thousand coins, and it should grind for the Monastery as much wheat as it needs." This does not indicate, with any certainty, that there were monks in that Monastery for a second time. It merely means that the priest, who was called an "abbot," would need flour for breads required in liturgies and joint meals, according to Sepsis' will. Galanos quotes Zolotas, saying that the traveler Thevenot, "saw in Agios Menas fifty monks, one-hundred and fifty at Nea Moni, and twenty-five at Agios Georgios Sikousis."

The information culled from the traveler himself, Jean de Thevenot, who visited Chios in 1656, is considered inaccurate. He speaks of various villages in Chios, among which is Agios Georgios Sikousis, saying, "I will mention here the major villages of the island of Chios, which I did not see, but of which I received information from a handwritten commentary which came into my hands." The only thing he wrote about Agios Georgios was that, like Vessa and Flatsia, it had two hundred inhabitants.

Therefore, working only with what has been written in this section, we retain serious doubts about whether the Monastery ever functioned again after 1518. Furthermore, as noted in a prior chapter, it seems logical that

Pantelis A. Mavrogiorgis

Sikousis – even after its decline – continued to be known as and written about as a monastery, and its priests were still called abbots. Sofronios Sepsis calls it a monastery in his will, so it is possible that one or two monks continued to live there at times. "Symeon, Ieromonachos and Abbot, and monk Gerasimos," signed a document dated September 7, 1644.

CHAPTER 7
Building Remnants of the Monastery

A. *O Stavros* (The Cross)

The intact portion of the monastery, *Pylonas* (gateway), is called *Stavros* by the village residents. It is a separate edifice 5.3 meters long and 10.5 meters high, built of stone, which gives the impression of a large apse, beneath where the entrance of the Monastery is located. Two poles – each 1.3 meters wide, 2.3 meters deep and eight meters high – lie sideways and support a level roof, but form an arch within. Above the roof, at symmetrical distances from the corners, a small tower rises to a height of 1.5 meters; it is orthogonally shaped, with three blind sides and the fourth closed with wooden window frames. It is covered with an inclined shard roof on whose peak an iron cross is affixed.

In the interior, a large portable icon of the crucifix is placed, which may be the reason for naming *Pylonas* "the Cross." I do not know if this entrance carried that name from the time the monastery was operational, after which a similar icon was positioned. A vigil lamp always burns before the icon, which can be raised and lowered with a pulley system located within the interior of the small tower. For the Agiorgousoi, *Stavros* is a sacred place.

In the olden days, before the opening of the road that runs alongside, the villagers were forced to pass beneath the apse of the Cross. They would then remove their hats, make the sign of the cross, and jump off the backs of animals they had ridden there. I recall gathering with others in this area for vespers on the eve of the holiday that celebrates the Elevation of the Cross on September 14. I remember the yellow colors of fall and the joyous light of day prior to sunset.

B. *O Pyrgos* (The Tower)

Piracy is as old as sailing, but there were times that it occurred with greater frequency. During the later part of the Byzantine Era and beyond, Arab Corsairs, Saracens, and Turks would sail the Aegean Sea and pillage the shores and the islands, causing great fear and dread to the inhabitants, who had to organize defenses to protect themselves, the animals, and the harvests of the fields and trees. So they built towers and castles and created fortified villages, such as *Mesta, Olympoi, Pyrgi*, and to a lesser degree Agios Georgios.

O Stavros (The Cross): entrance of the old Monastery, 1928
The fortified wall of the monastery is visible on the right
(Photographer: P. Papahatzidakis)

Besides on the shores, above high hills, cylindrical structures are still preserved to this day as a type of windmill, known as *vigles*. Those who guarded the *vigles* came from nearby villages and would scour the waters of the sea for suspicious signs. To alert villagers of impending danger, they would light torches to create signal fires at night or smoke during the day.

The inhabitants would then either arm themselves with weapons or take refuge in the towers, which existed in most of the villages. The towers and smaller towers had been built during the Genoese period and were at Kambos and near other countryside homes, which were at a great distance. Today we are able to see the ruins of those towers in Sklavia, Krina, Notso Kipos, and elsewhere. The towers had thick walls with openings for guns and to allow the guards to spill hot oil on the enemy below. They were structures of two to three levels, where ammunition, food, and water would be stored. There were towers even at the monasteries, such as Nea Moni, Panagia Halandron, and at Agios Georgios Sikousis.

> *"There were very many round and high towers and little towers all along the shoreline at specific locations, and there were forty large, square towers, the most fortified located at Agio Gala, Kardamyla, Mesta, Agia Eleni, Pyrgi, Karyon, Agios Georgios* **Sykeou** *of Penthodos (Petsodos), overseen by Genoese head guards."*

One portion of the Tower of Sikousis, 6 meters by 10 meters, is still standing today, abandoned. It is approximately 30 meters from *Stavros*. Between these two structures there must have been a tall castle wall, which surrounded the entire interior of the Monastery. I actually recall seeing one piece of that wall, which leaned against the Pylonas at an elevation. The villagers decided to tear it down, because they wanted to construct a side road to avoid passing beneath Stavros. The Tower was built with large, unchiseled stones, between which is a mortar-like substance strengthened with mud-bricks. The corners are fashioned from carved, cubed stones. The first floor is ground level, and the preserved portion is intact, covered with an arched roof of mud-bricks that appear to be nailed, each one adjacent to the other, giving the impression of a single span. On the second floor, the sides are in ruins; in certain places rifle holes can be distinguished. The floor on this level gives the appearance of stones made of iron. The Tower, in later years, seems to have been used as a storage room for the Monastery. The codex offers only one excerpt regarding the Tower, and it comes from a dispute between the Board Members and a village parishioner.

> *"On January 7, 1635, the Abbot of Agios Georgios Sikousis was present, along with the noble rulers, Miser Simous Gioustinias,*

O Pyrgos (The Tower)
The ruins are visible in the center
(Photographer: Cathy Mavrogiorgis)

and Miser Visentzos of the late Miser Brinou. Being inside the Monastery due to some issue and noticed an exterior door blocking the door of the church tower. Michalis Alamas has land adjacent to the Tower and had constructed it. Therefore he promises not to prevent anyone – whom the abbot of the monastery wanted to send to the tower – from entering.

In truth, the present document was created with the following witnesses:
Priest Ioannis Kouloumbos, ex-abbot of this church
Simous Gioustinias
Vitsentzos Gioustinias
Priest Georgios Mavrokalos
Monios Tornaris
Georgios Koukias
Niamonitis Allages"

C. The Church

The Church of Agios Georgios, according to the archaeologist Georgios Soteriou, was a copy of the *katholikon* of Nea Moni, like the churches of *Panagias Agiogalousainas, Krinas, Sikelias*, and *Agioi Apostoloi* in *Pyrgi*. It is octagonal with a dome. The basic characteristic of this design is the change from the square-shaped floor to the circular one, where four large arches stand – one at each side of the building – and four, hollow spherical triangles fill in the corners between the four arches. The support of the dome is the result of the combination of these enormous arches and the spherical triangles. Thus, the upper side of each triangle has an arc equal to one fourth of the circle, thereby allowing for the transition from the square floor to the circular base of the dome. In the octagonal design, where there are no columns to support the dome, the whole area is open and one can see the entire architectural composition of the church. The Church of Agios Georgios was constructed of stone and does not seem to have had an external brick facing, which can be seen at *Panagia Krina* and *Agioi Apostoloi* in *Pyrgi*.

Due to the fact that a portion of the southern side and the eastern side of the church with the altar remain, it is possible to describe the church as it would have been centuries ago. The walls of the interior side contain three high, horizontal belts in a repeated pattern. The first is comprised of three blind apses, and the wide middle one has two lobed windows. The side apses are decorated at the edges with two pairs of little columns, one pair at each edge. Moving up the wall, the second belt contains three semi-cylindrical conches,

Pantelis A. Mavrogiorgis

The rear of the sanctuary of Agios Georgios
Teacher & historian Alexandros Galanos is visible
Source: A. Orlandos, "Monument Byzantis de Chio," 1910

concave surfaces, the middle one being the largest of the three. The uppermost or third belt forms the support system of the dome, along with the arches and spherical triangles.

Professor C. Bouras determined that the architect of Agios Georgios retained the characteristics of the octagonal island form apparent in Nea Moni and only simplified the support of the dome on the eastern side, with the elevation of the arch of the altar replacing the shallow conch. The dome is approximately three meters in height, wherein three repeated circular belts can be distinguished. The first, higher one, contains skylights with colored glass; while the second is unadorned but allows for iconography. These converge upwardly and end at the dome-shaped ceiling, upon which is a more recent fresco of the *Pantocrator*. The exterior of the dome has a ceramic tile roof, at the peak of which is a Byzantine cross. On the eastern wall of the church, the three conches of the altar are preserved, the middle one widest and containing a three-sectioned window.

This old Church of Agios Georgios must have had frescoes, as we can infer from seeing similar churches of the same time period. The marble revetment seen on the walls of Nea Moni did not exist at Agios Georgios, though, which had neither the wealth, majesty, reputation, nor the beauty of the Monastery of Nea Moni.

[Editor's Note: In the past few years archeologists have uncovered exquisite icons below the plaster covering the walls of the church. As of June 2018, the archeological work is ongoing.]

D. Other Outbuildings

Several meters outside of the Church, on the north side, a chapel – which according to oral tradition was dedicated to Agios Ioannis – is preserved. The Agiorgousoi believe that this church is much older than that of Agios Georgios. Anastasios Orlandos, Professor of Christian Archeology, who visited the village, decided that the chapel was actually built more recently than the church, based on the construction of its walls. The chapel has a wooden roof, which is ten to twelve meters long and five to six meters wide. Had the conch of the altar not been preserved on the eastern side of the church within the clamshell, it would be difficult to recognize that the building had ever been a church.

While I do not know when it ceased functioning as a place of worship, several decades prior to 1951 it was an elementary school classroom. It was here that my teacher, Georgios Dellas, taught me my first letters, and also where I was taught by Christos Vekios, my fourth grade teacher. In the past few years,

Agios Giannis: old church of the Monastery

the room has been renovated and used by parishioners, following religious memorials.

On the west side of this building are two adjacent, two-story buildings, which are probably from the same period, judging from the construction of their walls. We do not know exactly when they were built or what needs of the Monastery they served. Each of these contains a windowless ground floor and a large room on the upper level. They may have been used as guest rooms or visitors' rooms for the Monastery, because from a document contained in the codex of the village (number 1043, in the *Koraïs* Library), we learn that the church provided a kind of hospitality.

> "1782, December 7. Present: Giorgis Kostaris, papa Giannis Syntaxaki [?]. They receive the vessels of the church of Agios Georgios into their hands: a silver gospel, a silver censer, a silver chandelier, six vigil lamps – one of silver, three small vigil lamps, four small silver vigil lamps, two large candles, three small candles, twelve rings, silver chalices, four blankets, four sheets, six napkins, one towel, 26 clay plates, nine cups, ten forks, and nine stamped spoons. All of these, which were placed into their hands, are to be taken care of as though they were their own, until the time they are turned over to a new Board. Furthermore, they were given one silver cross and eleven aslania, and 30 grosia from the tameio (money box)."

These large rooms were used as classrooms for the elementary school grades, and the church of Agios Iouannis was used that way, as well.

When we pass the *Stavros-Pyli* (Cross-Gateway) and proceed eastward beneath the current courtyard of Agios Georgios, we encounter old, low, half-abandoned houses; and somehow it makes one consider that they may have served as cells for monks. As far as the homes which papa Sepsis, in his will, claims to have built, there is no data to help us locate them. In fact, on page 20 of the old codex, edifices are referred to as being "near" the Monastery, but we cannot prove that.

> "Agios Georgios Sikousis has **in the outer yard** (courtyard) nine homes with yards and vineyards behind them. There are three mulberry trees, and an olive tree next to the houses and the Church. And with these are one field of five modia with one pear tree, a vineyard of three modia, an orchard with 20 fig trees, five apple trees, one pear tree, all next to the houses, the castle (Tower), the path, and the church. At the same location one field of 15 modia, with four olive trees, one almond tree, one walnut

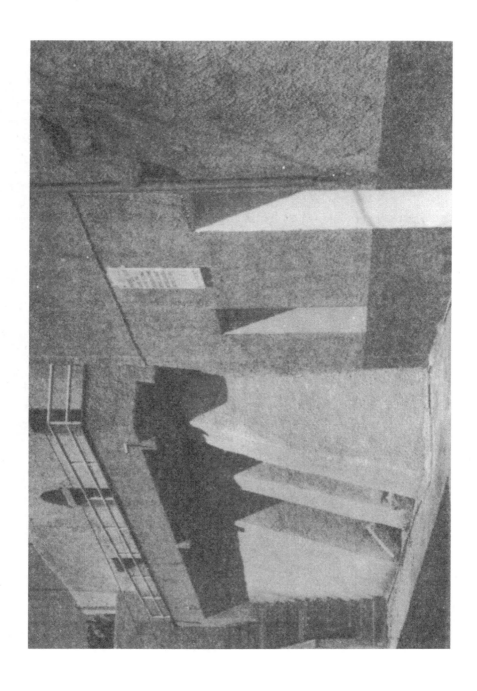

Buildings of the Monastery: site of the old school
(Photographer: Cathy Mavrogiorgis)

The Village Agios Georgios Sikousis

tree, and one oak tree.

He pays (as a tax) five yperpyra (gold coins)."

Using these facts to define the internal area of the Monastery, with the Stavros as the starting point, the possible boundaries are as follows: the southern side is defined by Stavros, the Tower, and its extensions. To the right of Stavros, past the covered streets, there is a narrow road which goes toward the mountain *Kalyvakia*, making this road the eastern boundary. To the north, there is a small road, which goes out to the edge of the village and serves as a boundary. Therefore, from this spot, the western boundary is created by the road that passes in front of the current courtyard of Agios Georgios, where the entrance is, and visually lines up with the tower.

Pantelis A. Mavrogiorgis

CHAPTER 8
Igoumenoi (The Abbots)

A. The Responsibilities of the Abbots

The Igoumenos (abbot) is the individual who leads and directs a monastery. He is an ordained celibate and bears the ecclesiastical title of Archimandrite, which means "leader of the spiritual fold." Aside from his liturgical, religious, and monastic duties, he oversees the lives and the ascesis of the monks, assigns them jobs, and – in cases of deviation – imposes penances, which is the "canon." The abbot strives to keep the monastery regulated, regarding the administration of the estate, the management of financial areas, and the handling of any problems which arise – the most serious of which he solves with the assistance of the members of the *Igoumenosymvouliou* (Abbot's Council).

The abbots of Sikousis after 1518, when the monastery was dissolved, had the primary responsibility of managing the estates of the Saint, according to the codexes. They would collect rents from those who leased their lands; receive the Monastery's share of produce, which they would proceed to divide into thirds; rent fields under other terms; grant property for the construction of houses; and function in the capacity of private owners of these properties, with the approval of the board members, whose role was rather symbolic.

> *"1637, September 9. The abbot, having the authority given by the noblest rulers* (members of the Board), *gives to mastrogiorgis Kountouris 50 dachtila (rings) of land for a house, in the location of Aloniou. Once the house is built, one chicken shall be given (to the Monastery) every year.*
>
> *The abbot, papa Ioannis Valagros"*

The role of the abbot is peculiar, especially considering that Sofronios Sepsis does not make mention of an abbot in his will. But he does specify that

> *"the residents should select a worthy, faithful person as an oikonomos (Steward) to provide and gather the income of the Saint and appoint priests and Board Members."*

Therefore, it seems as though the abbot is actually performing the work

---

designated for the Steward. In referring to Sepsis' will, Ioannis Andreadis writes:

"These counsels and directions of Sepsis were completely fulfilled."

However, we cannot accept this viewpoint unquestioningly. **The codex even refers to instances of irresponsibility and mismanagement** as indicated in the following document of the old Codex:

"1623, April 14. I, the below undersigned, served for four years the Great, Holy Martyr Georgios Sikousis, finding a debt of sixty-thousand aspra, which is for purchases first made in the Ammoudarian from the late abbot-papa kyr Georgios Avasgas, which included his animals, vineyards and fields – both arable and uncultivated. They also bought from Georgoun of Kourmouzis, at Agios Ioannis o Kontos, a small, terraced field with a fountain and cistern, olives, mulberry trees, and other types of fields and trees – arable and uncultivated. For these debts, I have had to give ten thousand aspra per year for the kefali (principal) and sixty thousand, separately, for the proventi (interest)."

The Sakellarios of Chios, Priest Manuil the Pantevgenos"

The payment system of this church appears rather odd. Obviously, Priest Pantevgenos must have been receiving all the income of the church in exchange for fulfilling his responsibilities. A similar incident occurred in 1740, when an "abbot" was appointed to the church of Agios Georgios during a general meeting. This "abbot," who was actually a Board Member, was given certain responsibilities concerning village festivities and was assigned an annual salary. The details are presented in the following document.

"1740, November 1. Today, the Elders, priests, and residents met to appoint Board Member Konstantinos, son of Michalis Kaligou, as abbot of the Church of the Great and Holy Martyr Georgios for a period of two years. He is to give 335 aslania each year, plus an annual gift to the priests of 45 aslania, and a gift on the feast day of Agios Nikolaos. Every Saturday and Sunday he is to cense bizouvi (i.e., with fragrant incense) *in the Church. Also, during the holidays of the Lord, and on the feast of Agios Georgios, he is to slaughter an ox, and to hire good chanters. On both Christmas and on the feast day of Agios Nikolaos, and at the troparia, he is to feed the priests and a few residents. Every Sunday and during the Wednesdays and Fridays of Sarakosti (Lent), he is to feed the priest and the elderly deacon. He is to also give Taxiarchis at Lithi*

Limena two aslania, and two aslania to Kalamoti also. He must also bring to the feast day of Agios Nikolaos two okades of wax, and to Agios Panteleimon another two, and leave four okades of wax at the Church whenever he collects it. And every week he must wash the vigil lamps.
Kostantinos Mitsoudis, Witness
Papa Antonios Giannakoudis
Papa Kostantinos Giannakoudis
Ioannis Kalimasiadis
Papa Michalis Livanis, and others."

Only in a later document of the year 1757, which is found within a newer codex (1043, p. 210), does it seem that the suggestions of SofroniosSepsis are followed to some extent.

"Today, 1757 November 7, *the members of the parish, the priests, and the Elders gathered and appointed the following Board Members, Nikolis Yiannakakis, and Yiannis Delakakis for two years. And* **when their terms are finished, they must give an accounting to the people** . . . *Also, it is determined that these same Board Members serve in the churches Agios Nikolas, Agios Panteleimonas, and Agios Thomas."*

There is an analogous action indicated in a document dated **1843**.

"On this day, the Board Members present at the church of Agios Georgios, papa Ioannis Soukas, and Michalis Barlis, along with several members of the community, found it appropriate to appoint new Board Members to the same church, to provide for and care for the church as is required. They appointed Antonios Mountis and papa Hatzi Vekion to be at hand to collect and provide for the dependencies of Kalamotis and for the countryside estates we have purchased. Thus, we have agreed with the public to serve for one year and to give an accounting to the residents at the end of that year.
Behold the witnesses, in the year 1843 March 3
Papa Georgis Toublis, I certify
Papa Georgis Akrakin, I certify
Papa Georgis Foustanas, witness
Deacon Dellas
Nikolaos Kakaridis, witness"

After a year we find written the account presented by those board members:

"1844 March 3, Today, Antonios Mountis and papa Hatzis Vekakin are present. Having worked in the Church for one year, gives a clear accounting to all of the priests and residents of the village, young and old, which indicates that he neither owes nor must receive anything from the Church or the estates.
Papa Georgis Toublis
Papa Georgis Akrakin
Papa Ioannis Soukas
Hatzi Anegnostis Vekios
Hatzi Stamatis, I certify"

B. List of the Names of the Abbots

From the documents found within the old codex, we have gathered the names of all of the abbots, providing their titles, the year they were appointed and, in parenthesis, we refer to the actual page within the codex where that information was found.

1. *Papa Giorgis Avaslis, 1620 (p. 32)*
2. *Igoumenos papa Giorgios Evagros of Agios Georgios, 1622 (p. 78)*
3. *The Sakellarios of Chios, Priest Manuil the Pantevgenos,   1624-1626 (pp. 85, 86, 93, 94)*
4. *Ieromonachos Mitrofanis, 1627 (p. 79)*
5. *Priest Ioannis Kouloumbos, proigoumenos (former abbot) of the church, 1629 (pp. 45, 47)*
6. *Igoumenos of the Saint, priest Ioannis Valagros, 1635-37 (p. 48)*
7. *Kathigoumenos Meletios, Ieromonachos, 1640 (p. 65)*
8. *Igoumenos Symeon, Ieromonachos of Agios Georgios, 1644 (p. 66)*
9. *Kathigoumenos Andreas Stavrinos of Agios Georgios, 1645 (p. 62)*
10. *Papa Georgios Avasgas, 1646 (p. 52)*
11. *Ierotheos Kylanos, Ieromonachos, 1655-57 (pp. 55, 56, 61, 72)*
12. *The Most Honored Kathigoumenos of Agios Georgios, papa Ioannis Kalargyros, 1665-69 (pp. 53, 67)*
13. *Kathigoumenos papa Konstantis Kouras, 1679, 1688 (pp. 74, 95)*
14. *Papa Ioannis Giannakoudis, 1690 (p. 99)*
15. *Papa Demetrios Giannakoudis, 1694 (p. 103)*
16. *Kathigoumenos papa Constantinos Zoufianousis, 1698 (p. 104)*
17. *Papa Constantinos, son of Manoli, 1699 (p. 105)*
18. *Kathigoumenos Iasofos, 1701 (p. 107)*
19. *Igoumenos papa Michalis Kouras, 1717-1718 (pp. 112, 114)*
20. *Igoumenos Georgios Tornaris, 1751, (p. 115)*
21. *Igoumenos Ioannis, son of the late papa Vasilis, 1751 (p. 122)*

CHAPTER 9
Foreign Travelers and Sikousis

Phillip Argenti and professor Stilpon Kyriakidis have compiled a three-volume work, *I Chios Para tois Geografois kai Periigitais,* containing the impressions and opinions of foreign travelers who visited Chios. I thought that I might find noteworthy information about our Monastery and village in these volumes, but that was not the case. There is quite a bit of information regarding Nea Moni, but nothing about Agios Georgios – which at the time was deteriorating and moving toward oblivion. On the other hand, the village was just coming into being but was unimportant and poor. However, the location itself and the scenery did attract some attention, and a few lines were dedicated to it in the books. I will present excerpts in their original translations, not because they illuminate the history of our village in any way, but to satisfy the curiosity of my readers.

Christophorus Buontelemontius (1422)

Hailed from Florence, Italy and came to Greece in order to gather codexes. He spent four years traveling to islands of the Aegean, and he wrote a book in Latin, with the title *Liber Insularum Archipelagi* (*Book of Islands of the Archipelago*) in the year 1422.

"Cumque ad Sanctum devenio Georgium de Sicosi . . .

*When I arrived at Agios Georgios Sikousis, at its foothills springs flow, dropping down to the depths, and immediately **a river, through a very fertile field, descends toward the sea.***

*However, when I turned to the right of the mountain, we saw **the great castle Recovera**, where the partridges are in abundance."*

Legrand writes almost the same thing, adding:

*"To the right of the location, **there is a large fort called Lefkovoura**, and after that there is another one called Kalamoti."*

André Thevet (1549)

A French monk who made many trips and remained on Chios for two months. He wrote many travel works in French. He was trustworthy and mixed many myths that he heard with all that he saw. Among other things, he writes:

> *"Towards the place called Agios Georgios, to the south one sees the most beautiful gardens in the world. To the southwest, the field of Kalamoti appears, with the best mastic."*

Nic de Nicolay (1551)

A French traveler who visited Chios, and wrote his impressions in the book, *Navigations et Peregrinations Orientales* (*Trips and Travels to the East*). And he speaks about springs and rivers.

> *"Furthermore, there is Agios Georgios, where many beautiful springs are born and spring forth, which all together become a* **main river that empties into the sea."**

COMMENTS:

1. The river about which Vuontelmonte and Nicolay speak is obviously our familiar *Kokkalas*, which springs from the mountains that surround the Kambochora and Kambos, and the Agiorgousika: Petsodo and Profitis Ilias receive rainwater from Dafnona and Anemona, which empties at Lefkonia, near Kontari.
2. In olden times this river was known as the River of *Soris*, from where the church *Panagia Soriotissa* (*Syriotissa*) in Kambos received its name.
3. The castle *Recovera* or *Lefkovoura* is the castle of *Armolion*. This is a noteworthy fort, built at the peak of the mountain *Lykouri* ("Lecouveri" in Italian), which was built by Nicholas Joustinianis. According to others, it is older and built by the Byzantines. It is also called the castle of the *Apolichnon*. Apparently, Vuontelmonte is exaggerating when he writes that from Agios Georgios he "turned to the right of the mountain" and saw the castle *Recovera* of *Armolion*.

Jean Thevenot (1656)

A French traveler who visited Chios in the year 1656. He wrote the related work, *Relation d' un voyage fait au Levant* (*A Reference to a Trip to the East*). He speaks about the mastic in particular. He mentions that there are twenty-two villages that have mastic trees, and they give 27,000 *okades* of mastic to the Sultan. Afterwards he writes about Nea Moni; subsequently about a few *Mastichochoria*. He also writes that Agios Georgios was inhabited by 200 people, as were Vessa and Flatsia.

Francisco Piancenza (1688)

An Italian professor who traveled to the East and wrote a voluminous geographic work about the islands of the Aegean in Italian. We don't know if or when he visited Chios. He writes the following about Agios Georgios:

> *"In the lower area, there are an infinite number of trees producing mastic, but also very beautiful springs, which unite with each other by Agios Georgios. They comprise a beautiful and **moderate river** which, irrigating all these fields, empties into the sea."*

Elsewhere he mentions, like Thevenot, that Agios Georgios and Flatsia have a smaller number of inhabitants than Koini and Vessa.

> *"Chiny da 300, Vessa da 200, S. Georgio e Flacia con minori numero."*

Vincenzo Maria Coronelli (1699)

A Venetian geographer who did not visit Chios, but who draws his information from various sources. He especially copies Piancenza.

> *"The lower area is filled with exotic and exceptionally delightful hills that abound with trees of mastic, which reach one hundred thousand. There are many springs that unite under the Kastilion of Agios Georgios, and comprise a **moderate river** under the name Bellosano or Bedosano which, flowing forcefully in the port of the Amiston, empties into the sea."*

COMMENTS:

Piacenza speaks about "a moderate river" and, likewise, Coronelli mentions a "moderate river" which pours into the port of *Amiston*. I am of the opinion that he is referring to the river which springs from the monastic lands *Lepro* and *Voukrano*, runs through the western part of the village (*Ponio, Potamia, Ammodaria*) and *Kartera*, so for this reason, it is called *Karteros*. It receives the waters of the *Tholopotami*, *Didymas* and *Patrika*, and pours into the Gulf of *Kalamoti*, where it is also called *Katraris*. Coronelli seems confused, since he writes that the waters flow into *Amista*, meaning *Mesta*.

Joseph de Tournefort (1701)

A French nobleman who studied the lives of the peoples whom he visited and wrote a work entitled, *Relation d'un voyage du Levant . . .* (*Report on a Trip to the East*).

Here is a section that relates to Sikousis:

"The Greek monasteries enjoy great incomes. The one of Agios Minas has 50 monks, and that of Agios Georgios 25. The most important is Nea Moni. This Monastery pays 500 skouda as a head tax; it includes 150 monks."

COMMENTS:

We doubt the trustworthiness of the information provided by Tournefort, who shows the Monastery of Agios Georgios functioning again around 1700 with 25 monks. This is quite inaccurate, as is his information about Nea Moni, when he writes: "The Monastery is in a place unpleasantly isolated in the middle of big mountains, completely naked." How odd! Who doesn't know that Nea Moni was located in those years in the greatest pinewoods in Chios? Tournefort continues: "Everything in the church is Gothic. The icons are abhorrently coarse, despite the abundant gold coverings." We do not believe that this information corresponds to the truth. Furthermore, in the previous list of the names of the Abbots of Sikousis, we observe that none of them signs his name merely as "abbot of the monastery," but as "Abbot of Agios Georgios" or "of the Saint," and one of them signs as "Abbot of the Church."

CHAPTER 10
History of the Village

A. The Founding

This chapter is undoubtedly superfluous, since it has already been made clear that the founding of the village occurred when Sofronios Sepsis invited and settled the first colonizers, whose names we read in his will, following the decline and abandonment of the Monastery. According to Kanellakis:

> *"The only one of the current villages whose age we know is that of Agios Georgios Sikousis, as is deduced from the document of 1518. The monk Sofronios Sepsis did not have any purpose for settling monks there; rather he sought to settle laymen in order to create a village."*

Due to some curious information on page 26 of the book *Neamonisia*, written by Nikiforos of Chios and Grigorios Foteinos – which has resulted in incorrect conclusions being drawn relative to the founding of our village -- this topic must be examined and the truth determined. The information given about the founding of Nea Moni by Konstantinos Monomachos (1042-1054) comes from an ancient text Nikiforos of Chios copied from an unidentified author.

> *"It was constructed during a twelve-year period and funded by royal expenditures while the king was still alive. Following the death of the king and especially that of Zoe, who preceded him in death, construction was temporarily halted. Through the divine love of the sister of the Empress Zoe (I am speaking of Theodora), whatever was incomplete regarding the construction was then added. At the end, a perfect and outstanding building had been created. During the second year that the church was under construction, the famous king offered substantial economic support to feed the monks and for **the village of the Great Martyr Georgios, surnamed Sykountos.**"*

This information, which claims that Konstantinos Monomachos offered **the village** of *Agios Georgios Sykountos* to the monks in order to support them economically by giving them food, is not accurate for the following reasons:

1. Nikiforos himself translates the text of the unidentified author and on

---

page 43 of *Neamonisia* we read that:

"Two years after construction began, while the monastery was still being built, the ever-memorable King Konstantinos Monomachos gave gifts of considerable income to feed those who lived in the Monastery."

2. Sofronios Sepsis called in farmers from the surrounding villages. If our village had existed at that time, wouldn't he have simply given the Monastery to the Agiorgousoi?
3. None of the historians of Chios pay much attention to this information. In fact, Konstantinos Amantos informs us that:

"The large village of Agios Georgios Sikousis started developing around the sixteenth century, since the cultivators of the estates of the Monastery of Agios Georgios began multiplying."

Georgios Zolotas writes this in his history:

"The Dependency of Sykeou, along with its cultivatable land and pastures and all the areas under its jurisdiction, served as the core of the village, according to Michail Paleologos."

Stylianos Vios clarifies this viewpoint further by saying:

"Before the village was inhabited, there was herein a Dependency of Nea Moni called 'of Sykeou' (afterwards 'Sikousis'), with the Church of Agios Georgios, around which the village was settled."

From all of this, we surmise that the history of the village begins from 1518. Through the years, after the initial inhabitants settled there, the village grows by attracting people from other villages who have no land of their own.

The *Igoumenos* (abbot) and the *Epitropoi* (Board Members) give the farmers arable and uncultivated fields, neglected expanses of land that have been returned to them, and homesteads, in exchange for which the farmers must then return anywhere from one-third to one-ninth of their annual produce. It is very possible that Greeks from the east took refuge at times in the village to avoid the Turkish yoke, since Chios was under the jurisdiction of the Genoese until 1656. Even later – under the Turkish occupation – the privileges offered by the Turks facilitated the growth of the settlement in Chios and, consequently, also in Sikousis. Another reason why passersby might have decided to settle there could be because the location was mountainous and fortified, which provided the inhabitants safety from pirates. So the village grew and became the second most populated village after Pyrgi in the Mastichochoria. Here are

Pantelis A. Mavrogiorgis

the population figures of our village drawn from various years:

1827: pop. 629 (*Chiakon Archeion* Vlachogianni, vol. 2, p. 25)
1831: pop. 386 (following the massacres) (Zolotas, vol. 3, p. 706)
1866: 264 families (A. Karavas, *Topographia*, p. 41)
1889: 260 families (M. Mougeris, *I Nisos Chios*, p. 32)
1901: pop. 2,010 (Kanellakis, *Topographia*)
1937: pop. 1,732 (S. Vios, *I Sychronos Chios*, p. 98)
1951: pop. 1,507 (Government Census)
1961: pop. 1,403 (Government Census)
1971: pop. 1,063 (Government Census)
1981: pop. 878 (Government Census)

B. Topographical Outline

The village was initially constructed around the Church, the *Pyrgos* and the *Periavlo* (courtyard) of the Monastery, and from there it spread from north to south, as I estimate, becoming 1500 meters long and about 400 meters wide.

Its general appearance is long and narrow, with three nearly parallel roads running along its length through three basic neighborhoods – *Kato* (Lower), *Mesi* (Middle), and *Piso* (Back).

The widest inhabited area, with the Church of **Agios Georgios** in the center, is known as **Mesa Chorio (Inside Village)** and its resident as a **Mesageitonousis** (Inside Villager). The Mesa Chorio includes a portion from the neighborhoods called Piso, Mesa, and Kato; and the neighborhood of **Prinos (Holly Tree)**, which received its name from its large holly trees. There is also **Plateia Mpou (Square of Mpou)**, probably deriving from the family surname Mpous or Mpougous (Mpouos - Mpous); the neighborhoods of **Agios Georgios**, **Stavros**, and the **Tenekekioi**, (a Turkish word that mockingly calls the area "poor village). Correspondingly, the wider area to the south and around **Agios Panteleimonas** is known as the **Oxo Chorio (Outer Village)** and its inhabitant as an **Oxogeitonousis (Outer Villager)**.

The distinct neighborhoods, aside from the *Piso*, *Mesi*, and *Kato* neighborhoods, include **Myloi**, where windmills once existed; **Oxo Geitonia (Outer Neighborhood)**, where the road for Tholopotami passes; and **Batsilis**, where the road leads to Vessa. The name of Batsilis probably came from a family surname.

From Prinos, the descent traverses the entire village with an abrupt slope called **Lakkos (the Pit)**, that becomes like a river on rainy days and empties into

The neighborhood of Prinos

The covered street "skepasto" gives the impression of a castle structure

Pantelis A. Mavrogiorgis

the little ***"Mpavla to aryaki" ("Bavla's Creek")***. Another, even steeper, descent going from the Mesi to the Kato neighborhood is known as **Manaouda**. Its name comes from the Manaoudas family, as seen in the old village codex, where reference is made to the Managoudon rural area.

C. A General Structural View of the Village

The village, even though it is younger than Zyfias, Tholopotami and others, seems older because it didn't suffer serious damage in the earthquake of 1881, thus it did not require rebuilding. It also survived that event well since it was built similar to the so called medieval villages like Mesta, Pyrgi, and Olympoi.

I think it will be helpful to present some general information on the characteristics of these "medieval villages." They were fortress-like in design so as to protect their inhabitants from pirates and other enemies; therefore the houses were attached to one another. The back walls were solid, like a fort, and the windows faced the interior. In the center of the village there was a strong, high tower, such as still exists in Pyrgi and in other villages, like Mesta, little towers were built at the edges. The houses were all approximately the same height, so that – in case of emergency – the roofs could be used as a continuous road.

The streets of the villages were narrow, and arched buildings known as *"Skepasta"* ("covers") were joined with the houses at both ends. Each medieval-style village had two to three large iron doors, which were locked at night or whenever there was a threat to the village. Vikelas, in his novel, *Loukis Laras* gives us a beautiful description.

> *"The villages of Chios were, and are fortified like forts and narrow as prisons. They don't have walls, but at the four external sides of the houses, their backs joined together comprise a ceaseless bulwark. The doors of the houses are placed in the village, while its central road traverses these houses and subsequently forms the gate of the fortification.*
>
> *Very narrow streets and edifices squeezed together complete the area, surrounded by the exteriors of the houses. In the middle are the towers."*

This approximates the style of the village of Agios Georgios. The village, of course, did not have a special castle, except that of the Monastery, nor did it have iron doors. I do not know on what facts Zolotas bases the following in his *Istoria,* when he writes:

Part of the "Exo Horio" (Outer Village)
The neighborhoods of Batsilis, Agios Panteleimonas & Miloi are seen

Pantelis A. Mavrogiorgis

"The village was fenced, at other times, by strong walls with a tower."

Vios, probably influenced by Zolotas, says:

"The village had, at other times, a fort wall with a tower."

My opinion is that some confusion exists over the Tower and the fortress wall of the Monastery, about which Rodokanakis writes that *"Agios Georgios of* Sikousis of *Penthodou* (*Petsodou*)" was also among the strong towers.

CHAPTER 11
The Genoese Period

General Information

Chios remained under the control of the *Genouvezon* (Genoese) for two hundred and twenty years, specifically from 1346 to 1566 A.D., at which time the Turks overtook it. Since this period is unknown to many, I will cover it in detail.

Genoa, at that time, was an independent small state like Venice and other cities in Italy with intense competition among merchants and seamen.

A. The Takeover

Chios was then a very sought-after center of mercantile and economic traffic in the Aegean and the East. In order that Chios not be overtaken by the Venetians, the Democracy of Genoa paid Simona Viniozo, the owner of a private fleet comprised of twenty-nine galleons, to take over Chios on behalf of Genoa. Viniozo closed off the port, and following a three-month siege, overtook the castle and forged an agreement with Ioannis Zyvon, Administrator of Chios, in the Cathedral church of *Agios Nikolaos tou Frouriou* (Saint Nicholas of the Fort) on September 13, 1346. This agreement included a general amnesty for the inhabitants, concerning their lives and properties, and freedom in the performance of their religious duties. Aside from that, any privileges that had been ceded to monasteries or to private Chians – noblemen known as *chrysovoullatous* – through imperial chrysobulls during the Byzantine Era were also recognized.

Due to the fact that the Democracy of Genoa was not able to repay the expenses of the expedition immediately and compensate Viniozo and his twenty-nine partners, in 1347 they allowed them to exploit the economic wealth of Chios for the next twenty years. Viniozo and his galleon captains jointly formed a merchant marine company to use in Chios and named it *"Maona,"* and its members were called *"Maonies,"* a name that similar Genoese companies also used in Cyprus, Corsica, and elsewhere. The word *Maona* comes from the Arabic *Maounach* and means "an industrial or mercantile company."

The *Maonies*, under the dominion of Genoa, undertook the administration of Chios and its defense from enemies. At a later point, the members of the *Maona* began selling their stocks, which prompted the need to settle the financial differences that appeared. Therefore, Genoa decided to lease Chios for twelve years to twelve businessmen, some new and others from the old *Maona*.

This new *Maona* took control of Chios in November 1362, with the obligation to pay off the debt owed by Genoa to the old *Maona*. It created an organization within the company and named it *Albergo dei Giustiniani*, which means "lineage (mainly foreigners) of the Justinians." The stockholders proceeded to abandon their family names and took "Giustinian" as a surname, which was handed down to their descendants over the years. Thus, a number of Frankish Chians are called **Giustounias**, even to the years of the Turkish Occupation, as shown in many documents in the old codex of our village.

In 1363, the Emperor of Constantinople, Ioannis the 5th Paleologos, recognized the rights of the Justinians in Chios. Therefore the Genoese control over Chios was made official.

B. The Justiniani Despots of Chios

Genoa appointed the administrator of Chios and gave him the title of *Podesta* (Commissioner). There were twelve administrators under this commissioner, who were either elected or appointed to oversee the twelve departments into which they had divided the government of Chios. The administrative building was housed in the Castle, which was next to the dark prison. For their defense they maintained a fleet of thirty warships and about 800 mercenaries.

At first the Genoese treated the Chians harshly, even inhumanely. Karl Hopf characterizes them as the "Despots of Chios." For example, the theft of mastic – on which the Genoese maintained a monopoly – was inhumanely punishable by anything from a monetary fine to the removal of one's nose or even hanging – all dependent on the magnitude of the theft. Unbearable taxes were levied upon the population; properties were confiscated; residents were forced to do heavy, unpaid labor; and there were instances of abuse and humiliation of both clergy and laymen – all of which forced some well-known Chians to form a plot against the Genoese in 1380, using the church of Agios Georgios near Varvasi as a secret meeting location which was named *"Tou Katadoti"* ("The Informant") because the plot was reported to the Genoese and the participants were captured during on of their meetings.

In religious matters, the Genoese did not meet the terms of their agreement. As Catholics, they made every effort to intervene in the ecclesiastical

---

matters of the Orthodox dogma of Chios. The *Potestatoi* of the island did not allow an Orthodox Hierarch on Chios. So for the duration of the entire Genoese period, the Hierarch was replaced by a clergyman, known as a *Dikaios*, by order of the Patriarch.

In other instances, the occupiers acted in a positive manner and set the basis for development in Chios. They repaired the fort, surrounded the port with a wharf, they built seaside towers, erected forts on hillsides, and constructed tall, fortified towers in villages to safeguard the inhabitants and the agricultural production of the island from invaders. They created majestic edifices and, particularly in the area of Kambos, they built Catholic churches and monasteries, and also founded a school, a shipyard, aqueducts, a hospital, and a hospice for lepers.

In time, the administration became milder, with a relaxation of harsher methods of governing. Therefore, the parameters for a better quality of life were set. It seems that the Justinianes were influenced by the reduction of the population, due to the harsh measures taken earlier.

There was a large population of noblemen and bourgeois from Genoa comprising a higher social order on the island, which contributed to the basis for financial and cultural developments. A second population element concerned the *Genoutochiako,* who originally came from Genoa but became Hellenized through intermarriages, and were known as *frangochiotes* "Frankish Chians." A third reason for progress was the presence of *chrysovoullatoi,* the former Hellenic noblemen. These three sub-sections of the population became so intertwined over the years that the only distinctions among them were dogmatic in nature, because from the 16th century until the middle of the 18th century, mixed marriages were very common; therefore sacred services were performed without distinction in churches of Eastern or Western dogma.

The segment of higher society, which lived in Chios at the time, affected the financial and spiritual dimensions of the island in a beneficial manner for centuries. The Chians founded schools, sent young people abroad to study in Italy and, in general, mercantile and shipping development began. These factors, I believe, were among the reasons that the Turks, who later occupied the island, handled Chios in a privileged manner.

C. Sikousis During the Genoese Period

In the prior section, we offered general information about the Genoese period of Chios, since it also contains a portion of the history of our village and because there is often talk at Agios Georgis about the Genoese, yet we know nothing about them. From the time that we were children we would hear that the Tower and the wharfs in the countryside location of Notso Kipos were Genoese. Our parents would also tell us the same thing about the towers and fields of Sklavia and Makri.

Rodokanakis informs us that the Makri and other estates in Sklavia belonged to the family of Fornettou Justiniane also called Tsikka. There are also buildings that still exist today in Krina, Plagia, and Kanavoutsato that are attributed to the Genoese, as well. It is not unlikely, in fact, that the Genoese repaired the tower and fortress wall of the Monastery of our village. Rodokanakis mentions that one of the forty large, square towers was also that of Agios Georgios, and that each tower had a Genoese in charge of it.

Contrarily, Katlas writes that the Genoese had guards managed by Maones in fifteen forts or towers, "Kalamoti, Mesta, Melanio . . . Volisso, Elata, Rikoveri," yet he does not mention Agios Georgios at all.

The village of Agios Georgios entered the historical arena in the year 1518, and for the first fifty years of its development it was under the domination of the Genoese. They undoubtedly contributed, to some degree, to the colonization of the village with the political control they exercised in the last decades, offering asylum to the Hellenes who came from Anatolia pressured by the Turkish expansion.

As the population of the village gradually grew, it followed that they would pay taxes, which other villages also paid. The "Tobacco Tax" was a tax of six *yperpira* per year paid to the government by the head of each family. We do not know exactly how much the Agiorgousoi may have paid, because that particular tax was smaller in the poorer villages. In Pyrgi this tax was four yperpira, whereas at Mesta it was only three yperpira. Another tax levied was the so-called "Acrostic," an amount analogous with the size of the estate. The fact that the Agiorgousoi paid taxes is seen also in the will of Sofronios Sepsis, who left an order that the Monastery must pay an annual amount of eight yperpira the "Authentian," to the Justinianes in charge.

It is not possible to discuss the mandatory hand over of mastic to the special agents of the Maona, since Sikousis was later considered one of the Mastichochoria. In the old notary documents, there is rarely any mention in the rental and sales agreements of any mastic trees. From everything I know, Michele Justiniani first counts Agios Georgios among the Mastichochoria in 1658. Undoubtedly, the relationship that the Agiorgousoi had with the Justinianes probably was no accident, as it occurred due to some kind of guardianship regarding the governing of the Church and the Monastery. Sgouros claims that:

"there are monasteries in Chios, governed for centuries by the

Justinianes, on the basis of 'jus patronatus' (right of inheritance)."

The Gioustounianes retained this right during the initial centuries of the Turkish occupation, as well.

I have formulated the theory, in all probability, that is the reason Sofronios Sepsis appointed Frangiscon Gioustinia, Peri Gioustinia, and Giouzepe Gioustinia as Board Members and overseers of the Monastery. Furthermore, Peri and Giouzepe came from powerful families in Genoa: Peri being the grandfather of Cardinal Oratio Ioustiniane and Giouzepe being the second cousin of Alexander-Loggou Ioustiniane, Duke of Genoa. The Gioustounians were Board Members at Agios Georgios until 1656, the last of whom was Kosma Gioustounia, son of Andrea, who signed a sale dated December 5, 1656, according to page 70 of the old codex.

Pantelis A. Mavrogiorgis

CHAPTER 12
The Period of the Turkish Occupation

General Information

Chios fell into the hands of the Turks in 1566 and remained under their domination until November 11, 1912. For years the Turks had shown great interest in Chios, due to its wealth and geographic location. The Genoese, in order to avoid any problems, decided to give the Turks 10,000 ducats a year. In time, there were clashes between the Turks and the Genoese, which opened the path for the occupation of Chios by the Turks. The Turks complained, because the Genoese had neglected to pay taxes to them for two years and also because the Genoese were offering asylum to slaves who were fleeing Byzantium. In the *Tourkograikia* of Grusius, we read the following:

> *"Bienni tributum dare negavissent et quod receptum ibi haerent captive qui Bysantiane effugissent."*

However, the basic reason for disenchantment was the Turks' suspicion that the Maonis were passing on information to the rulers of Europe about the movements of the Turkish army and navy. According to the Turks, this caused Piali Pasha's failure to capture Malta. Thus, the Sultan, Suleiman the Magnificent, ordered Piali Pasha to capture Chios.

A. The Occupation

On April 15, 1566, Piali Pasha, allegedly a friend of the Genoese, arrived in Chios with 120 galleons. The following day, his army disembarked with swords hidden beneath their clothing. The premise was that they would buy food, since he had invited the Genoese governors of Chios to a reception on his flagship. During a conversation regarding taxes, without hesitation he had the governors bound in chains, and proceeded to take over the Administration Building in the castle with his army. He lowered the flag of Agios Georgios of Genoa and elevated the Half-Moon flag during blasts of the ships' cannons. In this manner, on April 17, 1566, Chios fell under Turkish rule without any resistance from either the fort or the countryside.

Following the takeover, thievery and pillages began. Piali himself usurped thirty-two orchards from the Genoese, including Krinas and twelve noble homes. Foteinos writes in *Neamonisia*:

> *"He grabbed quite a bit of money, fields, and homes to liberate. But, deceptively, he did not do that. On the contrary, he sent many of the Genoese to Constantinople. Besides that, he also sent twenty-four young men as a gift to Sultan Selim."*

Those young people suffered much torture, and for that reason the Western church numbers them amongst its saints.

Aside from the official and unofficial acts of thievery and pillage committed by the Turkish army, Islamization of Catholics and Orthodox occurred during the first period of the occupation, until the "privileges" were granted. Western churches were converted to mosques. The Catholic cathedral in the fort became a mosque and there is a plaque on the wall to this day commemorating the capture of Chios. Fortunately, by the order of the Sultan, no slaughters took place. Maybe it was destined for Chios to be under the knife of the Turk in 1822.

B. Privileges and Administration

The Sultans, Selim the 2nd (1567), Murat the 3rd (1578) and others bestowed *achtinamendes* (decisions or privileges) to Chios which initially improved the tax and penal legislation in existence during the time of the Genoese. The Sultans granted those privileges because the occupation of Chios took place without resistance and also because Chios had noteworthy men in Constantinople who had power in the Sultan's environment.

When Chios became a district of the Ottoman Empire, the Bey – later known as *"Muselimis"* – was its official administrator. He represented the authority of the state, which also included an interesting financial structure. He would buy the incoming taxes of the island for two years at a cost of 40,000 gold coins.

The *Zoumbasis*, who was a policeman and leader of the guards, would assist the Bey in carrying out his responsibilities. The *Kadis*, which was a stronger arm of law enforcement, represented Turkish justice. The *Kadis* brought tax and penal matters to trial and also presided over the religious court, where decisions were made about significant sales, *hotzetia* (ownership titles), and other civil matters. The First Secretary, known as the *Naitis*, assisted the *Kadis*.

The most important privileges given to the Chians were the inalienable rights of life and property. The *paidomazoma* (gathering of children) and forced Islamization were forbidden, freedom was given to perform religious ceremonies, and churches that had been destroyed were rebuilt. Chians were given the right to have their own notary offices and to compose notary deeds

Pantelis A. Mavrogiorgis

that stood up "before every rule and authority."

The *Kefalition* (head tax) and the estate or land tax upon the private countryside estates and homesteads were maintained, but the ten percent tax on farm produce was abolished. The secondary trade taxes for importing and exporting still applied. Maintenance of the privileges was quite arbitrary, as it depended upon the corruption level of each Turkish official, the Chians resorted to the Turkish custom of bribery.

Of great importance for the *Dioitikiti Praktiki* (Administrative Practices), in actuality, was the recognition of the self-governing system, with elected leaders (archons) – the *Demogerontes* (Elders of the community} – whom the Turks called *Moutarides,* and whose authority was overseen by the Turks. An annual election, certified by the *Mouselimis*, was held to select three to five leaders to serve for one year in the municipalities as *Demogerontes.* Their authority was administrative, judicial, and partly executive. They regulated situations that arose between citizens, they strove for keeping the customs of the people, had oversight of the schools and philanthropic organizations, and also had a voice in ecclesiastical issues. They organized conventions, appointed judges to the *Emborodikeio* (Trade Court) and the *Naftodikeio* (Naval Court), appointed *symvolaiografous* (notaries), and – together with the *Mouselimis* – set the taxes of the Chora and forty-two villages within their jurisdiction, since the Mastichochoria had their own administrators.

There were two bodies (of authority) which minimized, to some degree, the power of the *Demogerontes*: the *Megali Synelefsi* (Great Convention) of forty to fifty Elders, and the *Mikri Synelefsi* (Small Convention) of five to fifteen. The facts are that the *Demogerontes* of the municipalities were chosen from the "notable families," and that these individuals were an institution of "aristocratic democracy." It seems, however, that they handled their responsibilities with conscientiousness and objectivity. More importantly, they were obligated to give an accounting, at the end of their terms – just as it was in the ancient Athenian Democracy. For these reasons, they were honored and respected and obeyed by the inhabitants under their jurisdiction. It must be noted that, within this privileged administration, the prestige of the Orthodox Church was also restored with the appointment of a Metropolitan from the year 1571, as opposed to the situation that existed under the Catholic Genoese, who had minimized our church.

The *Demogerontes* many times used bribery to request that the tax collectors – who were consuls of Chios to Constantinople – bring various concerns before the Sultan and the Queen Mother in the *Ypsili Pyli* (Porte). It is characteristic that the *Demogerontes* were offering to Capoudan Pasha alone, the military administrator of the Aegean, 25,000 gold coins per year and were undertaking the responsibility that whenever a captain of the guard, an administrator or translator of the fleet arrived in Chios, they would pay their hospitality expenses for two to three months.

Nevertheless, under the conditions of the privileges of self-administration, and the restoration of the authority of the church through the appointment of a Metropolitan from the year 1571 on, the people of Chios – with their intellectual ability and efficiency – were able to cultivate education, develop trade and shipping businesses, and make Chios – after Constantinople and Smyrna – the most cultured land in all of the Turkish state.

C. The Mastichochoria During the Turkish Occupation

We will examine the history of our village during the years of slavery under the Turks within the framework of the history of the Mastichochoria. Since Sikousis was a newer village than the others, it was natural that the cultivation of mastic trees and the production of mastic were delayed, as we mentioned before. For this reason, Zolotas' claim that Agios Georgios was put under the jurisdiction of the administration of the Mastichochoria during the Turkish Occupation is justified. This favor was done not so much for the production of mastic, but because the Agiorgousoi were obligated to **supply the required lime**, and other materials used as fuel, to the Turks for their public buildings and fortifications. In 1810, Dominico Luigi Santi writes:

> "Of the twenty-one Mastichochoria, the most famous are Pyrgi, Nenita, and Kalamoti. Less prominent is the village of Agios Georgios, which is part of the Mastichochoria, but mastic is not currently produced probably due to the quality its mastic trees which are not as productive. Instead, the inhabitants of this village are occupied with the **making of lime**."

Independent of every other opinion, our village is correctly counted among the *Mastichochoria* since it also belongs to that region geographically and because, today, mastic is one of its most important products.

During the Turkish Occupation, the mastic was the criterion regulating the specific structure of governmental authority for the Mastichochoria, which comprised a second administrative area. This area had a loose association with the Turkish authorities and had no relationship at all with the Demogerontia of the city. Due to the production of mastic, the area was dedicated to the mother of each of the Sultans, resulting in the exercise of authority by eminent Ottomans appointed by the Porte. The most powerful ruler was the *Agas*, also known as *Sakiz Emines*, whose basic responsibility was the collection of mastic and the delivery of the product to the seraglio of the Sultan.

In the Mastichochoria, the legislation, the fees, and the taxes differed from the rest of Chios. These villagers were given the right to ring the bells of the churches during the sacred services and to wear white turbans like the Ottomans, whereas other villagers had to wear black ones. Despite all of this, life in the Mastichochoria was more torturous, due to the mastic. Fustel de Coulanges, a French traveler, says that:

> "The Chians don't rejoice over the most beautiful part of their wealth. This precious and unique gift of nature, which the popular religion attributed to the blood of a martyr (Agios Isidoros), didn't seem to be a blessing for a section of the island, but merely a cause of oppression."

D. The Production and Delivery of Mastic

Mastic was cultivated and produced exclusively for the Turks. From the production of almost 50,000 *okades* (62,000 kilos), 21,000 *okades* were destined for the Porte as an annual tax. The authorities set the tax on mastic for each of the villages and each individual producer. If the yield of a villager was insufficient to pay his tax, he was required to make up the difference in cash. When the yield was higher than the assessment imposed, the remainder had to be sold to the Agas, who set the price. Only small quantities made their way to the black market, since the penalties if one was caught were steep and could result in death, as had been the case when the Genoese were in power.

The villagers were told to gather in the village field to hear what the Agas had decided regarding the mastic. The day the Agas was due to come was called "*the feast of the Emine.*" He determined the exact day when the piercing of the mastic trees was to commence and the day all mastic in the villages was to be harvested. During production, locals and foreigners were forbidden from entering the mastic field areas, where the Agas would place guards in all of the important places.

Following the production phase, the mastic villagers transported the product, using their own animals and at their own expense, to the Kastro. As the historians inform us – from the age of the Maonese – it was the custom whenever the "*mastic tax caravan*" set forth from the villages, it would be accompanied by villagers playing drums and musical instruments all the way to the Administration Building. From a document from *Kalamoti*, we learn of the amount of mastic given as a "gift" (*kaniski*) by the villagers to various individuals, during the delivery of the mastic.

"1712: The secretary messier Bastias took 73 okades of the best quality mastic from our village to give to Minis. And the secretary said that, from the 73 okades the Agas took 15, the bolombos 12, the Koskinistis [siever] 12, the Konaxis [head guard] 2, the Turkish secretary 2, Mise Bastia helpers 2, chavala 2, Mini's helpers 2. The secretary kept 23 okades for his gift. Thus the Elders Kostas of Angerous and his companions told us.""

From a document in a codex of *Pyrgi*, we are informed of the villagers' obligation to use their own animals in the service of the Agas.

"Today the Elders of the village, the priests and residents, are present all together for one purpose: for the Agas to inform the Board Members of the following. Every day that the Agas is in our village, six animals should be at his disposal. And if the Board Members prevent or delay this from happening (alikountisoun) and a homeowner does not abide by this or appears to be disobedient, the Agas will punish (paidevgetai) them. And, at times, whichever group of Elders (gerontiliki) seeks to invalidate the present letter, that group should give the current Agas 500 silver coins (aslania) I say five hundred.

This was written in the year 1791, December 8th, with the following as witnesses . . . .""

E. The Self-Administration of the Mastichochoria

At the time of the Turkish Occupation, administrative authority was held by the Elders, *Demogerontes*, a type of self-government similar to the island's *Demogerontia*. Every year, two to five Demogerontes were selected and given the responsibility of attending to issues that arose during their one-year term. I cannot ascertain how these selections were made or who had the right to be chosen. It does seem, though, that these men were villagers and, in particular, those who we referred to as "good citizens" until recently. I was also not able to find out whether all of the village residents had the right to vote, or if that privilege was only given to the more affluent. I also do not know whether they were selected during a general meeting in the village or were appointed just as the church Board Members were. And in considering those Board Members, we must note that in the documents of various villages, the Board Members also had community duties that were mainly financial. They were considered colleagues of the Demogerontes and members of the *Gerontosymvoulio* (Council of Elders), as we learn from an 1878 document from Tholopotami:

"Since the elected Board Members are also considered members

---

of the Gerontosymvoulio, it was necessary for them to have half of the seal of the village and the privilege of working with the contemporary Elders in order to prevent injustices and assist with the implementation of justice."

Nevertheless, we must consider these Board Members as leaders within the village. I noticed that both the Demogerontes and the Board Members were usually present and signed as witnesses when wills and dowry agreements were made in our village.

The main task of the Demogerontes was the collection of taxes, the undertaking of hospitality – known as *Turkofagia*, for Turkish notables who would arrive in the village – *Paroikada* (the collection of money and chickens) from the residents for the expenses of the administrative offices of the village, the gifts, and the tips.

In addition, the Demogerontes worked to reconcile the differences amongst the *paroikoi*, to mediate in disagreements between Turks and Christians, to oversee agricultural safety, and to take an active part in village matters – both general and specific – in cooperation with the members of the Board and the *Vekilides*. They also had to arrange village meetings in order to make decisions on various matters. The *Vekilides* or *Eforoi* were two elected archons with more authority than the Demogerontes, since their jurisdiction extended to all of the villages comprising the *Demos of Mastichochoria*. The mastic villagers were involved in common meetings in *Koini, Sikelia*, or *Armolia*.

The Demogerontes of the villages elected the Vekilides for a term of one year. From among ten individuals presented to them, all of whom hailed from the most notable families – like the Stamoulis of Kallimasia, the Mogiadis of Vessa, and the Moulos of Agios Georgios – two were selected. Secondarily, the Vekilides had the powers of the Elders and the responsibilities that the Demogerontia of Chios had for the non-mastic producing villages. They gathered in the *Koino*, a special building in the *Kaloplytou* area of Chios, and they represented the Mastichochoria before the Turkish authorities. Here is an example of that session:

"In the name of the Lord, Amen. Today the priests and Elders and the common people of Kalamoti are gathered, and according to the old custom of this village, they appointed the following Board Members of the village: Kostan Glaftron, Stefanon Maïstron, and Ioannin Kynigon, who shall serve the village for one year from today in any capacity and any work which may arise. Those who signed above and below will remain to give the Board Members and the bosses 45 silver coins for whatever expenses they have in

the village. If the village has no other expenses, only they should take one chicken from each inhabitant, as per this order.
(The present document was written and read aloud in the Livadi (Meadow) in the year 1686, February 9, third day, second hour)
The protopresbyter, the Gerontes (Elders), and several village residents are signing this with their own hand."

Here is a decision made by the Vekilides that relates to the dress code for girls:

"Elders, Board Members, and men and women of the twenty-one Mastichochoria, we hereby give you notice that a complete and fervent decision was made by the presently undersigned individuals that from today, according to a strict order, we are writing that your daughters are not to wear gold, woven clothes, nor silk dresses, nor silk head scarves – that is, "caps" – nor thick, silk, flowery dresses to the feasts of celebrations, neither at any marriage nor any other day . . . If the elders in charge of each village appear negligent or learn or hear that such things were worn and they do not take action, they will receive double the punishment due to them.

October 15, 1850
Ioannis Tzourias, Vekilis
Stamatis Tziliakos, Vekilis"

Pantelis A. Mavrogiorgis

CHAPTER 13
The Revolution of 1821

A. Tobazis With a Fleet in Chios

The Proclamation of the Revolution of 1821 finds Chios unprepared and somewhat numb, because its geopolitical position is near the bloodthirsty mouth of the Ottomans, and

> *"because a great number of Chians dwelt in Smyrna and Constantinople for trade reasons,"*

as Konstantinos Koumas, the esteemed professor, who was teaching there at the time, wrote. However, there were not only commercial and economic factors that connected Chians with Turkey. Some prominent Chians held important governmental positions – officially or unofficially – in the *Phanar* and in the Sultan's court.

The peculiarities of the local conditions were major reasons Chios, like other Greek areas, initially remained outside of the movement for independence. Nevertheless, the tragic fate of Chios emerges at the dawn of April 27, 1821 when Captain Tobazis – with a fleet of eleven boats from Ydra, seven boats from Spetses, and three from Psara – all docked at the *Pasha's Vrisi* (Fountain), in order for Chios to take part in the national uprising. The captain sent a messenger to the villages with a proclamation but did not get the expected response.

Following this event, the Turks closed themselves in the fort, took as hostages Metropolitan Platon along with thirty other eminent individuals, and locked them in the dark prison inside the Kastro. This caused Tobazis to abandon his plans. This is what he wrote in his diary:

> *". . . an escaped worker from the capital city came and told us that the nobles and the Bishop are in the Kastro and that there are thirteen Anatolian guards outside the castle guarding it and that the Turks are running to the villages to find and confiscate weapons."*

Tobazis' decision to abandon the effort was strengthened by an event that occurred that same day. Two Greek ships sacked a Turkish ship that was taking pilgrims to Mecca, the sacred city of the Ottomans. After killing the pilgrims,

---

they threw the corpses into the sea and began arguing amongst themselves over the distribution of the spoils. Here, Tobazis notes:

> ". . . the disorder on these two ships, the capture of prominent people and the Hierarch in the Kastro, and the difficulty of conversing with them, made us abandon the expedition to Chios in order not to do harm, instead of benefit".

It seems that, secretly, Chian Demogerontes visited Tobazis and enumerated the dangers facing the island. Filemon's work, *"Dokimion peri tis Ellinikis Epanastaseos"* ("Essay about the Greek Revolution"), quotes the concerns of the Demogerontes: "Several notables, such as Michalis Vlastos and Ioannis Patrikousis, joined us and presented the extent of the dangers faced not only by the entire island, which is without weapons, but also by the Chians living outside of Chios."

Neofytos Vamvas was an eminent professor at the *Scholi tis Chiou* (School of Chios), and a member of the *Philiki Etairia* (Secret Society of Friends). He was in Hydra then and was the main initiator and promoter of the Tobazis Plan for the revolutionary expedition, which was proven to be a wrong move at the time. Once the eminent Chians had been imprisoned and the villagers had surrendered their weapons, terror was rampant, especially when armed Turks arrived in Chios. Not a day passed without murder, thievery, and harsh words. The authoritarian administrator Vachit Pashas, who had been sent from the Porte as a special envoy, ordered thousands of people to open the *Souda* (moat) to increase security in the castle. Thousands of people, practically slaves, worked toward the opening of the Souda. Mamoukas likens Vahit Pashas to

> "another Pharaoh, an overseer who tyrannizes the workers, depriving them of food and drink, in order to complete his diabolical plan to clean Souda."

In addition to the humiliation, the Demogerontia was forced to pay the expenses of the Turkish guards and Vachit Pashas, as well.

B. The Revolution of Chios

The success of Lycurgos Logothetis' revolution in Samos, inspired other patriots to revolt.

> "For this reason, certain Chians, Lesvians, and Cypriots, seeing the present time as suitable, gave of themselves for the liberation of their homeland. And the protagonists of the Chians – Ioannis Rallis, Nikolaos Mylonas, and Neofytos Vamvas – cooperated with

their entire souls".

Ioannis Rallis, a member of the Secret Society of Friends, arrived in Samos in order to cooperate with Lycurgos Logothetis for the revolution in Chios but, not finding the conditions appropriate, they postponed the campaign. Lycurgos wrote the following to Ypsilantis:

> *"I postponed the Chios campaign for better circumstances, although some patriots from Chios were urging me to go ahead with it."*

Nevertheless, at about the same time an officer in the French army, Antonios Bournias from *Pyrama* in Chios, along with others from Chios, persuaded Lycurgos to plan a landing on Chios. According to the historian Kokkinos, this movement would result in the destruction of Chios. He says, with austere criticism:

> *"Logothetis saw in this campaign only the possible gains, without considering the more grievous results; and this without communicating with the government* (in other words, Ypsilantis)."

On March 11, 1822 Lycurgos and his co-leader, Bournias, landed at *Mega Limniona*. After the failure of the initial skirmish, the Turks locked themselves in the Kastro. In a rush of success, villagers took clubs and guns and joined Lycurgos the following day. Lycurgos positioned canons to attack the castle more effectively, he replaced the Demogerontes with a group of seven "superintendents," he both sent and sought assistance from Psara, Hydra, Spetses, and the central government,

> *"because they were deficient of armaments, explosives, canons, and – even worse – food."*

The effort was haphazard. The Psarians sent gunpowder, bullets, and six ships. But the arguments that occurred between Bournias and Logothetis worsened the situation. In the mean time, they sent an ultimatum to the Turks with a demand to surrender within three days and with a promise that:

> *"They will not harm the inhabitant Ottomans, who will be allowed to travel to the East without being charged. The Turks found themselves in an untenable position. The governor, Vachit, was so unsure of what to do that he sought the counsel of others, some of whom advised that he surrender the city. But, in the end, an oulema's (clergyman's) suggestion prevailed, when he said, "We must answer them with the language of fire and with the mouth*

of the sword."

C. The Catastrophe of Chios

On March 30, Holy Thursday, a strong fleet of 7,000 men under Admiral Kara Ali disembarked, uniting with their fellow Turks. After their initial resistance, Lycurgos and Bournias were without supplies, therefore they had to abandon their siege on the castle and withdraw. After another disagreement, Lycurgos went to Lithi and Bournias to Nea Moni.

From this point forward, the tragic fate of Chios began. Vachit ordered the garrison to attack the "infidels." Hordes of barbarians poured into the city and slaughtered men, women, and children; they set fire to the churches and philanthropic institutions. A characteristic sample of this butchery, was committed here when the Turks killed seventy lepers who lived at the leper colony. Three of these people escaped and hid beneath a little bridge. *"Much wailing and crying was heard."* Frightened out of their minds, multitudes abandoned their homes and fled from village to village in an attempt to escape. They hid *"in caves and holes in the Earth."* The western shores filled with people, their hearts in their mouths, as they awaited sailboats on which to escape.

On April 2, the day of Pascha, the tale of the holocaust in the Monastery of Agios Minas is written in blood. There the Turks slaughtered 3,000 Chians, whose bones exist to this day, causing visitors to shudder.

The following day, a new attack took place at Agios Georgios, where Lycurgos Logothetis had taken refuge. The massacre spread to Nea Moni, Anavatos, and Kavo Melanio, while the Samiotes fled the island and sailed to Psara. On April 17, Kara Ali announced that the inhabitants would be given amnesty only if they would return to the cities and villages they had abandoned. Ambassadors from Austria and England undertook the responsibility to present this proposal to the inhabitants and persuade them to accept it. So the villagers, trusting these envoys, fell into the trap laid by the Turks and met bloody deaths. Among these tragic victims are Metropolitan Platon Frangiadis and sixty-three noblemen, all of whom were hung in the *Plateia Vounakiou*. These are some of Mamoukas's recollections.

> *"On the 23rd of April, a Sunday, around four o'clock in the morning, they began to take them out: first the Metropolitan and another nine; subsequently, ten at a time. They hung the fifty-five hostages of the Chora within an hour and a half."*

While Kara Ali disagreed with the hangings, Vachit Pasha ordered him to do it in order to "satisfy the thirst of his soldiers." Vachit admits to sixty-three

Pantelis A. Mavrogiorgis

hangings in his memoirs. Chios was at the mercy of the Turks.

The fleet that the Greeks had assembled at Psara to strike the Turkish fleet at Tsesme did not undertake the intended attack due to disagreements among the fleet admirals and disobedience from the sailors of the fleet. The heroic people of Psara could not endure the misfortune of Chios. They were near enough to see the smoke from fires that the Turks had set in Chios and could hear the sighs of the multitudes who had fled to Psara to escape the carnage. According to Nikodemos, a group of Psarian sailors one night made a vow on the icon of the Virgin Mary to burn the Turkish fleet right in front of Chios. Two fire ships – with Admiral Konstantinos Kanaris on the Psarian ship and Admiral Andrew Pipinos on the Hydrian ship – accompanied by four other ships to assist once the Turkish fleet was burning, set out from Psara on the night of June sixth to seventh and approached the Turkish armada. The Turks, unsuspecting, were celebrating the great feast of Bairami. Kanaris skillfully maneuvered his ship and set the Turkish admiral's ship afire, causing more than two-thousand Turks to die, together with their fleet admiral, Kara Ali, whose tomb remains in the castle to this day.

The Turks, enraged, went into the Mastichochoria the following day with 20,000 troops and totally destroyed them. The Chian population, once numbering more than 100,000 was now reduced to a mere 2,000 souls; some 40,000 escaped to the Cyclades, Pireas, and the Peloponessus. Vachit Pashas, the human monster, boasts thusly in his memoir:

> "During the whole duration of the skirmishes, 600 Islamists died, and many others were wounded and became incapacitated. Modestly, I declare that 1109 heads of priests, officials, and other rebels were taken by the sword; and 25,000 boys and 5,000 girls were taken as slaves."

Following these events, Vachit lost the title of Pasha and was exiled to Thrace; Lycurgos Logothetis sent a written apology to the Greek government, and Bournias was left indigent. Regarding the destruction of Chios, each of these men shares a portion of the responsibility.

D. Agios Georgios and the Massacres of the Revolution

After the slaughter at Agios Minas, the Turks launched an attack against the village of Agios Georgios on April 3. There were 2,300 revolutionary Chians who had taken refuge there, according to Trikoupi, who says that

> "quite a few armed Samians, including Lycurgos who were there also (in Agios Georgios), fled in hopes of resistance."

The Turks closed off the village from three sides, Dafnonas, Zyfias, and Sklavia. After a battle, they entered and completely slaughtered the people, among whom was the mathematician Tselepis, a famous professor from the School of Chios.

To further inform our readers, we will present excerpts from the official narrations of various individuals.

1. From the *"Apologia"* (Defense) of Lycourgos Logothetis

"After all that, we came to Lithi, where we safeguarded the strongest positions. Throughout the day, March thirty-first, we did not see the enemy. This morning, Hatzi Antonis Bournias also came and urged us to go to Nea Moni, where the Vrontadousoi are standing with weapons, and once we meet with them we should unite for battle. But we did not judge that place as suitable. We found Agios Georgios Sikousis to be much more appropriate, because we could freely communicate with Psara from that location.

On April third, at eight o'clock, three groups of enemies – numbering about one thousand – appeared, each coming from a different location in order to surround us. We were approximately a group of four hundred soldiers, and we opposed the enemy. We struck and we fought, but then we retreated, as it was impossible to continue. We then scattered here and there, and fifty of us took the road to Psara.

All the villages raised the Turkish flag. This was actually the main reason we decided not to continue to fight and rushed to flee Chios. We had enemies both internal and external."

(Logothetis, in his "Apologia" is using harsh words when he speaks of "internal enemies," whom he refers to as "Grecoturks" in other sections of that same document.)

2. From the *Memoirs* of Vachit Pasha

"Suddenly, we heard that Logothetis, the rebel leader, was encamped at the village of Agios Georgios and boasting that – according to the information he received from the leaders of the revolution in Peloponnesus – 150 Greek ships, with a large amount of food, explosives and supplies, will arrive within days and they

Pantelis A. Mavrogiorgis

should not despair after one or two attacks. This was said so the villagers would not lose courage but, instead, should keep their rebel weapons trained on the respected government of the Great Sultan, their leader.

Our own soldiers did not hesitate to attack this village, either, although it was defended by the rebels – as directed by Logothetis – until the rebels retreated under the onslaught. O, woe to the Infidels. Much blood has flowed here from the Infidels after six hours of stubborn resistance from these besieged ones."

3. From the *Memoirs* of Grigoris Foteinos

"On March 30, 1822, Holy Thursday, the Ottoman fleet appeared (This is a reference to the armada of Kara Ali) *on a religious day, during which the Christians receive Holy Communion. Just as when a wolf appears before a flock of sheep, causing them to scatter in fear, thus it was with us Christians, everyone fleeing far from the enemies to save ourselves. On that same day, the Samian fighters ended the siege, and the entire army deserted and gathered at the village of Agios Georgios Sykountos, where most of the teachers and priests had taken refuge – and where most were brutally murdered. The thoughtless and haughty Lycurgos, without ever fighting, had deserted the victims and fled to the village of Agios Georgios.*

That same day, we abandoned our priceless items by putting them into deep holes and proceeded to Agios Georgios Sykountos, taking only those things that were absolutely necessary. There, most of the inhabitants of the cities of the Katochoria (Lower Villages) *gathered, along with the Samians. We remained here on Holy Friday and most of Holy Saturday and subsequently learned that our enemies were moving toward the neighboring villages and suburbs, mercilessly committing the same atrocities. Therefore, we decided to move on to Lithi in order to find a ship.*

We arrived in Lithi at night and discovered endless multitudes in the countryside. We remained there for the night, but set out to return to Agios Georgios again the next day. On the Monday after Pascha, those who had already destroyed Agios Minas and felt courageous as victors, attacked Agios Georgios, coming not by the usual road but over a mountain pass from Zyfia. We learned of this strategy quickly and left for Makri and Eso Kipo,

---

then ascended to the east of the Karteros River through the Kondylopou, and we arrived at that large village, Pyrgi, which was crammed with fugitives. Those who attacked Agios Georgios plundered, slaughtered, and imprisoned."

(Foteinos was only ten years old when these events took place, yet he actually wrote his memoirs at a very old age.)

4. From a Letter Written by Argenti to His Brothers

[June 30, 1822] *"From the day that the Turkish armada arrived, the greater portion of inhabitants left for Psara and other islands. Since the wretched Samians followed their evil and unlearned leader, Logothetis Lycurgos, who first fled before the armada had even docked, they never fought any battle. It is true, though, that while some of the northern villages attempted to hold onto their areas, the criminal Lycurgos – moved by the tears of his compatriots – gathered some of the deceived soldiers at the village of Agios Georgios, in order to at least open the road to Kambos, in order for us to get to the towers and retrieve our supplies and food, so that we and they do not die from hunger. But what resistance could be given by people deprived of food and supplies?*

It is very odd for me to add that, while the Turks were already ascending to Agios Georgios, the spokesman of the criminal Lycurgos was requesting lead items – that could be used to make bullets – from the villagers taking flight. He did this while simultaneously deceiving us with nonexistent news. He prevented us from leaving the village until, at last, we saw the Turks descending from the peak of the mountain. And then a great multitude of people, us among them, fled. However, very many perished in this place."

(Augustus Argentis is writing *"under the pressure of events as they are happening,"* and that is probably why he uses those particular characterizations regarding Lycurgos. Some information is also imprecise. It is a fact, as witnessed by Vachit Pasha, that after the appearance of the fleet, the revolutionaries battled in Trouloti and obstructed the fleet.)

5. From a Publication by Vik. Koukouridis

"My grandmother, Despina Fragakis, who was the ten-year-old daughter of a priest in Agios Georgios Sikountis, remembers

Pantelis A. Mavrogiorgis

seeing one evening, through a crevasse in the high mountains of her village, flames rising from the burning flagship of Karali's flagship. Around noon on a nice day, several days after what happened in the sea, hordes of Turks, seeking revenge, stormed into the village. A few of the residents fled to the mountains and the shores.

My great grandfather, a good man, petitioned the God Almighty to defend the country from its enemies and to safeguard it 'from fire, sword, sudden war, and the invasion from foreigners.' His prayers were those he was accustomed to reciting in church services during the blessings of the five loaves of bread, yet he was unable to flee and was killed. He believed unshakably, from the manner in which he was raised and from his work as a priest, in the power of the Divinity to protect him from evil.

After the slaughter of his family and the torching of his home, he was hung in the narthex of his church after being ordered to step on the Crucifix. The Turks, enraged at his refusal, **impaled this unknown Christian martyr** *– whose name I can no longer recall – to a pole, to be known only among the angels and be adorned with the crown of a martyr."*

(This martyred priest, whose name was found in the Codex of the village, number 1043, was named papa Antonios Fragakis. He signed a document in 1818 as a Board Member of the church of Agios Georgios.)

6. From the *History of Chios*, by G. Zolota

"The Turk, Sali Agas, hated the head priest of Agios Georgios and took revenge upon him in the following manner: He took the priest, put a harness in his mouth, sat on him, whipped him, and rode towards the town, promising to grant him azati (liberation of a captive). *Arriving at Chora three hours later, an elderly lady who was following this caravan all the way to the River Kaloplyti, heard the rider saying to the 'horse,' 'Oh, Priest, we are nearby.' Dismounting, the driver placed the priest on the ground and said, 'Behold, your freedom, filthy priest,' and he cut off his head."*

7. Narration of Gianni Zacharia (from *Agios Giorgis Sikousis*)

"I was twenty years old during the giourousia (attacks). *When the Turks showed up, I was at home and I hid. My father was in Mesta, where the Kastrinoi* (the inhabitants of the Kastro) *– who*

had gone there with their families – gave him letters. But they caught him together with Nika and took him to Mpanio.

My mother and I stuffed ourselves down into the Kato Pigadia in the cave above the Tsoumbari, where no one found us. At the time that Kanaris from Psara and Nikolis Pantelios from our village burned Pasha Gementzi (Kara Ali) along with 800 Turks, we spent twenty days hiding there, without bread. But at night we would come into the village, where piles of corpses were laying, because 70,000 Turks (the number is a figment of his imagination) *had came to this location. I could see them from our hiding spot.*

In Kartera, a Moros (black/dark/Arab) *went to kill a Liapi* (Arvanitis)*, and they both fell into the deep part of the river* (the Karteros River) *and died. When night arrived, I discovered three kosaria* (a kosari is worth twenty grosia) *on the body of the Liapi.*

Right after this ortaliki (incident)*, we gathered five comrades and went into the village. An infidel, Ali Tselepis, was astride his horse and was putting obstacles in the way of the people. I'm surprised that no one killed him. All five comrades were hidden on top of Lepro mountain." We climbed down forty steps and descended to what might have been an old hermitage. There, at Lithi and at Avgonyma, we went down and took supplies; food.*

In Mpou (the village Square)*, there were two Turks who were taking down doors from houses and setting them on fire in order to bake bread. At that point, Panteliaros said to Savlas, 'What are you thinking, Savla?' They charged these Turks and killed them both in the attack of six years later."*

8. Narration of Kostantis Kalagyros (from *Agios Georgios Sikousis*)

"The Kalagyroudes were of the old inhabitants of our village. The family included two priests, Papa Giorgis and Papa Pantelis; and also Hatzi Kostantis, their brother.

In the Revolution of 1821, the Turks invaded Chios without countering any resistance. When Kanaris burned the Armada, the Turks became angry and began slaughtering residents throughout Chios. Those who were able to escape hid in the mountains and in caves, because the Turks were hunting them as though they were goats.

The Turks caught the two priests outside the village in Koukoumos, put ropes around their necks and dragged them, using a piece of wood, until their heads split open. All the while, the priests screamed, "God be merciful to me!" They caught the priests' brother, Hatzi Kostantis, on a mountain, along with another three men. They rounded them up and took them to Agioi Viktores, the church in Droposi.

When the Turks fell asleep, Kostantis Kalagyros nodded to the captives, indicating that they should escape, but they refused to do so.

Therefore, Kostantis, my great grandfather, left by himself and found his wife up at Lakki. Her throat had been slit, so he pressed on the wound to keep her alive. He hoisted her onto his shoulder, where she died. Afterwards, he took her to Fa, where he had a field. He created an opening in a wall and pushed her body into it so that dogs would not defile it. Afterwards, he left from Lithi and went to Andros."

(The Kalargyros family were in fact from the old inhabitants of the village. On pages 66, 67 of the old Codex Ioannis Kalargiros signs rental agreements the as Abbot of the Monastery for the years 1665 to 1669. In addition, on page 51 of the same Codex on another rental agreement Georgios Kalargyros signs as a witness. On another document he signs as Kokkinokolos a nickname which was passed down to the narrator old-Konstantis Kalargyros whom I had known in the village.)

9. From the Impressions of Traveler Anton Prokesh von Osten

In 1825, he departed from Nea Moni in order to visit Agios Georgios:

"We descended through a dangerous path to the village of Agios Georgios, which appears to be a wealthy area with well-built homes made of stone. Logothetis, after the evacuation of Nea Moni, continued his retreat to this village, which is not more than two hours from there.

The Turks had attacked the inhabitants, and nearly everyone was murdered. Only a few homes were then (1825) inhabited anew. We visited one of those homes, and we found the people to be hospitable. There was a little girl there who was about four or five years old. She had beautiful eyes and was happy, and I especially liked her. If I had not been ashamed of my entourage, I would have given her a big kiss.

Agios Georgios had been one of the Mastichochoria, but from that time on, the mastic trees had lost their strength."

(Von Osten has made a number of errors here. These are that Logothetis retreated from Nea Moni and went to Agios Georgios, that Agios Georgios was prosperous, and that it had **once been** one of the Mastichochoria.)

10. From Folklore

The Destruction of Chios

"Listen for me to tell you of the suffering of our Chios.

Such Greek enslavement never before existed in the world.

In eighteen hundred and twenty-two the Samians decided to take over Chios. Samians decided to assume the leadership, but they didn't have ordino (help) *from the three islands* (Hydra, Spetses, and Psara). *Logothetis and Bournias gathered the askeri* (soldiers) *and informed the Chians that they have seferi* (a state of war).

They disembarked at Thymiana and made preparations to take Chios, the worthy city. When the Chians heard this, they went and worshipped him. The poor people took courage, believing that they would be liberated. They worshipped him like a god, and they glorified him like a god, and he urged them to hail him by shouting, Zito, 'Hail!'

The Greeks asked for the keys to the castle, so that they could occupy the castle to force the Turks to worship the Greeks. On Holy Thursday, the Turkish Armada showed up. When the Samians saw, they were terrified. They abandoned the tapies (fort), *they left the cannons, and they spent the day mourning their fate, like beautiful peacocks. They ran to the mountains like wild goats. They went to the shores to find boats. Then they saw a green flag at the castle. Woe, what a sigh occurred that day.*

The castle door opened, and the Tangalakia (unruly, harsh, barbaric Turks) *emerged. They drew their swords and took to the streets. They cut Touloumbatzides* (the firemen) *the brave lads, taking women slaves, with their infant children.*

Beautiful girls, holding their hair, were taken to the East by the

Tangalakia. They took over mansions that contained an abundance of silver and diamonds, and were as noble in appearance as consulates. My Chians, of noble blood and considerable education, who sat on your horses like Janissaries but did not condescend to set foot on the ground. You did not descend stairs so as not to make yourselves sick. You have now suffered great evil, you unfortunate ones. They send letters to France and to Russia of the harm they have suffered and they are seeking protection. Everything has been destroyed nothing remains standing. There is only the black smoke that comes out from Chios.

Little birds of Mise Meni and Deli Thanasi no longer chirp – because Chios has perished."

CHAPTER 14

From the Massacres to Liberation

A. The Campaign of Fabvier and Some Other Events

With a short description, we will attempt to draw a picture of the most important events to bridge the time difference from the destruction that occurred in 1822 until November 11, 1912, the day that Chios was liberated. From the approximately 35,000 Chians who had the good fortune to escape the Turks, the farmers gradually began to repatriate southern Chios.

The Turkish administrator, Yiousouf Pashas, promised the mastic villagers that they could return to their homes and properties. However, the Turks did not extend that same privilege to the merchants, businessmen, and industrialists of Chora; they did not allow them to return. Nevertheless, one contingent of Chora dwellers who had not taken part in the revolution – either due to their absence abroad or because they had fled to Asia Minor during those critical times – did return to Chios freely. Thus the Chora was not completely devoid of inhabitants, so the Turkish administrator appointed Elders, according to the previous administrative system.

All of those individuals who had been off the island, especially the active and patriotic merchants from Syros, undertook the initiative to organize an expedition for a French colonel named Favbier, who then headed the army that landed at Megas Limionas during October 17 - 18, 1827. The main contingent of Turks had already withdrawn to the fort, following some minor resistance. However, they continued to receive supplies by sea, because the blockade was incomplete. Yiousouf Pashas, commander of 2,500 Turks, attempted to escape from the fort but failed. The long siege on the fort (by Favbier and his troops) was discouraging to both the Turks within the fort and the Chians, who were still traumatized by their recollections of the massacres of 1822. On March 1, 1828, Favbier was forced to order a retreat to Mesta, due to a lack of weapons and food, combined with the appearance of the Turkish fleet under Tachir Pashas.

Around 1830, when the free Greek state began to organize itself, Chians started returning to their homes with a feeling of certainty and security, and life in Chios once again returned to normalcy. However, **in 1850**, a dreadful frost destroyed the citrus trees, killed the mastic trees, and affected the olive, almond and fig trees.

In 1866, due to the interest of the residents of the countryside in taking part in the administration, the institution of Demogerontia was abolished. From then on, numerous administrative duties passed to the Metropolitan, who together with the tax officials oversaw the philanthropic institutions and schools, and also had the responsibility of hearing cases involving family and inheritance disputes.

B. The Catastrophe (Earthquake) of 1881

I can recall hearing villagers and others throughout Chios speaking about the earthquake, which took place on March 27, 1881. That particular day left such an impression of massive destruction that it was unforgettable to the people. In fact, they would refer to themselves in terms of the earthquake saying, "During that catastrophe, I was [for example] ten years old." A total of 4,869 individuals were victims of this dreadful event; of those 3,558 died and 1,311 were wounded. It resulted in the destruction of the city of Chios, the Kambochora, as well as the southern villages of Kallimasia, Tholopotami, Katarraktis, Nenita, and Mesa Didyma.

However, in Agios Georgios, due to the mountainous terrain of the village, the destruction was minimal. Houses in the *Mesa Geitonia* were either totally ruined or became uninhabitable.

K. Papamichalopoulos in his book *From the Ruins of Chios, 1881* on page 26 exaggerates regarding the destruction of the village when he writes that:

> *"We were above Sklavia, a village occupied by Westerners [Catholics]. Stones make the roads impassable. From here, the **village of Agios Georgios** appears. We can distinguish houses standing here and there and a mill, which has been spared, still working."*

N. Damianos writes in his report that there were 34 dead, 13 wounded, and 1,520 who survived. Dr. Stamatios Konstaninidis crafted a powerful image of the destruction:

> *"I was on the bridge of Varvasi when a fearful underground noise with seismic tremors startled me. The sides of the bridge opened and closed with the forward-backward movement that occurred. Thick clouds of dust covered my eyes. From end to end, a noise could be heard beneath the ground. Homes were being torn down, the dying and wounded cried out, there was desperation in the sounds of the wailing from those who were crushed, and there were loud shouts and the shrieking of dogs, continual thundering*

Earthquake ruins in the neighborhood of Lakos

Pantelis A. Mavrogiorgis

*from beneath the Earth – which was a constant and indescribably
weird noise that mixed with the cries of despair."*

Spyridon Paganelis who visited Chios on March 25, three days after the earthquake wrote:

*"The earthquake took place on Sunday at 1:45 p.m. It came with a
roar of thunder that passed from east to west. The ground above
shook, then more dreadful tremors followed, taking a semicircular
shape. The ground on the eastern shore was ripped apart, and
water poured forth from various points within the streets of
Kambos. The sea appeared blurry, and the waters had risen. The
city was destroyed, and the magnitude of destruction leaves one
without the strength to even think."*

Elsewhere:

*"As I ran on the road toward Kambos, I saw a multitude of people in
the middle of a field. Approaching them, I burst into tears. These
unfortunate souls were performing the service of the Salutation
of the Panagia. They had placed a table there and set the icon of
a saint upon it, and the priest was reciting the salutations with
passion, as the multitude cried out to God for mercy. That scene
was both majestic and tragic!"*

For many years, Chians rang the bells in mourning as liturgies and litanies were performed, and they fasted in commemoration, even forgoing oil.

Since the people's way has always been to express hardships genuinely and emotionally, with spontaneity in both verse and song, we will close the chapter with a related poem.

C. The Earthquake of 1881 (Verse)

*"With what heart, with what soul can I open my lips
to write in pen of the destruction of Chios?
In one-thousand eight-hundred eighty-one
I take in hand the paper with the grieving pen.
Trembling, I hold it to write the misfortune –
our unjust death, to cry from the heart.
It was a Sunday, on the twenty-second of March
a great earthquake occurred; Tsesmes and Chios were lost.
It was one-thirty in the afternoon,
and Chios began trembling with all its villages.*

You could hear the Earth grunting and the walls falling.
It kills young men, it kills young women, it crushes fine lads.
Young, old, were running in the streets to escape,
and the walls are falling and mightily crushing them.
All poor and wealthy, and those used to a good life,
in the cold are staying up at night, naked, or not dressed warmly.
No matter who escaped, you see them sad:
they were crying and mourning for those killed.
Mothers wailing for their children, and children their mothers.
Well married women cry for their good husbands.
A telegram was sent to the entire universe:
Save, brother Christians, poor Chios!
They immediately telegraphed Turkey and Russia,
France and America, Prussia and England.
Austria also learned of it. Athens and Italy.
Everyone helped wretched Chios.
The Greek excavators came and helped.
With their heart and soul they supported everyone,
among whom were twelve doctors who came from Athens
and freely gave medicines to the people.
Two hundred sailors came from boats
to take bodies out of the ruins.
They put the wounded bodies into their boats,
to Smyrna they took them to heal them.
Elsewhere they amputated arms and elsewhere the legs.
Truly, the little children, woe, the poor creatures!
They removed their smashed little bodies.
You were not there to see what mourning occurred:
beautiful girls, like lilies, now dead.
Markets and neighborhoods all became ruins.
Five-and-a-half thousand people were killed.
And nine thousand brothers were wounded.
Two hundred Ottomans (Turks) at the castle murdered.
Forty-five Turkish women had been in one house,
and they were reading in their own faith.
There, where the poor things were reading,
the house crushed them, the evil-fated ones.
You were not there to see, in the cemeteries
where they were putting ten bodies together into one tomb.
Brave-hearted people were digging the graves.
Without the six-winged cherubims and the cross
they were burying the murdered ones.

Pantelis A. Mavrogiorgis

Oh, my famous Chios, who was the envy,
and now you ended up black and withered.
Where are your flowers? Where has your beauty gone?
Where did your people and their possessions go?
Twenty-eight villages besides Kambo,
together with Chora, ruined and all of Vrontados.
Tsesmes also ruined with so many other villages,
Alatsata and Kato Panagia were ruined.
O, my famous Chios, the star of the East,
your throne, your ancient Kastro, was ruined.
God, all-powerful, show compassion,
and have mercy on the innocent, small children.
God Almighty, cease the vengeance
from this horrible earthquake and give us Your blessings.
God Almighty, stop your wrath,
and save your people from the horrible earthquake.
God Almighty, great is Your name.
No leaf falls from a tree without Your will."

D. The Liberation of Chios

At dawn, on November 11, 1912 – the name day of the patron saints of the Chios, Agioi Viktores – in the narrows between Chios and Oinousses, a fleet of Greek ships appeared. "They're coming! They're coming!" the Chians cried out. They were certain that their liberators were arriving, since they knew that Lesvos had been liberated a few days earlier. That afternoon, fast-moving cruisers and the troopships *Sapfo* and *Patris*, with 2,500 men and their leader, Colonel Delagrammatikas, docked at *Kontari* since earlier Zichni Bey, the Turkish administrator, refused to relinquish command of the island.

The landing took place at Kontari – where a memorial bust currently exists in honor of Ioannis Chrysoloras and Emmanuel Pothitou - the first to be killed in the battle.

The following morning, the liberation army took the shore road and headed to Chora. The welcoming cry of the inhabitants was wildly enthusiastic. The mayor, Nikolaos Kouvelas, welcomed the army personally at the entrance of the city, saying,

> *"Where were you, lads? We have been waiting for you for five-hundred years!"*

The following day, the Greek flag was raised at the Administration Building, and a doxology was held at the Cathedral.

The Turks withdrew to the northern heights above the city. Flushed with victory, the Greek Army rousted the Turks from Karyes, forcing them to occupy the central mountainous area of Chios, the Piganio Mountain with the Monastery of Agios Markos, Nea Moni, and Provateion Mountain with the Monastery of Agion Pateron. Meanwhile, Chians and non-Chians band together into volunteer groups to assist the regular army at Vrontado, Kardamyla, and at the Mastichochoria – centered in Lithi – where the Agiorgousoi certainly joined this effort.

We will avoid describing the battle of Aipos – Aipos being a mountain, at the peak of which a marble pillar has been erected in memory of Lieutenant Nikolaos Ritsos, Ensign Pastrikakis, and the others who fell in battle. We also will not discuss the events at Kardamyla, Pityos, and Volisso, in order to refer more extensively to what relates to Agios Georgios Sikousis and its surrounding areas.

Delagrammatikas, the Administrator of Chios, made a decision to isolate the majority of the Turkish forces in the mountainous and barren areas of Chios in order to force them to surrender. With that in mind, he sent an infantry battalion under Captain Papakyriazis, to occupy Agios Georgios on November 14, where the inhabitants offered him all kinds of assistance, and he subsequently took Dafnonas, as well.

As the situation at Aipos and Kardamyla evolved, Papakyriazis set out on the morning of November 16 with two platoons from Agios Georgios and overtook the mountain Kakia Rachi in order to march toward the Monastery of Agion Pateron. He was unable to succeed with this plan, however, since the enemy's strength was far superior, and their positions were fortified. In addition to that, the artillery of Papakyriazis' troops was rendered useless, since the irregular terrain caused the artillery to constantly overturn. Therefore, Papakyriazis was forced to return to the village. The battle had lasted until nine o'clock at night. Nine Turks and two Greeks were killed. The bones of the two Greeks who lost their lives are buried in the village cemetery under a marble slab upon which the following inscription appears:

"Herein lie the Soldiers
Ioannis Polykarpos of Siatistis, Macedonia
Vasileios Koultsiotis of Melistiou, Corinthia.
They were killed on November 16, 1912
at the Mountain *Kakia Rachi*."

Following the liberation of the northern villages, the Turkish army was limited to the central, mountainous area of Chios. In the meantime, Greek reinforcements arrived, and on December 20 Colonel Delagrammatikas ordered a general attack from Lithi, Karyes, and Agios Georgios. Papakyriazis' battalion charged forward from Agios Georgios and occupied Koumarous, Saliakomyti, and Stavro – thus uniting with the forces that had set forth from Lithi. Following a painful journey, these troops encountered the enemy, which had holed up at the Provateion mountain, and a fierce battle commenced and resulted in the Greek Army occupying the Monastery of Agion Pateron. The Greek contingent from Karyes was able to occupy the Monastery of Agios Markos, resulting in the Turkish commander Zichni Bey to realize that he was surrounded and any resistance would be in vain. He negotiated a surrender, which was completed on December 21, 1912. Chios, liberated from slavery for the first time in 346 years, begins its march toward progress and follows the historical destiny of the Greek State.

PART TWO

VILLAGE LIFE
&
FOLKLORE

CHAPTER 15
The Houses in the Village

A. The Houses

From the beginning, attached houses were constructed in the village, since the general design was of a fortified area to safeguard the inhabitants from danger. Except for houses built in recent years, the older ones are made of stone. Their exteriors are not covered in plaster, so that from above or afar, the impression is one of a beautiful, picturesque, gray "dry stone wall."

In order for a house to be secure, an animal must be slaughtered and buried when the foundation is first dug. Thus, the Agiorgousoi, after the foundation of a house is blessed with holy water, would slaughter a well-fed rooster and throw it into the open foundation. This fascinating act comes from our ancient folk tales, according to which during the construction of the building, some sort of life had to be part of the foundation, depending upon the size and the purpose that the structure was to serve. This is illustrated in the well-known folk song that refers to the "Bridge of Arta," which was built upon the beautiful wife of the master builder. Since this refers to a custom adhered to by idol worshippers, the alternative solution became one of placing a cross, made of reeds, at each corner of the structure.

1. **The One-Family House.** This very basic house consisted of a long, narrow room that served all of the family's needs. It functioned as a bedroom, kitchen, and storage room, as well.
   a. **The Walls**. The walls were made of irregularly shaped stones, held together with a compound made of lime, sand, and water. Only on the corners there were chiseled stones called *kantounia*. These walls were half-meter or more in thickness. The builder, using a hefty hammer, would adjust each stone to fit amongst the others. With a trowel, he would fill in any empty spaces with a mixture of mud, pebbles, and small bricks.

   The head mason, using string and the arrow of a compass, aligned the walls both vertically and horizontally as he worked. The *Pourgoi* were the helpers who prepared and carried mud and stones to the craftsmen. The *Pelekanoi* or *Lixoxooi* (stone cutters) would use a heavy hammer and a chisel to shape the

Old, stone houses

stones geometrically, create the *kantounia* of the structure, and design the slabs for the doorway and window-doors. As the height of the wall they were building increased, they would fashion scaffolds of wooden beams and support them on wooden poles inserted into the wall under construction. Once the scaffold was removed, the holes in the interior of the wall would be filled with plaster and whitened with lime. However, the *tryposcaloi* (hole steps) remain on the exteriors to this day.

b. **The Doors.** The doors of the houses were not very tall, and their tops were arched. Sometimes the area around the opening was rather plain and other times adorned with columns they called "masks," chiseled of Thymianousian stone, which was then topped with a horizontal stone lintel. A bow-shaped, small glass skylight was often created above the lintel. The threshold consisted of a wide area of stone, accessed by two to three steps for entering and exiting the house. The doors were made of wood and were single or double panes. The single door many times had a moving part the "panoporti" allowing for the upper portion to be opened during the day like a window.

c. **The Windows**. In the oldest houses, the windows were small openings high up on the wall, which could be opened and closed with a piece of wood or a reed. Later on, larger and lower openings closer to the floor were created, protected by wooden shutters and iron rods in front. The windows were placed on the front side of the house. For those privileged few whose houses extended farther back, openings were then made in back, as well as in front.

d. **The Floor**. Special sand with pebbles were strewn over the floor of the structure, soaked with water, and pounded into a compact state with iron rods. In newer structures, a bed of cement would be laid to form a type of floor known as "*astrakies*."

e. **The Ceiling**. In the interior of the house, the ceiling was arched, but the exterior, called *vota*, was either curved or level. Every year, the residents would coat the vota with *votochoma*, a leaden dirt that would waterproof the house. A few homes had a flat, cement ceiling and several had a small, double-shingled roof. Using *anemoskales* (movable wooden ladders) or rope ladders, the residents would ascend to the vota through the small trap door in the ceiling, known as a *klavani*. The flat *vota* was generally used as a sun porch, but occasionally it also featured a *fengitis* (skylight) that served to brighten and aerate the house.

f. **The Smokestack**. The *fouflaros* (smokestack) protruded from one corner of the vota, issuing smoke from the fire burning in the fireplace inside the house. The *fouflaros* is characteristic of these village houses.

2. **The Development of the One-Family House**. Walls would often be built inside, along the width of the one-family house. Their dimensions would vary from ceiling height to only halfway up to allow air and light to reach the back portion of the house. If the height of the structure allowed, a type of second floor, like a loft, would be constructed. This was done by using thick, wooden poles across the width of the house upon which boards were nailed, with a protective railing placed in front. To access this area, either a stationery or movable wooden stairway was used. This additional space was where the girls of the family generally slept. Occasionally, some houses created several rooms on this level, connected by doors that allowed passage from one room into the next.

3. **The Two-Story House**. Better and far more spacious houses were

One family house

the *dipata* (two floors). Stone steps, which were built either in the interior or the exterior of the house, led from the lower to the upper floor. Beneath the stairway was a room the *"koumasa"* (an arch). Similar stairways were sometimes constructed in the one-family houses to allow easier access to the roof.

a. In some of the two-story houses, the stairs led to the *pounti*, a balcony, also known as a *liakoto* or *xato*. Behind this balcony one or two rooms would be built. These "good homes" were where foreigners were welcomed and offered a place to sleep.

b. Some houses had three floors: *anoï* (upper), *katoï* (lower), and *mesiariko* (middle). An internal staircase allowed one to get to the middle floor. A small window or skylight would be created to illuminate the otherwise dark area as one ascended to the upper floor.

c. No architectural plan existed. Houses were simply built according to the plot of land and its inclination. Houses in the village were not complete. Very few houses featured an external yard, an oven for baking bread, or a well for water. Some houses had steps on the outside, either for one's animals to ascend or for

Pantelis A. Mavrogiorgis

the occupants to sit outside in summer.

4. **The Stable.** The stable for the animals and for the storage of wood and animal feed, was sometimes a room connected to the house, or it could be a separate structure next to the house or even a rented old house.

All parents were obligated to provide a dowry for each of their daughters when they were to be married. Depending upon the parents' financial circumstances and the number of daughters in the household, a dowry generally consisted of one or two goats, land, and at least one house.

B. Foreigners' Impressions of the Village and the Houses

1. **Hubert-Octave Pernot,** was a French Professor of Linguistics and a fervent friend of Greece. He traveled to Chios in the summers of 1898 and 1899. He visited many villages, among them Agios Georgios, which did not leave him with a favorable impression.

> *"For anyone thinking of visiting the southern part of Chios, the village of Agios Georgios offers little interest. It has just a few wretched habitations worth seeing. The only access is through a door, from which air and light both enter. The climate in Chios must be exceptional for people who live there and subsist on merely a tomato and a few olives daily to live under such conditions.*
>
> *I explored one of those houses speaking with an elderly woman who was seated on the porch outside her door. One cannot imagine anything more primitive. To the left was a two-meter square covered with dung. Also, there was an area for a donkey or mule. Within the depths of the house, an oven could be seen. The old lady occupied the remaining free area."*

Pernot exaggerates in his description. From a mere one or two observations, he makes generalizations. What made him think that the only food Agiorgousoi would eat on a daily basis consisted of one tomato and a few olives? He is the only one who would be able to answer that question.

Pernot does not limit his judgment to one village. Of Lithi, he writes that:

> *"the inhabitants are profiteers. The only good recollection I have is of an exceptional lobster they caught among the rocks of the shore."*

Regarding Kalamoti, he says,

"Unfortunately, the women of Kalamoti are beautiful; but as beautiful as they are, they are that much unlikeable."

His thoughts about *Pyrgi* are as follows:

"They called it a noble home! One would enter from the stable . . . and a stone staircase began from the corner of this stable, uniting the ground floor – which was the dwelling place of the animals – with the first floor, the residence of the people."

2. **Arnold Smith** describes the homes in the villages.

"Only in Agios Georgios Sikousis and in Lithi can you see one-story houses. In Lithi, this seems natural, since so many of the people are fishermen, and they don't need stables. At Agios Georgios Sikousis, many of the single-story houses have stables in the rear, so the animals must pass through the rest of the house in order to get to their own area. However, large animals like cows or mules are not kept in these stables. There are only smaller, domesticated animals there like goats, sheep, and especially chickens.

The type of construction that prevails for these houses features a stone-domed roof, which rests on stone walls. The compact dome has thick sides filled with pebbles and lime-laden mud. The exteriors often have a small protrusion in the center, thus minimizing the thickness of the sides."

3. **Hedwig Ludeke** an Austrian visited the village in 1935 to collect folk songs. This is what she wrote.

"Our small car was climbing the abrupt ribbons of the road toward Agios Georgios Sikousis. The village has suffered destruction from an earthquake some decades ago and, furthermore, one part of it was abandoned, whereas many charming little homes have taken the place of the old ones.

The view from up there was indescribably beautiful. Down low, gardens, the capital, and the port surround it. Further, the deep, blue, wavy sea, and the vast panorama of the mountains of Asia Minor, with their snowy peaks.

They took me to a house. After they treated me with something warm, figs and homemade raki, I sat and wrote the most beautiful things and various songs for two hours without stopping. The spirituality and fine poetic sense of these simple people impressed me. What wealth of their souls is revealed there, and how wondrous it is, with all their primitive and deprived lives, for these people to feel the blessings of poetry as something self-evident and necessary in life.

After the wonderful sunset, which dressed the site with soft yet brilliant colors, I left the good people, who granted me the treasures of their songs, and I returned to Chora."

C. Carved Decorations in front of the Houses

For the protection of the home, the ancient Greeks would write phrases above the doorposts of the pillars, such as:

"Noble Hercules, the child of Zeus, dwells here."

They would place their house under the protection of our familiar hero Herakles. Elsewhere, they might write, *"Let no evil enter in."* The Byzantines continued this custom, writing upon plaques they would fasten to their outer doors phrases like,

"O, Lord, bless our entrance and exit. Amen."

Oftentimes, icons of Jesus Christ, the Virgin Mary, or a saint would be painted above the door.

The Franks generally rendered the likenesses of saints in the form of statues, rather than icons, as we did. When the Genoese had control of Chios, their influence upon the local inhabitants resulted in the continuation of the Genoese custom of inserting small marble or stone slabs with carvings into the front walls of churches and homes. Upon these slabs – either simply or quite skillfully carved – were the faces of saints or geometric or plant designs, sometimes containing the name of the artist or the owner of the structure and the date of its construction. The purpose of these items was to ward off evil.

These carvings, especially at Agios Georgios, impressed the Byzantinologist, Giorgos Sotiriou.

"In almost all of the villages of the island, most beautifully at Agios Georgios Sikousis, one notices the use of carved slabs. For example, on the front side of Nikitas Vafeias home are seven plaques inserted into the wall. They depict Agios Georgios, Archangels, the Neamonitida Theotokos, and others."

The particular house mentioned above is situated behind the church of *Agios Panteleimonas*. Nevertheless, in newly constructed houses these plaques no longer exist. What visitors will see these days are Byzantine crosses, with each of their arms ending in a three-leaf design, carved in doors above the upper floors of the houses. Other, more complex designs feature crosses surrounded by *anthemia*, a leaf motif. For example, in the small square of Agios Panteleimonas at the house of Antonios P. Patounas, in the upper window is a carved decoration composed of a small crown of twigs bearing long, narrow leaves. On these tiny branches two birds stand facing in opposite directions. There are two ribbons to the right and left of this design, and their narrow sides combine for a three-part leaf. One ribbon contains the year that the home was built, "ΕΤΟΣ 1935," and the other ribbon has the owner's initials, "Α.Α.Π."

Nearby, in Sarantis Psyllos' home, is a framed double-headed eagle formed from two helixes, connected by a three-leafed *anthemia*. Between the eagle's two heads is a crown, under which the owner's name and date have been carved. It reads: "ΓΕΩΡ ΨΥΛΛΟ, 1858, ΙΟΥΛΙΟΥ 24."

D. The Household and Housewares

What we refer to as "housewares" are the necessary pieces of furniture and utensils required by a family in the village for the needs of daily life. For the ancient Greeks, the center of family life was the *"estia"* (the hearth), a fire lit in an altar dedicated to the goddess Estia, in the belief that she protected the family. There is a broader meaning to the word, however, as it encompasses a home and family life. *"Anestios,"* on the other hand, is the person who wanders without a home and family of his own. Even today, the word "hearth" is a metaphor for a gathering place.

The ancient hearth, minus any religious characterization, was basically a *pyrostia* or *parostia*. Families in the village would gather around their homes' fireplaces as kindling burned to warm their bodies and souls. In winter, the fire was lit both day and night, the housewives cooked food, and the families sat together at their tables for the noon and evening meals.

1. **The Kitchen and the Fireplace.** The *tzaki* (fireplace) was usually built within an inside corner of the house. Beneath the base was a trivet, which supported a kettle, *"stenetai to tsoukali,"* for cooking above the fire. The Agiorgousoi would characteristically say, *"Pao na steso to tsoukali mou"* ("I'm going to stand my pot"). The arched covering that spanned the two corner walls was set one meter above the fireplace itself. Nearby, the housewife had stacks of cut, dried wood and

Pantelis A. Mavrogiorgis

kindling to keep the fire going. The fireplace narrows as it ascends, leading to the *fouflaro* (smokestack) that cuts through the rooftop.

The lady of the house would keep various cooking implements near her: clay pots, metal kettles, frying pans, large spoons, and other spoons that oftentimes had been made in the monasteries. Some of the spoons and forks hung on the wall, and others were placed, together with knives, in the spoon holder. A *luserna* (lantern with multiple wicks) – and, later, an oil lamp – hung on the fireplace wall to illuminate the area used by the housewife when she cooked. What enormous difference electricity makes in today's world.

2. **The Interior of the House.** Within the home's interior, two or three *therides* (indentations) were created during the construction process. These areas served as shelves for items used while food was being prepared. A funnel for dispensing oil, boxes and bottles with various supplies, pots, earthenware jugs, and pitchers of water were placed inside the *therides*. There would also be a *therida* that had built-in shelves and a little wooden door that closed to form a cabinet. In those, the family kept bread, a bowl of olives, a bowl of cheese, a bottle of wine or *raki*, and anything else they wanted to keep handy. Either on a wooden pole or a wall would be cords to hang small tomatoes, onions, garlic bulbs, and herbs like oregano and sage. That year's olive oil and olives and cheeses were each kept in large jugs, with smaller portions to be used for cooking kept in separate smaller jugs, and the pots were stored in wooden barrels. They would pour the *raki* (*ouzo*) into large, glass bottles and place them into *bousedes* (woven wicker receptacles) to prevent breakage. A wooden frame separated into compartments was hung on the wall, with a shelf above it, all of which provided a storage place for good plates and cups, small plates for preserves served with a spoon, and *flitzania* (coffee cups).

3. **Tables, Chairs, and Meals.** The simplest type of seat was the *Takos*, a cylindrical, thick section of a tree trunk, 30-40 centimeters high with two level circular surfaces. One circle served as a table surface and the lower one as a seat. These were mainly used for small children. There were also basic stools made with four wooden legs and a woven reed seat. Very few families had a *sofras*, a low, round, wooden table with a thick pedestal. Most had low, square or orthogonal tables and sat around them taking food from a pot placed in the center.

Meals were generally eaten with slices of bread; there was also a dish made of chestnut wood and filled with olives, and a jug of wine. This paints the most frugal and simplistic picture of mealtimes. More affluent families had high, round tables and chairs with a back, used mainly for specific family rituals or when they entertained guests.

4. **Beds and Bedding.** Within the house, either a corner or the area beneath a staircase would be where a couple would house their double bed. The bed itself was nothing more than two *stripoda* (wooden poles) laid on the floor, upon which boards were placed horizontally. The mattresses, which were strewn on these boards for the couple to sleep at night, were rolled up again in the morning. A more sophisticated bed – known as *carriola* in Italian and used for guests by the few villagers who owned them – was a four-footed, iron one decorated with gold-colored coverings. The mattresses were filled with rags or hay, and the sheets were either store-bought or woven on the loom at home. The women also wove woolen blankets, but the extremely thick *paplomata,* winter quilts, were generally purchased from *paplomata* makers.

A long, narrow pillow, *maxelaromana,* ran from the left to the right end of the bed and the couple's two pillows would rest on it. In some homes, the residents would drape a type of bed skirt around the lower portion of the bed to hide whatever was stored beneath it from the eyes of visitors. High on the wall near the bed would be the *eikonostasi*, a wooden frame to hold icons, palm crosses, small bottles of holy water, the Four Gospels, and the framed *stefana* (wedding crowns) of the couple.

5. **Traditional Furniture.** It was natural for modern technology and craftsmanship rendered quite a few pieces of furniture and various household utensils obsolete. An example of these items is the *sentouki* – which was a long, narrow trunk, often made of almond wood and, more rarely, decorated – into which underwear, festive clothing, sheets, and other such things were kept. In the wealthier homes, a bureau made of good wood, festooned with decorations, had four drawers and a marble top that supported a mirror in a carved frame.

6. **Utensils.** The *gdi* (*goudi* or *igdion)* – the mortar, a pot fashioned from hard stone – allowed people to grind coffee beans, using a heavy iron pestle. In order to roast their coffee, they would use a *kavourdistiri,* a closed, cylindrical container with a thin metal rod threaded through it that functioned as an axle, which they twisted to rotate the container over the fire. Another old device was a *cheromylos*, a hand mill made of two thick, round, smooth stones. One stone remained motionless on the floor and had a vertical, metal rod in the middle that went through the center of the top stone. When the housewife turned the top stone,

using the attached wooden handle, it would revolve and grind wheat to prepare *chondro* or *pligouri*, to use in different dishes instead of rice.

Another obsolete device is the *skafi* or wooden *pinakoti*, which had three to four compartments and was used for kneading bread. The dough placed upon it was allowed to rise, then it was rolled out with a thin rolling pin. Presently, there are very few homes where you can find metal *skafes* that were used to wash clothes and/or to bathe and shampoo one's hair, since almost all of the houses in the village now have electric appliances.

CHAPTER 16
Farm Work

A. *Fyteia* (Planting)

The rural area of Agios Giorgis is mountainous and barren, and the plots are small. For this reason, life was always difficult there, and a feeling of deprivation prevailed. Therefore, the Agiorgousoi were forced to climb the slopes and create farmlands there, to "crush rocks to make soil." These hardworking farmers, who did their jobs under such harsh conditions, enjoyed their meals earned by the sweat of their brow and the blood of their souls.

They would awaken in the middle of the night, way before the rooster would crow to signal daybreak, pack bread, figs, olives, and water in their *tourva* (sack), and set out to create arable land. Their tools were an axe, a hoe, a sledgehammer, a crowbar, a shovel, and a rake to gather stones and pebbles. To create an arable patch of land, they would take a sledgehammer to the slope of the mountain. The farmer would first spit on his hands to firm up his grip, and would strike the area repeatedly. As they used a crowbar to pry rocks from the ground, their sweat would run like a river and their breath would be expelled in gasps. This work would be done horizontally for one to two meters.

Since the area was a mountain slope, they would build retaining walls with stones, spread soil, and thus create the first *Skala* or step. They would proceed up the mountainside, making a terraced pattern of ever-ascending steps. The Agiorgousoi had a few flat fields, but most were terraced, so they would ask one another, *"Poses skales echei to chorafi?"* ("How many steps does your field have?")

Once the mountainsides had been cultivated to create arable land, trees would be planted, and this new field would be called *"Fyteia"* ("Planting"). To plant rows of mastic trees, pits would be dug and several shovels full of dung would first be thrown into those pits. They would plant small branches for fig trees, and they would also plant olive trees and almond trees this way. In the widest and most fertile sections, they would fertilize the land with dung and create vineyards.

Planting was only one part of the work of the farmer. But those who did the planting cared for their plants as tenderly as one would care for a child. This involved watering the fledgling trees and sometimes fencing them in with wild and prickly bushes to keep goats and sheep from entering and picking at the growing trees. If the farmer had no other tasks, he would spend entire days and nights near his plantings.

He would eventually dig a well, in order to water his vegetable garden, and he would build a hut for shelter from rain and thunderstorms. When the exhausting but productive job of planting was complete, the Agiorgousis was filled with pride, as he was able to obtain a field for his children and their offspring through his hard labor.

Today, this arduous task of planting no longer continues. Life is much more comfortable. The farmers fought the land with their hands in the old days, making things right with themselves and with God.

B. *Spora* (Sowing)

The task of sowing the land is by no means a simple one. It is quite complex and extends from September 14, *tou Stavrou* ("the Day of the Cross"), until the beginning of the Christmas season. In sowing, the hopes and expectations of the farmer for a good harvest are contained. In those years, a good harvest meant "bread" for his children and life for his family. There is also something mystical in the process, as the seed represents the sacrament of reproduction and results in a new life. Therefore, the ancient Greeks created myths around this process and associated it with the Goddess Demeter or Dimitra and with the Eleusinian Mysteries.

When the ancient Greeks celebrated the *Thesmoforia* in the month of *Pyanepsiona* (mid-October to mid-November) to honor the Goddess Dimitra, who taught people the way to sow wheat, they only allowed married women to participate in the celebration, as they were seen as a source of fertility – therefore similar to the earth. It was thought that, just as the sperm of a male enters the female and results in the creation of a new life, thus the seeds of wheat and other plants enter *"Mother Earth"* and create a new plant that will blossom and continue the everlasting circle of fruitfulness and life. Subsequently, with the introduction of Christianity, sowing continued to hold onto many rituals and customs. Our Church, in order to bring attention to the process, designated one Sunday during the month of October for the passage of the sower to be read:

"The sower went out to sow his seed."

More recently, farmers tend to call October or November *"Sporias"* ("Sowing"), as they call August *"Trygitis"* ("Harvester"). Agios Georgios *"tou mesa krevatiou,"* as it is called in our village and whose feast day is on November third, is called *"sporiaris"* ("the sower") in other parts of Greece. On November

21, the feast day of the *Panagia ton Esodion* (The Entrance of the Virgin Mary) is known as the *"mid-sower,"* since that date coincides with the middle of the sowing season.

1. **Preparation for Sowing.** Nearly all of the residents of our village were farmers, with plots of land that varied in size. Their initial task was to discern which wheat was the best of the crop and collect seeds from those specimens; the seeds had to be full of nutrients, not hollow. As far as beans went, whether they were broad beans, lentils, or chickpeas, had to cook easily.

   However, it was not sufficient to merely select the best seeds for sowing. They needed to imbue those seeds with divine power. So every housewife would place platters of seed samples on a small table together with an icon, perhaps of *Agios Tryfonas*, and a small amount of water for use by the priest who would come to the house and perform a holy water service. The priest would sprinkle the sanctified water on the seeds and read a special prayer *"for the blossoming of the fruits of the earth . . . ."* These blessed seeds would be mixed with the rest of the seeds to ensure that divine grace would infuse all of the seeds that would be sown in the new year.

   In most of Greece, the preparations made prior to the sowing of seeds are combined with the feast of the Cross on September 14. Every farmer places seeds on a napkin and leaves it in front of the Holy Side Door of the church to be blessed and to be sprinkled with holy water from the feast of the Cross. The farmers would say, *"Stavrone kai sperne"* ("Make your Cross, then go and sow").

   The ancient Hesiod in his work *Works and Days* advises his brother Persi, when the sowing period begins, to pray to Zeus and the innocent Dimitra for the land to fill with wheat, the nourishing, sacred fruit of nature. He cautions him to listen for the sound of cranes in the month of September, as well. Here is what he writes:

   "Pray to Zeus of the Underworld and to the innocent Dimitra so that her sacred shore will sprout abundantly from the first plowing. Listen for the annual voice of the cranes above, from the clouds, because it is the signal to plow and the harbinger of winter to come."

   There is no precise date for when seeding is to begin. The farmers would await the first rains to soften the earth, in order for the fields to be plowed. Whenever drought conditions came to Agios Georgios, the families of the village, along with the priests, would perform a *litania* with the icons, going around the village and through the fields asking for God's help and mercy in ending the drought. It was less important whether this ceremony resulted in rain; it was more significant that these simple villagers, who unlike many people today, had such strong faith.

2. **The Wages of Sowing.** Before dawn, *"Bri vali gyali,"* as the Agiorgousoi would say, meaning before the light of day touches the glass of the windows, the villagers are awake and ready to work. The village is alive and "buzzing," and it resembles a very noisy beehive. The housewife lights the fireplace to boil soup made with broad beans and chickpeas, while her husband saws wood for the fire and gives water and food to the animals. Later, he will shovel dung from the stable into *koprotsouvala* (dung sacks) to use it as fertilizer in the fields. Once the food – along with olives, garlic and onions, and *raki* or wine – is ready, the farmer will sit at the table – where he is joined by his workers, who work for food or money or are borrowed temporarily – and *"chew his food with great appetite, emptying the pot to the bottom."* Not only the workers known as *sypsomoi* go to the farmer's house to eat.

The farmer then makes his cross, loads his animals with the sacks of dung, ties the goats and sheep to the frame of the saddle, hangs the sack containing the seed and – taking some figs, bread, and water – he sets out with his rake and axe over his shoulder. As you see all of these farmers leaving together, you'll hear them speculating on the weather – especially if it's a cloudy day – and their experience will be sufficient for them to produce a "weather bulletin" for that day.

Their journey, on foot,may take up to an hour. They unload their supplies, scatter the dung with shovels across the entire field, and the owner of the plot uses his axe to divide the land into portions called *spories.* When they first plow that area, they toss wheat or barley seeds into the furrows, then they cover them with soil. Their phrase for this simple way of planting crops was *"kopse – rixe"* ("dig and sow").

The process for planting *koukia* (broad beans), was far more complex. First they would plow row by row from one side to the other along the width of the field, which would create an *orgo*, a small ditch. The work of *koukisma* then called for them to toss broad beans into the furrow, one by one at even distances. Usually the women did this to allow the men to dig at a quicker pace. And, thus, they proceeded until the entire field was planted.

Revithia (chickpeas) were planted later in the season. In order for them to ripen, more systematic work was demanded from the farmers. The chickpeas were planted far deeper, thus the name *vathi,* for "depth," described the planting method. They would say, "*To doulepsame to chorafi*" ("We spent a lot of time working the field.").

Throughout the day they would dig, taking a short break for a snack or a cigarette. Other times they stopped for a meal provided by their owner's wife, when this was a part of the arrangements made in advance for *taïstous ergates* – those who worked to be fed, not paid.

Agiorgousoi referred to the process of digging and planting as "I'm doing." They would ask one another, "Where did you do today?"

The end of the day was marked by sunset. They would look at the sun and remark: "Two statures ("statures" refers to the height of a man). We still need one more stature for it to be sunset. Let's leave, because we will end up on the road at night." Back home, thoroughly exhausted, they would drink *raki,* eat roasted figs, and wish one another, "*Kai stous karpous. Kai tou chronou,*" "To the harvest, also. Next year, as well."

3. **The Plow.** The plow is an ancient farm tool used to plow fields. From Hesiod's time it has continued to be used in the same way until tractors finally replaced it.

At Agios Georgios, we called it an *aletri,* and we referred to the related task by saying, "I am plowing" or "I am cultivating" – "*Aletrizo*" or "*Zevgarizo.*" Since the Agiorgousoi did not have large expanses of land they "*Zevgarizan*" only the lower areas in *Zyfias, Xerokambos,* and wherever the fields were flat.

The basic parts of the plow were the **hand lever**, the **foot**, the **seal or bating**, and the **yoke** – which we will refer to later with its ancient name to prove how long ago it existed. The word *cherolavi* comes from the ancient word "*egcheri*" (hand lever), a wooden handle held by the plowman, who controlled which direction the two animals tethered to the yoke went. Much depended upon how he held this *egcheri.* If he directed it in a straight line, the furrows were straight; if he allowed it to sink too deeply into the ground, the animals tired quickly; and if it didn't create deep enough rows, the seeds were not able to germinate and bear fruit.

The *elyma* or foot of the plow is the lower, curved, wooden piece that provides the framework for the plowshare. This foot is connected to the hand lever. At the point of connection, there is a hole into which the *"gyis"* or *"goula,"* a piece of curved wood or bating, is inserted. This bating comes out from the side and faces upward, where it is joined to the *Matisma*, a long piece of wood with nails at the edge for fastening the yoke. The yoke is a circular piece of wood made from a section of a tree trunk or the thick branch of a tree and is about twelve spans ("span": the hand from thumb end to pinky end) in length. At each edge, the yoke has two holes with *zevles*, arched switches, threaded through them to form a pillow-like rest for the yoke at the point of contact with the necks of the animals to prevent wounds. The *zevles* firmly tether the animals' necks to the yoke.

The plowman holds the hand lever with his left hand to direct the plow; and along with his verbal commands to the animals, he grips the prod, a long rod with a sharp point, with his right hand to move the animals in the direction he wants them to go. The digger assists by digging the edges, filling the narrow ditches, tossing in the seeds, and flattening the dirt.

4. **The Harvest.** After the sowing or planting of seeds, the harvest or threshing is the second most important farming job, since it is the second phase of the process of producing the fruits of the earth. June is known as the Harvester Month, since the work is done during that time.

The farmers get to their fields before sunup, so that the "heat doesn't eat them up" – *"Min tous fa i zesti."* The ancient poet Theokritos, in his first *Eidyllio* (poem), verses 50-51, writes the following about the harvest:

> *"Begin the harvest with the first flight of the lark, and end when the lark returns to its nest to sleep in order to avoid the burning heat."*

A commentator, writing about Theokritos's work, notes:

> *"The lark is the first of the birds to arise and the last to sleep."*

Hesiod offers this advice to his brother:

> *"In the harvest season, avoid shady spots and sleeping until dawn, as the sun will scorch your body. Get up early and get busy to make certain that you will bring home the fruits of*

your labor."

The Agiorgousis men protected themselves from the sun by wearing a straw hat or a *fakioli* (turban) on their heads, and the women wore thick white *mantiles* (scarves) on their heads as they set out to harvest. When their fields were at a considerable distance, they often left from the evening – along with workers they borrowed or paid. After a short nap, they would begin their work at dawn. The work is laborious and requires speed and many farmhands. In the village, a popular expression was *"Polemo"* ("I'm fighting"), since farm jobs were akin to going into battle. A typical question at that time was, *"Where were you fighting today?"*

The basic harvest tool was the scythe or sickle. It is composed of a wooden handle to which a semicircular metal blade, about two fingers wide, is attached. Its tip is sharp, and the blade is thin at its center in order to cut the sheaves. The scythes were made in different sizes, depending upon the strength of the harvester to heft the tool. The process involved him grabbing as many stalks as possible with his left hand and shearing them with the scythe in his right hand. After he cuts three to four handfuls this way, the women gather them into a bale for the harvester to bind. The harvester has prepared and brought from home wicker ties for this very purpose, fashioned from long stalks of reeds that he softened with water and joined together.

Working quickly under the burning heat of the sun, the Agiorgousis will take a quick bite when hungry, a sip of water, and wipe the sweat that runs from his face with the edge of his apron. It is important for him to get as much done as possible before noon, as the job only becomes that much more difficult as the sun goes higher. Aside from the heat, he is constantly inhaling the fine dust that issues from the cut stalks and affects his breathing. Other hardships the farmer faces are that the bristles from the wheat stalks stick to his face, and his hands often become bloody from the thorns and wild greens that tear his skin. It is understandable then, that when the farmer is eating his bread, it has not only been made possible by the sweat of his brow but also by the blood of his body and soul.

The bales are then loaded on the animals and taken to the threshing field and piled together into a haystack. We did not have any particular customs for the harvest at Agios Georgios. I only remember that when the stalks were ripe and the head of the fruit blackened, pieces would be cut and a cross woven for the promise of a good year. This cross would be placed on the *eikonostasi* in a corner of the house until the sowing period began again, at which time it would be broken up and thrown into the new seed for good luck in the new year.

5. **The Threshing *(Alonisma)*.** According to the Greeks, July is *Alonaris* ("the Thresher"), since that is when they threshed the wheat. This period is the final stage of production for the farmer, so his work and his struggles end at this point. In the village, the *aloni* or threshing floor was up high in an area that would catch the cool night air. They would draw a circle of five to six meters in diameter on the ground and clear the area of stones and vegetation, flatten it, and create *cheilia* ("lips") – a border of either fieldstone slabs or hardened soil mixed with moss – to define it.

The owner of the *aloni* would allow his fellow villagers the use of the threshing field, so there would be bales for threshing visible in the surrounding areas. Often, a handmade wooden cross would be placed at the top of the haystack. Every year, those who had threshing fields would take their families along and repair the aloni. They would sweep it clean, spread moss over the interior, and soak the area with water while trampling it for the moss to absorb the water. This would provide a clean, protective covering on the threshing floor. Since it was also necessary for them to be sure that the border was solid as well, the work they did was referred to as *cheiloma*.

When it was time to begin the threshing, the farmer and his family would spend the entire day at the threshing field. They would carry bundles from the stacks, cut the stalks into smaller pieces by hand, and spread them all across the threshing field, up to the borders or "lips." The actual threshing process would begin at ten o'clock in the morning and end at about five to six o'clock in late afternoon. The reason for this was that the cooler air of very early morning or evening would soften the stalks too much to allow them to be cut.

Before the animals, either oxen or horses, were yoked in the threshing field, they would be allowed to eat a few of the stalks. After that, a *fostoma* – which was a muzzle made of woven wire or sewn cloth – would be placed over their mouths to prevent them from further eating the stalks. When threshing was done with a pair of oxen, they would be harnessed to a yoke similar to that used with the plow. A thick, wide board was suspended from the middle of the yoke, and it had sharp, metal teeth beneath it to cut the stalks.

This ancient type of saw is known as a *loukani* today, but in ancient times, it was called a *tykani*. The plowman, *zevgolatis,* stands on the *loukani* and directs the oxen around the threshing floor with ropes in his hands, and gradually the stalks turn into hay.

If the threshing is being done with a mule or donkey, two wooden cylinders made from the trunks of trees – instead of a *loukani* – would revolve around the metal axle that is inserted through both cylinders, which have protruding metal cutters similar to those of the *loukani*. Someone then uses a pitchfork to collect stalks from the area outside of the threshing floor and to pitch them toward the cutters.

Every few hours, the "turning" of the threshing field occurs. While the animals are kept outside of the area, the workers use metal and wooden pitchforks to turn over the half-ground stalks. Then the animals are brought back in to pass over them with the grinder.

6. **Winnowing *(Xenenisma)*.** When a lot of hay has been gathered, the animals are removed and the hay is stacked, where the wind will blow, into a pile called a *Sarma*. (The word *sarma* comes from *sarono*, "I rake.") So once the *sarma* is set up, both types of pitchforks are used to lift and toss the hay high, so that the wind is able to separate the "kernel of the wheat," which is heavier and falls straight down, while the lighter hay blows away. Helpers use brooms to sweep away the hay that gathers around the pile of wheat. The wheat is then sifted through a sieve with large holes to separate "the chaff from the wheat."

The wheat is then put into sacks, measured by the *koilo* (24 *okades* equals one *koilo*), brought home, removed from those sacks and spread on level ground to cool off and dry. In a month or two, after it has completely dried and further ripened, it is ready for use.

The task of threshing and winnowing requires many workers. If the wind abates partway through the process, the farmers end up spending the night there.

In some areas of Greece, sometimes also in the village, on the last day of this work, the farmer will make the sign of the cross over the pile of wheat, plunge the thick-toothed pitchfork into the center of the pile and say, *"Kai tou chronou"* ("And next year"). This is a long-standing custom. Theokritos writes:

"May I thrust a large shovel into Demeter's pile of wheat on

the threshing floor next year"

When the work is complete, everyone gathers at home. The housewife has prepared fried dough balls *(loukoumades),* and over a drink of *raki,* they wish *"Nanai kalofagoto"* ("May it be well eaten").

C. The Production of Mastic

Mastichi or mastic comes from a semicircular bush – *skinos* – with a short, thick trunk, long branches that have a downward incline, and thick, deep-green leaves that remain that way year round. Due to the shape and thickness of the foliage, it is difficult for both sun and rainwater to adequately nourish it at all times. Entire terraced fields *(skales)* are covered by these bushes, which occupy a significant amount of space and do not allow room for the cultivation of other trees or plants. The process of producing mastic has several phases, which occur over a period of two to three months.

1. **Preparing the *Skinous*.** The first job at the end of June is to take care of the trees *(skinous),* working around and under their trunks. For that step, the Greeks use the expression, *"Isiazo"* or *"Siazo,"* ("I fix up"). To prepare for that, the grass around and beneath the trunk must first be cut with small, sharp trowels. The ground is then "scratched" with an *amnia* (ancient word: *ami*) – a wooden-handled device with L-shaped metal hooks that removes stones and other impediments. Thus the expression, *"Xio skinous."* The ground beneath the bushes is then flattened until it resembles a small threshing field that goes from the trunk of the bush to the outer edges of the branches.

2. **Whitening the Ground.** Once the scratching is complete, the ground is swept clean and *asprochoma* (white soil) is sprinkled over it to prevent the pale mastic from becoming soiled as it drips down. *"Asprogeiazo,"* ("I make the ground white"), is what this step is called. Since this "white dirt" was scarce in our village, the Agiorgousoi would get it from an area in the southwestern villages that they referred to as "white soil," also nicknaming the inhabitants of those villages "White Soilers."

3. **The Piercing *(Kentos)*.** From July to the beginning of September, men and women use a special piercing tool to prick the trunks and thick branches of the *mastic* trees. The *Kentitiri* is metal, sharp, and spiked in front. Depending on the endurance of a tree, the number of times it can be pierced ranges from twenty to thirty. Following this

process, a sticky white substance begins to flow out of the pricked areas, quite similar to how resin comes out of evergreen trees. These drops gather on the "white soil" and take various shapes, or they may remain on the trunk and dry up to resemble a tear or a pearl. The piercing is done twice a week for a period of five to six weeks, after which the first "gathering" begins.

4. **The Gathering.** This work is mainly done by the women, who sit on their knees beneath the bushes, gathering thick pies of mastic that have fallen onto the white soil with their hands. They also use a metal tool that has a triangular shape and wooden handle to collect the beads that are either beneath the trunk of the bush or on its branches. They place the mastic in the *kavki*, small, woven wicker baskets – the interiors of which they have coated by sprinkling a special type of mud that prevents sticking. After that, they empty the *kavki* either into two-handled shallow baskets or into copper trays and take them home. At home, the mastic is spread out in a cool area to prevent it from sticking or forming a ball.

5. **The Cleaning.** Once the mastic has dried, it is then spread upon *sinia* – large, round, copper trays – from which women, seated on stools, examine and clean each mastic bead by hand. This "selection of mastic" is called *"Dialego mastichi."* Each piece is washed twice with soap and water and then sifted through progressively finer sieves, which allows the women to then separate it all into different categories. There is the pie, the *floiskari,* the fine mastic, the yellow mastic, the mastic "dust," and the *petikas* – which is actually the bark of the bush with mastic stuck on it. After this process is complete, the mastic then goes to the markets through the local *Synetairismon* (Cooperative) and the Union of Mastic Producers Cooperatives.

D. The Production of Figs and *Raki*

Apparently, our village must have been surrounded by fig trees in ancient times, thus the name of Agios Georgios Sikousis ("of the fig"). Today, we still have fig trees there but hardly enough to justify the name of our village. This is a result of the Agiorgousoi turning to other jobs and abandoning farming.

The fig tree grows and develops quite easily, even in mountainous and rocky soil. Its trunk is large and thick, and its branches grow out to the sides with large, thick, green leaves that split into three or four "tongues" at their ends. An unusual characteristic of the fig tree is that its branches and leaves emit a thick, white liquid which, when it comes into contact with a person's skin,

The gathering of mastic

will cause itching. The tree also exudes a horrendous odor that makes one's sleep agonizing.

The villagers believed that after Judas betrayed Christ, he then regretted it and hung himself from a fig tree. Therefore, it is thought that anyone who sleeps beneath this tree will wake up in a bad mood.

1. **The Piercing *(Riniazma)*.** There are wild figs in Greece called *erinoi*. In June, women and children will hang bunches of *erinoi* on the fig trees, since they harbor fruit flies which help with the fertilization of the figs. While the figs will ripen without erinoi, they are considered to be "unpierced" figs, which are not quite as tasty and may even be totally sour and tasteless. Today, erinoi are no longer used. The word appears in Homer's *Iliad* as *Erineos*.

2. **Figs Suitable for Eating.** From the beginning of August, the figs begin ripening. They are a very tasty and sweet type of fruit, particularly in the early morning hours while they are still cold when picked from the fig tree. When there is fog or any dampness, a grooved, striped pattern forms on the peel. The villagers call them *"lourata"* ("striped figs") and consider them to be the best.

   All figs are not suitable to be eaten fresh. Those that are best are the figs with the black peel, the long-tipped or long-stemmed ones, the *Mytelinian* ones, and the *avosyka* (a compound word referring to "oxen" and "figs"), which are large figs. The short-tailed figs are best when dried and baked in the oven. The first figs of the season appear during the threshing period, so they are called *therites* (of the harvest), while the last ones to come out are known as *strounelia* (derived from *ysterinelia* and *sterinelia*).

3. **Gathering and Sun-Drying the Figs.** When figs overripen, they turn yellow, and our fellow villagers call them *"kounelia"*. *Sykologima* is the term used for gathering the figs. Any figs that have fallen from the tree are collected. Branches are pulled lower, and the yellowed figs are cut with a hooked instrument. Then the collection is taken back to the village in baskets and immediately spread over the *vota* (roof) to sun dry them.

   A few days later, the women go up to the rooftops, select the figs that have dried, and separate them into two categories: those to be baked in the oven, and those to be distilled for the production of *raki*. The evening sight is quite striking, as the women hurry to gather the figs, especially if it is expected to rain.

Pantelis A. Mavrogiorgis

The spreading of figs on the vota (rooftop)

4. **Baking the Figs in the Oven.** The figs selected for baking are placed either on metal sheets or in large pans and left in the lit ovens until they redden. They are then removed and put into containers or large jugs, then pressed down to prevent them from becoming worm-infested – as these figs are preserved this way for the entire winter season. In the village, in the old days, the farmers and their families used figs for multiple reasons: as school snacks for the children, as a handy food for the farmers, and for the farmers to enjoy with their raki at night, after a hard day's work in the fields.

Some women made *pastelaries* with the figs, which were served as treats to visitors. To make these, they would open and flatten the figs, sprinkle spices on them, sandwich them together in pairs, and bake them. Sometimes, they would use the largest figs to make *patita*. To do that, they would dip the figs in boiled water for fifteen minutes; strain them by pressing them with a cloth, after which they would place them in a sunny area for about a week to dry. The dried figs would be put into a container and pounded until they were white and sugary. The final step, pounding the figs, earned them the name, *patita*, in Greek.

5. **Boiling and Distilling.** The figs considered to be of secondary quality – because they were deformed, bitten by crickets, or partially eaten by birds – would be distilled to make *raki* or *souma*. This process took place in a type of distillery equipped with large *maerikes* (jugs) and barrels, in which the figs could be mixed with water and a special type of yeast. The openings of the jugs and barrels were hermetically sealed to prevent air from entering. This was the first preparatory step, aptly called *"vreximo ton sykon"* ("wetting the figs").

It took fifteen to twenty days for the sugar of the figs to be transformed into alcohol. At the same time, any impurities would come to the surface as it bubbled. A faint whistling sound signals that "the figs are boiled" and ready for distillation. The boiling is done in a copper cauldron over a fire fed by evergreen branches in a fireplace. The pot is filled with wet figs and covered with an *ambikas*, an arched lid that resembles a crown. This entire process is known as *lambikos* or *rembikos*; and so *rembikairno* means, "I boil in the cauldron." The *ambikas* has a tube on its side, which becomes narrow at its end and is connected to a spiral pipe that is inserted into a water supply, the *tagari*.

The figs are heated in the cauldron over the fire, and the alcohol

The distilling of figs

that they contain is released as steam. As this steam fills the arched *ambikas*, it is discharged through the pipe and is transformed into liquid by the temperature of the water in the *tagari*. Now a liquid, the *raki* moves through a little tube, the *loula*, which is outside of the water reservoir.

The distiller, who tastes the *raki* on an ongoing basis as it moves through the process, through his knowledge and experience is able to discern the quality of the product and whether the temperature of the contents of the cauldron needs to be adjusted. Depending upon what he determines, he may lower or raise the fire in the fireplace, and is always cautious that nothing sticks to the pot, or *"Na min tou kollisi to kazani,"* as they say.

In the early phase of the process the "steam is thick," so the alcohol content of the *souma* or *raki* is very high. When the alcohol drops to 16 degrees, the distillation process is halted and the cauldron is filled with figs again for a second "boiling in the pot." The special instrument used to determine the alcohol level is an *araiometro* (*grado*). The *raki* (or *sykosouma*) is poured into large round flasks called *bousedes*.

To prepare *souma* of better quality, they boil the souma in the pot for the second time. They add aromatic spices like mastic, anise seeds, and *anetol* to add a kick to the taste. To drink this good *raki* a lot of water needs to be added and it's called *metavgarma*.

E The Production of Wine

According to the Holy Bible, *"Wine gladdens the hearts of men."* Wine is actually the most ancient of alcoholic drinks known to mankind. Such is its value that a divine origin has been attributed to wine. The Old Testament teaches us that Noah first planted a vineyard, while Hellenic antiquity associates the vine and wine with the god Dionysos, just as wheat is associated with Dimitra.

In keeping with that tradition, the first King of Chios was Oinopoion (The Winemaker), whose name reflects Chios' relationship with wine. The wine of Chios, *Ariousios*, was familiar to the entire ancient world, and Greek and Roman authors spoke about it. Mnisitheos distinguishes three qualities of *Ariousios*, saying,

> *". . . for the one is very strong (brouskos), while the other is sweet (glyko), and the middle one of these is called aftokratos."*

The Church blesses "the bread, the wine, and the oil." The *"anama"* is the special wine used for Holy Communion.

Today, in Agios Georgios, I think that there is not even one single vineyard. In the early years, the farm areas of *Afaloti, Manourades, Lakkos,* and the *Mesa* areas, in general, all had wine-producing grapes. A good homeowner had to have a vineyard. Wine and *raki* were necessary at the table. The jug of wine was right next to the people as they had their soup at night. They considered *krasopsychia*, bread dipped in wine, as something to always have on hand to "support" (*na stylosoun*) their stomachs.

The village used to grow black grapes, not for eating, but for the production of wine. In order to create and maintain vineyards, the farmer had to take extra special care, as digging, fertilizing, pruning, and sulfurating were all necessary. In September, when the grapes ripened, harvesting began. We had no special harvest customs in Agios Georgios, nor did this event cause families to hold celebrations over a number of days as was customary in other parts of Greece where vineyards flourished.

The process involved cutting bunches of grapes from the vines with sharp sickles, filling baskets, and spreading the grapes out for several days in the drying area under the sun for the *moustos* (unfermented juice of the grapes) to become sweeter. The villagers then used their feet to trample the bunches of grapes in a *patitiri* (in ancient times: *"Leno"*) that was located in the end room of their home. This area was formed with a wall stretched across the narrow portion of the room comprising ten to fifteen square meters, it's length similar to that of the room itself (two to three meters), with a depth of 20 to 30 centimeters. The floor had flat stones with an inclination toward the outer sides to allow the wine – after the *patima* – to spill into the *ypolinio (polimi),* a round pit, through which the *moustos* flowed through a hole. Instead of a pit, the *moustos* could also be allowed to run into a large, clay vessel.

Once the trampling had been done, the *"kalamoti"* and the *"styraki"* were used to strain the *moustos* from the clusters of grapes. The *kalamoti* is comprised of rhododendron switches joined together with string. The trampled grapes would be thrown into the hollow of the *kalamoti*, which was placed on the stationary base of the *styraki*. They would squeeze the *kalamoti*, using ropes, and the grapes would be mashed into a solid cylindrical form. After removing the *kalamoti*, the base of the *styraki* would be maneuvered with the help of a pulley, and through turning and squeezing, the final portion of *moustos* would be expelled from the chunk of grapes in an action known as *sfeiridiasma.*

From the *patitiri*, the *moustos* was poured into jugs or *maerikes* (large jugs), where it would be left for forty days. For good luck over the year, the housewife would take a little bit of the *moustos*, strain it to remove impurities, place it over the fire, then mix it with flour to make a grape pie. This was laid out on plates and topped with cinnamon and crushed walnuts, then brought as a treat to the homes of relatives. This *moustalevria* was one of the most attractive and pure sweets of our village.

F.   **The Production of Olive Oil**

1. **Olive-producing trees and olives.** I don't know how olive trees always cause me to become emotional, to the point that my feeling is almost religious in nature. I can't understand why the olive trees, motionless in the night, gave me such an impression of a Biblical area, or why the hollows of the elderly olive trees seemed like a victory over the passage of time.

   In any case, it is true that people and seasons have distinct types of relationships with olives. In ancient mythology, the Goddess Athena gave a precious gift to the city of Athens, an olive tree; from its branches, which spawned yet more olive trees, come the *"Ierai elaiai,"* ("sacred olives"). The victors of Olympic contests were crowned with branches of the "wild olive tree of Hercules." When the Bible refers to Noah and the flood, it was a dove with an olive branch in its beak that delivered the message of calmness and peace. Christ, in His hours of agony, prayed in the Garden of Olives. Oil in the holy vigil lamps illuminates the *eikonostasi*, oil completes the sacrament of baptism, and oil is the basic element when one is given Holy Unction.

The olive tree is considered "the Mother of the Poor," the tree that supports every farmer in his time of financial need. Therefore, when the farmer sees the first blossom of the olive tree, he worries that bad weather (too rainy or too hot) will burn the blossoms. Everyone asks if the trees have yet blossomed and if there will be olives and oil that year.

In Agios Georgios, the farm areas contained numerous olive trees, and there were more in the *kato meri* (lower areas). I remember, in the village, that the farmers during the first rains would gather *xeronia*, dry and shrunken olives that contain very little oil, sell them to the middlemen to earn their first pocket money. Before the olives even ripened, the farmers would cut the thick, green olives from the trees and crush them to reduce their bitterness, and then salt them; these olives – called *"tsakistes"* – are very tasty. Other green olives that were also eaten were the *"machairotes"* ("knifed ones"), cut down with a knife and placed in a briny solution. Another type of olive meant to be eaten, known as *"tou ladiou"* ("of the oil"), was left to ripen longer to increase its sweetness.

Around November, the blond *"kourmades,"* are sweet and tasty and can be eaten right from the tree. They are truly the most beautiful and edible olives, and I doubt that they are produced in any other areas. Until December, when the rains would spoil them by making them oily, the *kourmades* were a very profitable crop for the farmers. When olives ripened and were blown to the ground by the wind, the Agiorgousoi would say, *"Stroma keinten oi elies,"* ("The olives lay spread"), and men, women, and children with baskets and panniers – which were huge baskets hung over the backs of donkeys – would go to gather those olives.

Today, since everything has been made easier, nets are spread around the trees and the olives are gathered in quantity. In the earlier years, we picked them up, one by one, as we sat on our knees or squatted. Many times we would feel frustrated until we finally succeeded in filling our baskets, especially when the olives were small. It was also hard for us when the ground was uneven or when it was cold

Pantelis A. Mavrogiorgis

enough to make our hands freeze. The gathering process lasted for months, until the beginning of March.

When the olives remained on the trees, the farmers would strike the branches with a long staff or climb up into the trees to shake the branches so the olives would fall down. From these, the women selected the ones with no bruises and firm skins, which they would then wash and toss into barrels or large jugs of salt water, where they remained for the entire year. They were considered to be a necessary food on a daily basis, and they were used especially during periods of fasting. The remaining olives were brought to the olive press for the production of olive oil.

2. **The Olive Press** *(Alaitrouveio).* In the village, the olive press was known as an *"Alaitrouveio,"* so they would say *"trivo elies"* to mean that they were pressing olives. There were two phases to the process of producing olive oil from olives: the pressing of the olive until it became mushy, and the squeezing of the mush until it released the oil. Each of these two phases occurred in one of the sections of the long, narrow building that housed the olive press. The crushing was done by the press, which sat upon a circular stone platform known as a *mandra,* that was about one meter high and two to two-and-a-half meters in diameter. The *mandra* rested on a level slate floor and had a raised, iron belt surrounding it and preventing the poultice from leaking during the crushing process.

The olives would be washed and spread on the mandra for crushing. Two wooden axles moved a millstone, a solid rock anywhere from 1.1 to 1.8 meters in length, which had a cyclindrical cone shape. The vertical axle sits in the center of the mandra, and its upper edge is attached to a beam supporting the roof, while the horizontal axle is merely a long stick that is supported by (either threaded through or nailed to) the vertical one. An animal, generally a mule, is harnessed to the horizontal axis. As the animal walks around the mandra, the movement of the horizontal axis moves the millstone and pushes it against the surface of the mandra, thus crushing the olives into a poultice.

Once the olives are pressed, *pessetiasma* follows, using *pessetes* that are square, loomed cloths made of animal hair. The olive poultice is spread over each cloth and the four corners of the cloth are folded inward to form a type of envelope. These filled cloths are then piled up in the *stiraki,* (press), and warm water is poured over them. The *stiraki* is made of iron, and the bottom portion, which is immobile, is the *katari* where the pessetes are stacked; and the top one is the *plakotari*, which moves downward through a vertical axle called an *argatis*. It takes the strength of two or more men, together with the help of a horizontal pulley, called a *Bozargatis*, to turn the *argatis*. As the pessetes are squeezed between the top and bottom portions of the *stiraki*, the oil and warm water – with which they often wet the *pessetes* – are extracted together.

This oil, in its impure state, runs through three successive troughs, rendering it purer with each passage, as the thick oil and the watery part drip. From that point, the oil is taken home in *ladotenekedes* (oil cans) and poured into the jugs and *maerikes* of the homes. The owner of the olive press receives payment in the form of oil, *"liniatiko."* To celebrate, the housewives make fried dough balls *(loukoumades)* and serve them with *raki*. The oil itself will be ready for use after a number of days, once the oil has settled.

The last of the olive presses to function in our village as we described were those of Stelianos Tsoflias (Tsarlatanos), Panagiotis Dellas (*Vrakas*), and Pantelis *Koilis*. Later, in our village, Stelianos Xenia's olive oil factory became automated. Today Dimitrios Koilis and the Cooperative of Olive Producers operate such factories.

CHAPTER 17
Occupations That Vanished

A. The Miller

The miller was the owner of a windmill, where the villagers would take their wheat or barley to be threshed. The millers tended to be meek and calm individuals, as they lived a somewhat isolated lifestyle in their mills, located on an elevated piece of ground outside of the village. The windmills depended on the force of the winds to operate. Today, these striking windmills no longer exist.

I remember the three functioning windmills near the new school, and due to their presence the area was named *"Myloi."* Pantela's windmill was in the same area, but it was abandoned.

The millers were: Nikolis Koumelas, whose mill was located where Dimitris Koilis' catering hall is today; Nikolaos Milonas, whose mill used to be where Milonas' restaurant now is; and Giorgis Koilis. The ruins of the mill which belonged to the old Monastery remain at the *Kalyvakia* mountain; and there are two other ruins on the road to *Tholopotami*: one being near Savlas' well. I had heard of another mill on the top of the mountain, which I recently heard belonged to Koilis'.

I've heard that there were other millers in Agios Georgios who rented mills in other villages, as well. This is probably likely since quite a few families in Agios Georgios have the surname *Mylonas*.

I would like to describe the windmill, both as I remember it and from the information I garnered from texts that I researched. I want to do this especially for the youth to have some idea of the way it was built and how it functioned, since windmills have completely vanished from Chios.

1. **External area of the windmill.** This is a spherical stone edifice with an external diameter of four to seven meters and a height of approximately four to six meters. The walls are extremely thick constructed with rocks, wood and lime dust which is necessitated by pressure from the weight of the mechanism itself and from the wind in the sails. These are also reasons for its circular shape, which has only a small door for access.

At the top of the wall of the building, there is a *"Stefani"* ("crown") made from pieces of wood known as *"proskefala."* This crown is supported by thick, hard pieces of wood known as *"bratsalia"* ("little arms") that are built into the wall to form an immobile frame called a *Mandra.* Above the crown sits the conical wooden roof covered with sheet-iron *lamarines* known as *"Travaka."* The roof contains two openings,*"klavanes,"* used by the miller to estimate weather conditions. In addition to its circular structure, crown, and *travaka*, we also observe the wind system that includes the antennas, the sails, and a portion of the axle that protrudes from the mill, in the center of which is secured a long, horizontal piece of wood called a *tsibouki.*

Within the six holes of the axle, twelve poles of chestnut wood – which are the antennas of the windmill – are inserted. They are secured with wedges of chestnut wood called *"Manes."* From the lower corners, the antennas are connected to one another with wire to increase durability, and their design now suggests a type of crown. The antennas are also fastened to the *tsimbouki* with another thinner wire that goes up to the *tsimbouki* and is known as *tsimboukoskino.*

To form each of its twelve "sails," three to four pieces of heavy *kannavatso,* canvas, are sewn together in the shape of an orthogonal (right-angled) triangle, and its edges are stitched with string called *"grandi."* The longest side of the sail is nailed to one of the antennas so that the corner of the right angle nearly reaches the tip of that pole. The surface appearance of the sails depends upon the strength of the wind. When the wind is weak, these sails open to their fullest extent.

a. **The Turning of the Mill.** The miller inserts iron cranks through holes in the *mandra's* housing to turn the *travaka* (the crown and the reel) in an opposite direction of the wind, which then hits the open sails and allows the windmill to function.

b. **The Interior.** Internally, the mill is comprised of three rooms. The basement is immediately within the entry door, and it is where wheat is left for threshing and for the production of flour. There is a second area, a type of auxiliary elevated room, called *"Patari,"* which has a wood floor and contains the "protruding arm," a horizontal piece of wood that holds the vertical iron axle of the millstones. The third area, known as the "upper room," also has a wood floor and houses the entire mechanism of the

Pantelis A. Mavrogiorgis

Windmill
(Photographer: Haviaras)

windmill: the millstones, the *xioni* (axle), the wheel, and the lantern. There is an internal stone, spiral staircase, which allows access to the upper rooms.

In the uppermost room, there is a large area where the two circular, smooth-surfaced millstones are located. The bottom remains motionless while the top one revolves. A wooden diaphragm protects them all around. The force of the wind on the sails turns the reel and the axle – a thick, cylindrical piece of cypress or terebinth wood that rests on the crown of the windmill and provides support for the antennas – in turn revolves. Thus, the entire functioning ability of the mill is based upon the revolutionary motion of the horizontal axle promoting the motion of the vertical iron axle called the *Lambada,* all of which occurs with the assistance of the Wheel.

The Wheel is a wooden cogwheel with sixty "teeth," positioned in the center of the horizontal axle and working in tandem with a smaller cogwheel called *Fanari,* which is connected to the vertical axle (*Lambada)*. The *Fanari* has a rounded conical shape and is constructed of twelve pieces of wood called *Pentodavria,* so as the gear teeth work together, the Wheel turns the *Fanari,* which then turns the *Lambada* and causes the millstone to revolve. Due to the disparity in the number of gear teeth in each of them, the *Fanari* makes five revolutions to every single turn of the Wheel with its sixty teeth.

c. **The Threshing.** The *Kofinida,* a pyramid-shaped wooden box, hangs from the roof above the millstones. The wheat is placed in the *kofinida,* and spills out through the *Goula,* a grooved board, to the millstones below. The miller checks the thickness or thinness of the flour by hand during the milling process, and he adjusts the position of the upper millstone accordingly. Due to centrifugal force, flour gathers near the millstones and is transported by hose from there to a wooden box.

B. The Lime Makers

In the old days, our village had many lime makers who built furnaces to produce lime. During the Turkish Occupation, the Turks needed lime for their public buildings and forts, so they granted privileges to the Agiorgousoi for lime production, since their ability to produce mastic was so limited.

Here, in a poem sung by mothers to her children, is a reference to this industry:

> *"Quickly, quickly, may you grow up,*
> *to be well-fed and strong,*
> *so I can give you the crowbar,*
> *the heavy, iron one."*

(The crowbar was used to move stone, remove rocks from the ground in the fields, and it was also used in the lime furnaces.)

The furnaces were operated in the summer and fall when the weather was favorable and not rainy. The job required five or six individuals called the *"Tsourmos"* or *"Parea"* (group). At least one of these men had to know the process of building and firing up the furnace and have enough experience to guide the others, who functioned as needed helpers. Some were tasked with removing stones from the ground, and others were responsible for *Koumbaniasma* – carting the stones to the location where the furnace was to be built. Another group of three, the *Partia*, would set out to get wood; two of them would collect and cut the wood; and the third person, the *Thetis*, would bundle it. Even though the other two men would ask the *Thetis*, as he worked, how many bundles he had put together, he would not respond – so as not to interrupt the rhythm of the work; but at night, he would let them know how many bundles they had produced that day.

The bundles would be brought to the furnace in order to keep the fire continuously burning and to "cover" the furnace to prevent the wind from extinguishing the flames, which they referred to as "Crowning" the furnace – *Stefanoma tou kaminiou.* When the crowning bundles would be used to feed the fire, they called this *"xevrochiasma."*

To build the furnace, a circular pit of 1.8 meters in depth and 3 to 3.5 meters in diameter is dug. Within that pit the furnace is constructed with a drywall in a semi-circular shape. The first line of stones upon which the *germa* (*tholos* or dome) will be built is known as *"Kavallaris"* ("The Rider"). Once the structure is completed, a wall is built above the surface of the ground around the entire building and is called *Poza*. The *Poza* is filled with stones, and the fire in the furnace burns at a very high temperature, turning the stones into lime.

In the front side of the furnace, known as *"Koutelo"* ("Forehead"), they create a door of about one-half meter in both height and width. The door is constructed of two vertical stones, *"Magoula"* ("Cheeks"), and two other long, narrow stones in the shape of a triangle; and the threshold is called the *"Podia"* (Apron).

The lime maker uses forked, wooden tongs to throw wood into the furnace, including the wood brought from the crown. In order to allow the workers to rest, the burning job is done in shifts over a period of about ten days, but the entire process requires approximately twenty days. The "cooked stone" is transformed into lime, due to being burned continuously at extremely high temperatures. Once the fire is put out, the lime is divided among the workers during the last stage of production called *"xekaminoma."* Upon completion of this final process, they sit together – as they did at the outset – and eat and drink.

Depending upon the load and how well the burning process succeeded, one lime furnace was capable of producing from 600 to 2,000 *kantaria* of lime. (Each *kantari* had 44 *okades*, and each *oka* contained about 1,250 grams.)

C. The Weavers

In Agios Georgios, five or six families were skilled at the job of weaving, from which their ancestors received the family surname Tsouvalades, and later on Sakoulades. Another family in the village owes its surname, Vafeiadon, to the business of dyeing local cloth and garments. The last of this family was Nikitas Vafeias, whose shop was located behind *Agios Panteleimonas*. The last of the weavers were the brothers Antonios and Nikolis Sakoulas, and a son named Antonios Sakoulas; plus the brothers Zannis and Dimitris Agouridis, brothers-in-law of Stelianos Sakoulas, who taught them the skill.

The weaving process has four stages: **separation** of the goat hairs used in weaving, **piling, spinning** of the hair threads, and **weaving**.

1. **Separation.** The goat hair would be purchased from the shepherds after the shearing of their goats. First, the weavers would separate this hair by color: usually white, black, red, and a dark gray-brown. Outside of these natural colors, the white hairs would be dyed red and green with artificial dyes to make the cloth more attractive.

2. **Piling.** There was a device called a *"Stoivastira."* It was made with two thin ropes: one was five meters long and the other was seven meters long. Each of the ends of these two ropes would be tied to four large nails embedded in the ground. They would grasp the center of each of the ropes and tie that to a wooden handle above. The handle would be used to shake the strings, which would then impact the hairs, resulting in a circular pileup of hairs behind the nails. This process produced the piles of hairs known as *"Touloupes"* or *"Tolypes."*

Pantelis A. Mavrogiorgis

3. Spinning. In order to spin thread *(otron)*, the craftsman would tie a *"Mesini,"* a leather bag, around his waist, put a *touloupa* of hair inside it, and stand in front of the *"Svya"* – a device consisting of twelve wooden spokes. Each spoke was secured to the revolving axle while its other end was tied to the other spokes with four strings, together forming the *"Trochos,"* a spinning wheel. The task of spinning was achieved by the craftsman taking piles of hair from his *mesini*, using three fingers from each hand, and walking backwards along the *svya* as it revolved and spun the hair into woolen strands.

4. Weaving. This final step is done on a type of loom, an *argaleio*, different from those used in the villages to weave cloth. It is set up according to standards of height or *"istos"* – the ancient Greeks used that word, taking it from the verb *istimi*. The loom is made from two wooden rafters, called "Ears," that are set up about two meters apart on the floor of the house and allowed to lean against the wall. There are grooves above and below those "Ears" known as *"Mesies"* or *"Antia,"* and the "Ears" are inserted firmly into those grooves. The craftsmen use a rounded staff that is anywhere from .4 to two meters in length and known as a *"Diasoverga"* and used to position the woolen strands from top to bottom on the loom. This process is called *"Diasimo."*

The *"Zachoverga"* is actually the shuttle of the common loom. It is a wooden spindle around which the woof (the threads or yarn running from side to side across a loom) is wrapped and then passed through other woofs. Therefore, the cloth is woven through the horizontal-vertical interweaving of warps (the yarn running lengthwise along the loom) and woofs and beaten with a *"Chteni,"* a comb-like tool that has teeth. Some of the items woven by the weavers were:

a. The **Pessetes** of the olive press: black and gray squares, with lengths of from 0.9 centimeters to 1.35 centimeters.

b. *Mesies* for the animals: strips of cloth that go under the bellies of the animals to secure the saddles onto their backs. One end of the *mesia* is sewn to the saddle, and the other end is tied to the ring of a hook on the opposite side of the saddle.

c. **Dipouzes:** ropes used to tie the front and back legs of donkeys and mules on either the right or left side to prevent them from going too far or jumping over the walls of fields when they were allowed to graze freely.

d. **Tsouvalia:** sacks used for hay, corn, or other things.

e. **Colorful strips:** made into decorative shapes to use in corridors of the houses.

f. **Rugs:** colorful for use on the floors of the houses during the winter months.

g. **Tourvades:** knapsacks a type of satchel in which farmers put small tools like saws and lopping shears, and a bag with dry foods like figs. When they went shopping in the *chora*, especially for the Christmas holidays, they would say things like, *"Pao na fero ton tourva,"* or *"E, iferes ton tourva?"* ("I'm going to bring the knapsack," and "Hey, did you bring the knapsack?")

CHAPTER 18
Responsibilities of the Homemaker

The women in the village carried the entire burden of household chores and family responsibilities. With kindness that approaches holiness, they made enormous sacrifices in order to raise their children, care for their spouses, and "worship" their in-laws. The women gave and gave, but never looked to receive anything in return. Those were the days, before the coming of modern times, when a wife would consider motherhood sacred.

We will not cover all of the tasks handled by the wife in the household, since many of these are familiar and common even to this day. We will only mention those responsibilities that changed due to the coming of electricity and modern technology or were rendered obsolete over time.

A. Lighting the Fire

With this simple example, we can illustrate just how difficult it was for a woman back then. In order to light a fire in the fireplace or the stove, *soba*, she would place kindling wood, pinecones, or branches from the thorny calico bush in the brazier and set fire to them. When the wood would not catch fire, she would grow frustrated and blow on it; and once the fire did start, the clouds of smoke issuing from the fireplace would make her eyes red and teary.

B. Preparing Dough

Each family, at that time, was an independent production unit. Therefore, the housewife would make macaroni, noodles, and other foods requiring dough herself. She would use a fine, mesh sifter to sift wheat flour of the best quality available, then add warm water and salt to knead the tight ball of dough she had made. She would press on the center of the ball to create a small depression and fill it with oil. Cutting a section of dough, she then held it up high in her left hand and used three fingers of her right hand to gently twist that dough into long, thin strands, *fides*, vermicelli noodles that she would drop onto a wide board sprinkled with flour. This was the process she used to make noodles that would first be allowed to dry before being used in soup. For macaroni, she would use the palms of her hands to wrap a small ball of dough around a dry spartium shoot, pull to widen it, and create a piece of circular macaroni with a hole in the center, called *"makaronia tou cheriou."*

The Village Agios Georgios Sikousis

At other times, she used a slender, cylindrical rolling pin, a *"Matsoverga,"* to roll out thin crusts on the board. Once she wrapped the crust around the *matsoverga* and then slipped the rolling pin out, the dough would remain curled, so that she could cut it into thin pieces called *"Koulourides"* or *"Mats."* For rice, the *"Chontro"* or *"Pnigouri"* – a thick wheat cut with the stone handmill – was used. This *"chontros"* was made into the most wonderful pilaf.

C. Roasting Coffee

This was an exhausting job. The expression, *"Kavourdizomai"* ("I'm roasted") was used to metaphorically express their feelings over any task considered to be really difficult. As referred in an earlier chapter, the roaster was a cylindrical, metal container; and its dimensions were approximately 0.15 centimeters in diameter and 0.2 to 0.3 centimeters in height. It had a small opening, with a movable little door that the housewife would open to put the coffee beans into the roaster. A thin iron rod passed through this roaster, with about 0.2 centimeters protruding from the right side, allowing the roaster to be supported over the coals of the fire; while the opposite side of the rod was bent upward for about one meter and arched like a handle. The woman would hold this "handle" with her left hand and turn the roaster over the fire with her right hand to roast the coffee beans. Thus the coffee beans were slowly roasted, in order for the *kopanisma* (pounding of the coffee beans) to follow.

D. Pounding the Coffee Beans

The roasted coffee beans were then put into a thick-walled stone morter and pounded into a powdery substance with an iron pestle. After sifting it through a thin, cloth sieve, any remnants that didn't pass through the cloth were pounded a second, or even a third, time. Once this was done, some of the coffee that looked to be the best was kept to make coffee for visitors. The remainder was mixed with roasted chickpeas and barley, since the coffee was very expensive. They tended to drink their coffee in large cups, as they did tea, and they would dip bread or *paximadia* (biscuits) into it.

E. Kneading Bread

Yeast was a necessary ingredient, and it was retained in a piece of dough saved from the previous kneading. It was subjected to chemical fermentation until it soured, and it became the yeast used to make bread dough rise. There seemed to be some superstitions among the housewives concerning yeast, because each woman refused to lend her yeast to another woman, and they

Pantelis A. Mavrogiorgis

never took it outside of the house at night, uncovered, as it was not "proper" for the stars to see it.

When they kneaded, they dissolved the yeast in warm water from a trough. They would "grab the yeast," as the expression goes, and pour in flour after putting it through a fine sieve, and then knead it again with their fists. Sections of the dough would be cut off, sprinkled with flour, shaped on a wide board, and put either into baskets or the *pinakoti*, which was a deep board with slots for bread. This process was known as *"Plasimo ton psomion."*

The loaves would be covered for an hour or two for the dough to rise, and then they would be baked in the oven. It was important that the yeast not cause the loaves to rise too much because the bread would be sour, but if it did not rise enough, then it would break into pieces while it baked. As they prepared all of this, they would occasionally leave some of the dough out, mix it with more water, and make *"zestopitti,"* which would be eaten with oil and sugar.

F. Baking Bread

The oven would be lit with branches, holly, brushwood, branches from the thorny calico bush, and so forth; and the woman would use a poker to move these objects around to keep the fire going and then remove the charcoal and any charred remains to a cylindrical container called a *"Tasi,"* with a tight-fitting lid, in order to extinguish the contents.

She would clean the oven bottom with a wet cloth. Using a *"fourneftrio,"* a type of wide wooden paddle, she would place the largest breads at the rear of the oven, followed by the smaller ones, and then she would put the pies in the front. She would close the oven door to ensure that no heat was lost, and when the breads were golden brown, she would remove them from the oven with the *"Katsouna,"* a hooked instrument, and stand them up to cool.

G. Making Cheese

The women had the job of milking the goats and sheep, both morning and night. They used this milk mainly to prepare cheese, calling the task "cheese cutting," expressed as *"Tyrokopsimo."* The milk was never wasted and was only given to children or sick people to drink, as it was considered to be medicinal. Adults dipped their bread into coffee or sage tea at breakfast or in the afternoon.

For the cheese-making process, depending upon the amount of milk used, the lady would select either a very large and wide kettle or a smaller metal cup, pour in the milk, put it over hot coals, and test its temperature periodically with her pinky. When it was lukewarm, she would put in a small ball of dough and, as the milk got warmer and the dough melted, she would stir the mixture with a large spoon. As the liquid boiled, it would separate, and she would scoop up the pieces of cheese with a holed spoon and deposit them into *tyrovolia*, little baskets woven from bulrushes.

To make *Mouzithra* cheese, she would continue to cook the remaining liquid, add more milk to make it stronger, and would constantly stir to prevent sticking. As a thin layer of cheese rose to the surface, she would remove it to a cheese basket with the holed spoon.

After all of the cheeses had dried in the cheese baskets, she would put them into a large basket for the wind to further dry. From there, they would be put into a barrel containing a briny solution. The cheese would be eaten with bread, but the saltier portions were cut into chunks to be put into soups or grated for use on macaroni.

Besides this "salty cheese," there was a drained cheese made with plain *mouzithra* and fresh cheese. It would be kneaded either in a kettle or trough and salted. It was then placed into jars or copper pots and vacuum-sealed, where it underwent chemical fermentation. *Kopanisti* or pounded cheeses of this type required much cleanliness and care to prevent spoilage. Therefore, the housewives would sometimes open the containers to check whether the cheese had remained clean and to sample it in order to taste whether it had become too spicy. In about thirty or forty days it was suitable for consumption. In cases where a household had produced an excess of cheese or *kopanisti*, they would sell it to village middlemen, who would then resell it to other villages.

H. Washing Clothes *(Bougada)*

The word *"bougada"* is either Italian or Spanish in origin. This was the name given to the task of washing clothes with soap, water, and ashes. Every month the housewife would "prepare the wash" by tying it into large bundles and loading them on the back of a donkey or mule. She would also put a cauldron right on the saddle and leave for a countryside area like the *Notso Kipos,* where there was a spring. Spring water ran from a channel and was collected in *gournes* (basins) placed beneath an arched portico to protect them from rain. This porch had *pezoules*, slate-covered parapets, on which to lay the bundle of clothes to be washed.

If there was a heavy load of wash, the lady would usually go to the springs at Notso Kipos. The clothing had to first be laid out. With thick clothes like suits and slacks, they would pile them up on the slab after the first washing

---

Pantelis A. Mavrogiorgis

and beat them with a *kopano*, a wooden paddle with a wide end, "for the dirt to come out." The second time they soaped the clothes, they would rub the fabrics together with their hands and then rinse them out, which was the basic part of the laundering process. To pour out the water, they framed a flat area of the ground with large stones to form a type of threshing field. They covered this portion of the ground with a large napkin or an old sheet, *"bougadopano."* The women would then pour boiling water containing ashes on each item of clothing in succession.

To have boiling water handy for this chore, the men would go out in the morning, cut a bundle of holly branches and, in preparation for washing clothes, the women would light a fire and "boil the cauldrons," as they would say. They would take buckets of boiling water from those cauldrons to pour over the clothing, which would then be left for one to two hours under boiled ashes, which would settle and form a thick layer on the surface of the clothes.

The final step, called *"neroperasma,"* was to rinse these clothes with plenty of clean water. Small and thin articles of clothing would be washed separately and spread out with the other items under the sun to air dry. The clothing would all become very clean and have a fresh smell.

I. Weaving

In those years, weaving was another task done by the wife. Using a loom, she would weave cloth for the home, underwear and outerwear for the family, rugs, wall hangings, and bedsheets.

The Homeric Penelope would weave day and night as she anxiously awaited Odysseus' return. In Homeric times, the "web" and the "loom," were primarily considered women's work.

When Penelope, mother of Telemachos, becomes very emotional as she hears Femio the Singer singing the "return of the Achaians," Telemachos advises her not to hate the singer,

> "...but to go into her quarters and tend to her responsibilities: the distaff and the loom . . . . "

To begin weaving, there are other things a woman must first do prior to placing the warp *(the lengthwise yarn held firmly on the loom)* or gathering the yarn to be wrapped around the bobbins. In order for sheep's wool to become thread, once the sheep were shorn, the fleece would be thoroughly washed and carded by hand to make it fluffy. *(Note: Carding is a process by which fleece is opened, cleaned, and straightened in preparation for spinning.)* After the carding

---

The Village Agios Georgios Sikousis

of the wool, it would be spun wisp by wisp, with the Distaff held high with the left hand, while three fingers of the right hand twisted the unspun wool. The woman would then move the spindle with her thumb and middle finger to spin the wool into thread. The Distaff, made with a reed or piece of wood, was the device upon which the tuft of wool was woven. In ancient times, this was referred to as an *"ilakati"* or loom, which we now call *"alekati,"* the name of the bush on which the silkworm weaves its silk cocoon.

The *Agdarti* or *Atraktos* (spindle) was a wooden contraption, thin at the ends and thicker in the middle. A wooden ring *("sfendyli")* was attached at the bottom; due to its weight and shape, it increased the revolutions of the spindle. The upper part of the *sfendyli* had a white metal overlay ending in a hook to support the thread of wool, and as the spindle revolved, the wool would become thread that was taken up by the *sfendyli* in loops. There was a piece of forked wood with a bobbin at each end to receive the woolen thread.

Another device used for spinning wool and weaving was the *"Anemi"* ("Spinning Wheel"). This is constructed with a vertical wooden axle made of reeds on a wooden base. A polygonal conical attachment with a hook revolves around the axle, winding the wool or thread onto the axle. The end of that thread is tied to the end of another metal horizontal axle, which is simultaneously turned by hand, so that it spins the bobbins. Thus, the vertical revolutions of the conical part become horizontal in order to wrap thread around the bobbins to prepare the shuttle of the loom for weaving.

1. **The Loom.** This device has four wooden beams that stand on the ground vertically, is one meter in width, with the beams spaced approximately two meters apart. They are known as *"Baloi"* and are connected at the top by four boards, *Rendines* or *Atropines*, inserted through slits at the edges of the four beams. At about one-half meter above the floor are another four beams also inserted into slits in the upright posts. Thus the structure of the loom contains four vertical and eight horizontal beams called the *"Strosi."* Above the loom are the various items necessary for weaving: the *"Antia,"* the "Door" or "Comb," and the "Shuttle," as well as other necessities.

The *Antia* are two cylindrical pieces of wood across from one another, supported by chocks added to the sides of the vertical beams. On one of the *antia*, the warp is wrapped, and the woven cloth is wrapped around the other. The "Comb" rests on two, large horizontal beams with two wooden sides, called "Swords" – which are attached horizontally at the bottom with two pieces of wood, between which the wooden combs are secured. The teeth of these combs support the main comb, through the teeth of which the threads of the warp pass.

The woman who is weaving sits on the board with the warp in front of her and moves the "Shuttle" through those threads with crosswise threads in order to weave. She uses the comb, moving it from front to back, striking the woven cloth in order to thicken it and make it firmer. There are other gadgets on the loom to assist the weaver, such as the "spools" and the "larger spools" above, the *zefles* (pedals) she steps on, and the *mitotires*, to name a few.

The job of weaving is difficult, but it is also a strong desire. Since the weaver had to sit at the loom for a considerable amount of time in order to do the work, she would often relieve her boredom by singing, which resulted in the "little songs" of the loom.

2. A Weaving Song

Whoever wants to get old,
let her buy a workshop.
And whoever wants to be young,
let her go and learn artistry.

•

In the tying and untying of the fabrics,
I don't want to love him.
I only want to sing and weave
in the middle of the cloth.

•

The embroidery is a pleasure,
and the distaff is a stroll,
but the loom is slavery,
very great slavery.

•

Golden is the cloth,
and the comb ivory,
and a graceful young lady,
who sings and weaves.

CHAPTER 19
The Water Supply

A. The Wells

From when it was founded up until 1926, our village suffered greatly from a lack of water. There was no running spring water for the necessities of the inhabitants, who at one time numbered 2,000 souls. How much could be done with the water that the women carried on their shoulders with clay jugs and bronze pitchers, considering that water was needed for drinking, washing, and for the animals?

In order to see to these needs in any way possible, the villagers dug a number of wells inside and outside of the village, creating community wells and private wells, which gave them a source of water or they gathered rain water in the winter months. Those who lived in the *Exo geitonia* got water from the *"Pigada"* – which can still be found on the road to *Tholopotami* – from the well of *"Koukoumou,"* southwest of the village, and from *"Kato pigadi."* The spring of *"Melanta"* is on the road and near the *Agios Panteleimonas square;* however that water is only used for the animals.

Those who lived in the *Mesa geitonia* had more wells. There were two in *Lakkos*: one across from Antonaros' house, and the other across from Patriarchis' home. Then another well was located across from Giorgis Vekios, next to Flouras; but they've since closed it up and that land is part of the road. A little further up from the church of Agios Georgios, *"Fardeia Pigada"* ("Wide Well") still exists. There is another in the *Plateia Mpou* and three or four on the road to *Lavidorkis*, further down from *Agios Charalambis*. These were dug by private individuals but were at the village's disposal. They actually belong to Zymnis, Smaïli's, the Turk, and Lambrinoukas.

Parenthetically, we'd like to say a few words about the wells of Smaili and the Turk's. I do not know anything about the Turk who owned this well, which still bears his name, nor was I able to get any oral information about him. Georgios Madias, the high school principal wrote:

> *"The famous well from which the hard-working Agiorgou sians drink, belongs to the Zychnis', a Turkish family who once lived in Agios Georgios. It is coincidental that it bears*

Pantelis A. Mavrogiorgis

the name of Zichni Pasha, who defended the domination of the
Turks over Chios (1912)."

I don't know which of the wells Madias is referring to, nor do I know where
he received his information. I wonder if the well he mentions is the one known
as "the well of the Turk." On the contrary, we do have specific information about
Smaïli's well from one of his relatives. That relative, the old man, Konstantis
Kalargyros, known as *"Kokkinokolos,"* gave written information to the school
principal Alexandros Galanos.

> *"Smaïli's well was dug by a fellow from the Kalargyros family who
> was made into a Turk when he was young. They called him Giannis.
> So Giannis Kalargyros was actually the hatzi Smaïlis, because his
> father took him to worship at the Holy Tomb at a young age, as
> many pilgrims did in those years.*

> *Giannis remained in Turkey as a slave and was called Smaïlis. He
> came to our village many times. He paid to have the well dug for
> the good of his soul, since the village did not have water. So, for
> that reason, it is called Smaïli's well.*

> *Whenever he came to our village, he would bring various gifts to
> his relatives. When he would leave, they would give him mastic,
> walnuts, pastelaries, and other farm produce. He never managed
> to leave on the day that he said he would. Instead he would delay,
> either because he wanted to receive more things or because he
> liked the village. Because of that, whenever someone says that he
> plans to leave but fails to do so, they say, "Hatzi Smaïlis is leaving
> again."*

I, myself, remember hearing that expression said about someone who
mentioned that he would leave but never did. To end our parenthetical addition,
we would like to say that a number of villagers had private fountains, and there
was also a small spring beneath *Agios Nikolas,* the *"Vigla,"* in which a little water,
suitable for the animals, ran only during the winter.

During the winter months, conditions were manageable. As we moved
toward the summer, though, especially if a drought occurred, problems
appeared. To have an adequate supply of water, two jugs would be put into
a net and loaded on donkeys – or else four gas cans in wooden boxes would
be taken – and those villagers would travel a great distance away to fill those
vessels with water.

The cranking mechanism of the well at *Ai Giannis o Prodromos,* required a rope of about fifteen to twenty meters in length to draw the water up from the well in a bucket. The well of *Nola Pigadi* is in the river near *Droposi*. My mother was telling me that one Christmas Eve, she took a mule to *Tholopotami*, a village about one hour away from Agios Giorgis, in order to get water.

Fortunately, our village had an active and inspired teacher, the ever-memorable Alexandros Galanos, whose appearance was imposing and who was a dynamic and action-oriented man. He advocated for our village to be provided with water from *Platanos*. Madias writes that Galanos put forth "undaunted effort" and was

> *"tall and slender like a tower, an unsurpassable obstacle for every reaction of the smart, but difficult, Agiorgousoi."*

B. The Water of *Platanos*.

Platanos, which is more than a one-hour walk north of our village, is considered a monasterial estate. It was first a Dependency of Nea Moni, and afterwards it came under the jurisdiction of the monks of the *Skiti ton Agion Pateron*. For someone making the journey on foot, there is a refreshing place to stop among the forested areas, including the isolated chapel of *Agion Platonos kai Romanou*, from which the name *Platanos* came. There was a thirst-quenching spring with abundant, cool water. Whenever we went to worship at *Agious Pateres*, we usually went down to *Platanos* to eat, drink, and refresh the animals we traveled with.

Relative to bringing the waters of *Platanos* to our village, this appeared in the issue 1594 of the *Panchiaki* newspaper dated September 1, 1923:

> *"Following the action taken by the town of Agios Georgios Sikousis, in which Mr. Alexandros Galanos, Director of the School, has taken a lead role, along with his praiseworthy brother, the former Myrsini businessman, Mr. Georgios Galanos, a Committee was formed consisting of the most eminent people of the community to collect funds to bring water to our village. The Ministry of Health and Human Welfare has approved the Committee."*

Members of the Committee, as we are informed by an article in the *Nea Chios* newspaper's October 25, 1924 edition, consisted of these fellow villagers: Panagiotis Nyktas, Stelianos B. Vafias, Nikolaos Patounas, Ioannis Kostilis, Georgios N. Soukas, the priest Stylianos Salagaras, Nikolaos Psaros, Ioannis Monioukas, Thomas Zymnis, Diamantis Papanikolaou, Ioannis Patounas, and Antonios Foustanas. This is the decision reached by the Community Council on

March 5, 1924:

> *"There are requests from the venerable Ministry of Transportation regarding the expropriation of spring water that exists near Platanos, belonging to the Stavropigiaki Moni of Nea Moni, which has granted the written rights of the farmlands and Spring to the Skiti of Agion Pateron."*

1. **The Expropriation.** Despite sporadic resistance from the *Agiopaterousoi* (monks of *Agion Pateron*), the government granted four-fifths of the spring's water to the inhabitants of Agios Georgios, leaving one-fifth for the monks. The following was written in issue 1743 of the *Nea Chios* newspaper on August 5, 1924:

> *"The inhabitants of our noble village, Agios Georgios Sikousis, were pleasantly informed, by our caring government, of the expropriation of the hotly debated waters of Plataniou for use by our village.*
>
> *The government, having decided this expropriation in favor of our villagers, did a just, Christian-like, and beneficial deed. It would have constituted a great injustice to have denied a village like Agios Georgios – with its more than 2,500 inhabitants thirsting for water – to remain without a water supply, while a short distance away the Monastery continued to squander abundant amounts of ample spring waters on fields and mountains, due merely to the stubbornness of two or three brothers in Christ.*
>
> *The water supply is more than sufficient. The monks, with their ration of one-fifth, will easily able to water the grounds of their estate while allowing the village of Agios Georgios the water they desperately need. Where was the benevolence of these venerable servants of God in this evangelical work? The government showed kindness in its decision regarding the expropriation of water for our village, Agios Georgios. The efforts of our Member of Parliament, Mr. Christos Rodokanakis, always eager to render patriotic services, and the government's understanding that this decision was within the rights of our good villagers, resulted in the expropriation of four-fifths of the water supply for our village.* **Already, through a document of the Ministry of Transportation**

to our Prefecture, it is made known that – based on the report of the appropriate Committee – the channeling of four-fifths of the daily water that flows from the spring of Platanos is granted to the Community of Agios Georgios, with the remaining one-fifth granted to the estate of the Skiti of Agion Pateron.

Based on these circumstances, we must extol the effort and the patriotic zeal of the Galanos brothers, from the village of Agios Georgios, who spared no effort and persisted with a strong and indivisible will, so that this great benefit for the village could be achieved."

2. **The Reaction.** It is a fact that even the most progressive and necessary work can stir up reactions born of narrow-mindedness, personal antipathies, and factions within the villages. Fortunately, very few Agiorgousoi had contrary opinions regarding the channeling of the water. Those who did oppose it did so either because they were relatives of monks, or due to their religious fanaticism, but more so, I think, from their political leanings. It is likely that these reactionaries simply did not like members of the Committee or the Member of Parliament who was assisting in the effort.

There was a local newspaper at that time named *Anagennisis,* which represented the negative reaction to this issue. I was not able to find the pages containing what had been written on the topic and which bore the signatures of "many Agiorgousoi." However, I did locate the answer printed in the October 14, 1924 issue of the newspaper, *Nea Chios*, in issue 1773 – as well as a letter written by the Committee in the same newspaper's October 25, 1924 edition, issue 1778, which I will present further down. I consider these articles very enlightening and illustrative of the spirit of the times.

"We are very frustrated by the lengthy essay in our sister newspaper 'Anagennisis' concerning the water supply for Agios Georgios Sikousis, both because of its Jesuit monastic tone, as well as the use of the anonymous signature.

'Many Agiorgousoi,' it tells you!!! Why not sign it then, since there are so many that it gives the impression of a great number of people? Even if it was a minority of inhabitants who had this opinion and wanted to be heard and hoped to persuade their fellow villagers to come around to their way

Pantelis A. Mavrogiorgis

of thinking, they still should have signed it. Or perhaps the naïve writer thinks that by using 'the signature of 'Many Agiorgousoi" it is more believable that it refers to a large segment of the villagers and not merely those who have a relationship with the cassock and only wish to divide the villagers and cause the issue to be abandoned. According to what we believe, it is impossible that there are Agiorgousoi – no matter what their party affiliations – who, with little thought, would react in this manner to an issue concerning the water supply for their village. This is the very reason why this evil-willed publication bears the anonymous signature of 'Many Agiorgousoi.'

As far as the sufficiency of the water supply in the spring of Plataniou, whether or not it reaches the village, we believe that the ones who are qualified to decide are others, and not 'these many Agiorgousoi.' **It is possible, of course, that the problem concerning the water supply will not be resolved** *as a result of the difficulties being presented. But the Committee and the good inhabitants of the village, who are so eager for this work to be done, will not be responsible for endless delays and much grief – since that is the work of the reactionary 'Many Agiorgousoi!!!' and the newspaper, 'Anagennisis,' is also to blame for taking a stand against the lives and very existence of the villagers."*

The above article resulted in the Water Supply Committee's answer below.

"To the Honorable Management of 'Nea Chios.' On page 1773 of the issue of the fourteenth of this month, relative to the subject of the water supply of our village, you write – among other things – 'It is possible, of course, that the water channeling may never occur . . .' At this point, we are pleased to categorically and officially declare that the only thing standing in the way of ordering the pipes necessary for transporting the water from the expropriated spring of Platanos is the lack of an engineer to perform the appropriate study that is required.

Once this difficulty has been resolved, and we hope it happens very quickly, a public bid will be announced for the supply of pipes – as the amount of money determined by the

---

Protodikeion (Lower Court) – 20,000 drachmas needed for the expropriation of water – was deposited in the Public Treasury. The venerable ascetics refuse to accept this, hoping to present an obstacle to the rapid completion of the work. They do not realize, it seems, that this action of theirs does not prevent us in any way from channeling the water, since we are now in charge, a factor of which they are well aware; but the need for water is so great that all of the village inhabitants will eagerly contribute to the success of the work.

They are deceived if they think that the reactionary deeds of the few, numbered on the fingers of one hand – along with the curses, excommunications, and exorcisms of the Most Venerable Abbot of the Skiti, Andronikos Karavanas, toward our fellow villagers abroad – will prevent them from contributing to the work or help to delay it or cause it to fail. This work will be performed quickly and safely. Everything is going well.

To the 'UNPREJUDICED' reporter of 'Anagennisis,' who cared so much and took a lot of interest in our water supply, we have to recommend that he would do better to cease being interested and imparting incorrect information regarding our issue. We are in the position of knowing our advantages better than anyone else, and we are not waiting for him to inform us about them. If he possessed even the most basic logic, he would realize that if there were a closer spring that could provide water to the community, we would not seek to transport it from a longer distance at a far greater expense. He would not mention the water from the 'Makri' spring if he were aware of the fact that it takes approximately twenty minutes for someone to fill a jug with water from that spring. As for the 'Peristera' spring, whoever mentions it should be pitied, since the flow from there is far less than the ouzo that flows from the pipe of the distilling vat.

In 'Anagennisis,' where the writer predicts discouragement that does not even exist, we are saving him from real disappointment when, despite his political interests, he sees that the work is quickly performed. It seems that our village is condemned to be used for political interests, even regarding our most important affairs. If Mr. Rodokanakis (the Member of Parliament at the time) *worked for our situation, should he then be worthy of indictment? Perhaps the support of the Director of 'Anagennisis' should have been sought? We'll leave that for his naïve Agiorgousis friends! who truly hurt on behalf of our village and do not seek accolades or positions and who have a monopoly on patriotism!!! May he rejoice over them.*

> *In Agios Georgios Sikousis*
> *On October 22, 1924*
> *The Water Supply Committee*
> *(Signatures)"*

3. **The Execution of the Work.** *Papa* Karavanas, the abbot of *Agion Pateron*, did not cease his threats of excommunication. The monks built a wall around the spring and prevented passersby from crossing it to get water. The relations between the Agiorgousoi and the *Agiopaterousians* had intensified.

As I heard, the Agiorgousoi destroyed the wall around the spring one night, and the following day a trial was to occur at that very location so that "temporary measures" could be taken. Despite all of this, the work was scheduled to be performed. According to my information, Antonios Kostalas, an engineer, assisted by Pantelis Aslamidis, an engineer from Agios Giorgis, completed the required technical report. The community undertook all expenses. The villagers abroad contributed; and the locals worked without pay for endless days, along with their animals, to dig the trenches and lay the pipes for the channeling of water from *Platanos* to the village.

We learn from the village archives that in 1924 the Community Council gave 10,000 drachmas from rented grazing fields to the Water Committee. In its decision of July 27, 1925, the Council

> *"imposes on the male inhabitants, who have completed the age of eighteen, the mandate for personal work of eight days towards the transport of water from the spring of Platanos. The community is unable to undertake the expenses required to pay for the creation of trenches to lay piping."*

In this way, the participation of the inhabitants was assured, and the villagers proceeded with the construction.

This is when *Gria Kori,* the elderly poetess of the village befittingly created these four verses:

"Forward, my brave ones,
and in front go your teachers,
so that you might bring us water
through the Field."

(By "teachers," she refers to the late Alexandros Galanos, and by "Field" to *Plateia Mpou.*)

The community continued to contribute money, while requiring personal work from the residents.

- 1926 – 30,000 drachmas are given; four days of personal work are required.

- 1927 – 32,000 drachmas are given; personal work is required *"for the completion of the job."*

- 1928 – 10,000 drachmas are given; four days of personal work are required.

- 1929 – 10,000 drachmas are given; four days of personal work are required.

With Decision 16, of September 9, 1928, the Community Council decided to construct a reservoir and whatever internal mechanisms were required in order to bring the water into the village. I have no idea why this decision was never acted upon and the work not completed. The piping had already reached *Lavidorkis,* across from the well of the Turk and a few meters from *Plateia Mpou.* So the water ran day and night, like a little stream, and we would go there to get our drinking water. I remember how tiring it was for those of us who were children living in the *Oxo geitonies* to carry water from *Lavidorkis* in jugs on our shoulders.

In order for the work to proceed and be completed, the Agiorgousoi of America also contributed money. The only data I have regarding those contributions comes from the *Panchïaki* newspaper published on April 24, 1936.

"The expatriate Agiorgousoi, in Lancaster of the United States, gathered $150 through Mr. Christos Mereos, which they sent through Kostis Monis, a fellow villager of theirs

Pantelis A. Mavrogiorgis

who recently arrived from America, for the water to be brought to the village. Likewise, those in New York sent another $35 through that same person."

4. **Networking the Water System in the Village.** For a period of about ten years, the water ran from *Platanos* to *Lavidorkis*. Finally, around 1939 the Community Council had Konstantinos Frangidis, an engineer, execute a study for the construction of a reservoir and the networking of the distribution of water to the village. The reservoir was constructed at the heights of *Lavidorkis* towards *Petsodos*, and pipes and fountains were placed on the roads by neighborhoods of the village. One fountain was put in front of *Agios Panteleimonas*, another in *Batsilis*, another in *Piso geitonia* – approximately halfway down the road – in *Prinos*, in *Mpou*, in *Mesi geitonia* where the Community Office is today, one in *Lakko*, and also in *Kato geitonia* – where it intersects the road to Chios.

Villagers would go to the fountain closest to their home and bring jugs or cans with them to fill with water. The only problems would occur during the summer months, since the fountains would only be opened for two to three hours a day, so it would get crowded as all the women went there to get water. Oftentimes, this situation would lead to arguments, and the women could be heard cursing or seen elbowing one another and pushing their cans forward in order to be first to get water.

When this happened, those who had little to do except observe their fellow villagers would watch these spats with amusement. I will relay just one such encounter, which is characteristic of the mindset and diligence of the women of the village. Giannis Frangakis told Thodora Mylonas, who delayed putting her can up to the fountain,

*"Come, **Kyria** Thodora, put your can there at last."*

But Thodora, offended by his use of the title *"Kyria,"* responded,

*"We're not **Kyries**, Gianni. The Kyria is your wife. We are women who work."*

Due to this type of thing happening when women went to collect water, an agreement was drawn up. Each neighborhood was to appoint one woman who would be paid to open the fountain and remain there to ensure that the process proceeded in an orderly manner. So the women of the villages would gather at the fountains in the morning, a beautiful and interesting sight, and sit in the shade waiting their turn. That was the place to learn all of the news of the village, the obvious and the secret, "the unspeakable and the improper," because the discussions were lively and the gossip flowed freely.

After using this system of water distribution for a number of years, faucets were installed in the homes during the 1960's, thus systematizing and completing the task of bringing water into the village. Since the amount of water was still insufficient, mainly in the summer months, a portion of the water from the *apano vrisi* (upper fountain) of Notso Kipos was piped to another reservoir in the village, whereas the rest of that fountain's water supply was given to the community of *Armolia*.

Pantelis A. Mavrogiorgis

CHAPTER 20
Religious Life

A.   The Saint of the Village

For older Agiorgousoi, religiosity and Christianity ran in their blood, having been breastfed these components along with their mothers' milk, due to the sacredness of the location. Let us not forget that the village was born from the Monastery and was, thus, dedicated to the worship of God.

The patron saint of the village was *Agios Megalomartys, Tropaioforos Georgios* (the Great Martyr and Triumphant Georgios). His presence was felt in the village so much so that the inhabitants in olden times would hear the galloping of his horse, as it ran through the village streets, in their dreams at night. In fact, there is a stone that remains in a particular road of our village and has never been moved. That road and that rock are known as "Footprint," because it is said that Agios Georgios would step on that rock to mount his horse. To this day, the rock is considered sacred and has been surrounded by an iron fence the villagers put up, and every day and night a vigil lamp burns to commemorate the piety and religious tradition of the village.

Mothers tell their children, who tell their own children the legend of the Princess as they look toward the bottom of the sacred icon of the handsome *Ai Giorgi* and see an untamed beast writhing beneath the feet of his horse. They tell this story to the children:

> *"Once upon a time, in a large city, there was a dragon whose cave was near a spring. This dreadful monster would not allow the inhabitants to get water or to water their fields if they failed to bring him a human victim.*
>
> *There came a time that the residents brought the only daughter of the King before the dragon. The maiden, dressed in silver, with dread in her heart, waited for the beast to seize her. Only a miracle would save her. Suddenly, a gallant fellow appeared astride a proud horse, which steps, but doesn't step on the earth.*
>
> *The beast rushed to the horse, but the Saint quickly thrust his spear into the mouth of the beast, which then lay wounded at the feet of the horse. The maiden was struck with wonder.*

The Footprint
(Photographer: Cathy Mavrogiorgis)

Pantelis A. Mavrogiorgis

The Saint revealed himself and counseled the Princess to build a church and place the icon of Christ and the Virgin Mary within that church. He also asked that an icon be created depicting a horseman armed with a sword and a golden spear."

From that time forward, that icon adorned churches and chapels built everywhere by the Greeks to honor the Saint whom the Vlachs, the Slavs and, even the Turks, honor. This icon, which depicts strength and daring, speaks to both young and old who approach to venerate. *"Ai Giorgis* is young, handsome, and he has an angelic face and well-built body. The battle of good versus evil is portrayed in the icon through the way in which the Saint directs his horse, the skill with which he thrusts the spear into the open mouth of the enraged monster, and the cape which waves with a flag-like motion on his shoulders. It all demonstrates the light that defeats the darkness, the hero who protects those who are mistreated and the weak."

For the aforementioned reasons, his icon adorns the polemic flags of the Greek Infantry. This same Saint grabbed and liberated a boy who had been about to serve his Turkish master. That is the boy we see many times seated on the hindquarters of the horse rather than the Princess.

The myths revolving around the killing of dragons have roots that go very far back in history. We are reminded of Perseus who kills the Medousa, a sea beast in ancient Greek mythology, in order to liberate Princess Andromeda, whom the inhabitants of the land had offered as a sacrificial victim to the beast! Furthermore, there is the familiar myth of Hercules, who liberated Isioni, whom her father, Laomedon, had sent as food to the fearful whale, which was obliterating the fruits of the land and devouring humans.

Independent of these associations, the action of Agios Georgios holds new dimensions in the spirit of the Christian religion. The slaying of the dragon is not interpreted merely as an heroic act but more as an expression of self-sacrifice, filled with the quality of love and, in general, that virtue which cares for all weak and scorned individuals.

In his "dismissal hymn," the Saint is not characterized only as a liberator of prisoners and champion of the poor, but also as a doctor to those who are ill. In terms of his medical role, I remember when we got dirt in our eye as children, we would close our eye, make the sign of the cross over it, and would recite the following beseeching prayer three times in all our childhood innocence:

> *"Ai Giorgi, rider of horses,*
> *and lady horse rider,*
> *give me your little key,*

to open my little eye,
for me to see what it has inside.
Whether it is barley,
whether it is wheat,
whether it is a gold pearl,
for the grace of the Virgin Mary."

B. Characteristics of Religious Life

The area of religious life would be narrow in both expression and content if it stopped with Agios Giorgis and did not consider the other saints. The Agiorgousoi honored young and old saints, and distinguished holidays as "major" or "minor" ones. When paying visits on Saturday nights, the women would neither sew nor patch anything, as Sunday was dedicated to God and was a day of rest for everyone. On Saturday night, the vigil lamp before the *Ikonostasi* would be lit in everyone's home, and the vigil lamps of the church burned brightly day and night. The people thought it shameful that the lights in front of the icons would ever be extinguished, so both male and female members of the Church Council would often go to change the wick in the vigil lamps, even at night. On Saturday nights, they would make every effort to light vigil lamps, even in the most remote chapels.

Traditionally, they ran their lives according to the rules of fasting. For the forty-day Lenten period preceding Christmas, the Great Lent before Easter, and during the first fifteen days of August, only the sick would eat *paschalino* foods (Note: *Paschalino* – Foods that are forbidden during Lenten periods, such as meats and dairy products.) Additionally, there were many others who fasted twice a week as well, on Wednesdays and Fridays.

They began each day by making the sign of the cross and ended the day with a simple nighttime prayer:

"Oh, All Holy Virgin and mother of God, to you I give myself night and day. When my tongue ceases to speak and my eyes no longer see, then Lady Despoina, come to my pillow" (to protect me during the night).

They would work hard all day and eat the bread earned by the sweat of their brows. They were pleased with life, with themselves, and with their God.

As I dug through old wills and dowry agreements in order to get to know the people of the past through these documents, it impressed me that in every case they would call upon God and the saints. All the dowry agreements began with the invocation of the Holy Trinity:

Pantelis A. Mavrogiorgis

"In the name of the Father and of the Son and of the Holy Spirit, Amen, and bless the present exchange (agreement)."

It was moving how they would preface a wedding to be performed.

"We will join our daughter in marriage according to the divine and sacred laws of our Eastern Orthodox Church."

They would subsequently determine the dowry. Their wills were filled with the awe of death, so they would proclaim at the beginning:

"Be ye vigilant, for you do not know the day nor the hour in which the Son of Man is coming . . . ."

Furthermore, the willmaker considers the ephemeral nature of this world and imprints it in his will.

". . . When the time of my death arrives, I hand my soul to its creator, while my body is buried according to the Eastern rite. I forgive everyone who may have embittered me, and I also ask forgiveness from those whom I have embittered. I leave first, for the salvation of my soul, 100 gold coins to Agios Georgios. . . ."

In composing his will, an individual had to stand among the more elderly people and Board Members of the Church, who were present as witnesses, along with one priest. The village had a multitude of priests and a number of *Hatzides*, who had been to the Holy Lands to worship.

One might say that the information I just presented indicates a superficial type of religiosity. However, I would like to point out that the Agiorgousoi, while not having very much formal education, touched the essence of the Christian religion with their religious upbringing alone. They were charitable and hospitable people. I remember, as a boy, seeing many poor people and beggars who went around to the homes of the village every day. It was considered a great sin for villagers to chase a poor person away from the doors of their homes. Something had to be given to that person to help him. *"Me ena kommati psomi . . . me ligo ladi."* ("With a piece of bread . . . and a little oil.")

They were honest, hardworking people who did not engage in thievery or adultery. Each person respected the wives and sisters of the others. In the village, you could sleep with your door open without fearing other people – only ghosts or *geloudes*. Bad people did not dwell in our village. Maybe some of the villagers were a bit discourteous and somewhat annoying – using sarcasm and taunting others; but deep down they were individuals with good souls, not so much as a result of cultivating that goodness as much as from their inherited religiosity.

CHAPTER 21
The Village Churches

A. The Church of Agios Georgios

We consider the church of Agios Georgios to be the cathedral of our village. In that church, all couples are crowned during the wedding ceremony, and the funeral service is chanted for the departed, as is the memorial service forty days after a death. These are not the only significant observances, though. There are special days throughout the year when the entire village gathers in the church of Agios Georgios to celebrate, such as the morning of Holy Friday when Jesus is taken down from the Cross. In the old days, we would go to church for the *Epitafion*, and to this day we attend on the Sunday afternoon of *Pascha* when the *Agape* vesper is chanted. On *Niotrito* (the Tuesday after Easter Sunday), there is a single liturgy, which is followed by a litany of the icons.

The church is on the northern end of the village and is the parish church for the M*esa Geitonia*. Its design features a wide, closed courtyard, enclosed on the west side by an iron fence. Two large iron doors lead to this outer courtyard with its beautiful, mosaic tile floor. The western and northern sides of the first monasterial church we introduced in an earlier chapter were taken down when the village population grew. That structure, designed in a Byzantine octagonal pattern, underwent a radical transformation, which altered the initial plan and left only the eastern and southern sides intact. The reconstruction resulted in a larger church, its internal section separated into two naves, the larger one on the right side for the men, and the smaller left side for women. There are two front entrances to the church with marble arched doors and colonnade buttresses on the sides.

Precisely above the more imposing door used by the men is the bell tower that – due to the manner in which it is built into the structure – appears to be a natural architectural feature of the church. The exterior walls have carved inlays, geometric designs, circles, and small arched windows. The interior walls are decorated with double-curved blind arches, plaster designs, and colored skylights. This renovation may have occurred in the eighteenth century, according to the opinion of Professor Haralambos Bouras:

> *"Even though it distorted the (design of the) Byzantine church, the*
> *final result was not disappointing, because this monument was*

Pantelis A. Mavrogiorgis

The church of Agios Georgios as it is today

---

given a unique, popular style, while the dome and the two sides remained untouched."

We now approach the issue of the reconstruction of our church, at the expense of the village inhabitants, since the Turks burned the original church during the massacres of 1822. It would be better if we read the appropriate excerpt from a letter by Sofronios, Metropolitan of Chios, which is dated August 20, 1848.

> *"Before the destruction of this island, the inhabitants of the village were paying an annual sum to the church (for the ecclesiastical estates they were renting). During that horrible period for the island, because the Monastery's church was set on fire then rebuilt by the inhabitants at their own expense, it was necessary to overlook the income expected from the residents for the sake of the renewal of the church."*

The appearance of the church today is the result of this second renovation. We must accept the fact that the exterior of the church was totally redone with plaster. The interior wall surfaces were beautified; and the wood-carved pulpit, Bishop's throne, and the exceptionally skillfully crafted *Ikonostasi* were all remade – as were the carved depictions above the small windows. In this newer construction, "the elements and the forms of the popular Baroque styles of the latter part of the Turkish occupation were used in the church."

1. **The Carved Lintels.** Above the center pillar of the church and between the two buttresses of the bell tower, a large gated alcove is formed and surrounded by an artistic, marble framework. Below, the foundation is level, and two small columns, connected by a double arch are supported above – with spirals among their vertical lines and plant carvings within their moldings.

   Within this beautifully crafted framework is a marble slab containing the carved icon of the Saint on horseback. His horse has one of its forelegs over the head of the winged dragon. On the hindquarters of the horse, the little boy who was liberated by the Saint is seated, and the Princess is shown in front of the horse's raised foreleg. Above, to the right, an angel crowns the Saint, and in a separate frame on the left side 'Ο ΑΓΙΟΣ ΓΕΩΡΓΙΟΣ' is written. The monster writhes beneath the feet of the horse, and the spear of the Saint protrudes from its mouth.

   There are three inscribed nameplates below this composition. From left to right, they read as follows:

The interior of Agios Georgios, with the carved ikonostasis
(Photographer: A. Sami Bey, 1937)
Shown L-R: The teachers A. Mavrogiorgis, S. Tsikolis & papa Stelios Salagaras

The Village Agios Georgios Sikousis

ENEKENIΣΘΗ'
'Ο ΟΙΚΟΣ ΤΟΥ ΑΓΙΟΥ ΓΕΩΡΓΙΟΥ'
'ΑΥΓΟΥΣΤΟΥ 1836

"Restored, The Home of Agios Georgios, August 1836". The entire area is framed with decorative designs of helixes, wide-leafed plants, fruits, and blossoms.

In the area where the women sit, Agios Georgios is depicted in a carving above the window, framed by a church-like structure. Its dimensions are rather small. In the southern entrance of the church, above a small arched window, there is a shell containing a carved icon of the Saint and above it on the left is the inscription, 'Ο ΑΓΙΟΣ ΓΕΩΡΓΙΟΣ'. The middle portion features the Saint riding his horse, which bears the following inscription beneath it:

ΜΑΣΤΡΟΦΡΑΓΓΟΥ
ΛΙΣ ΒΩΛΙΣΙΑΝΟΣ
ΚΕ ΠΕΤΡΟΣ

Carvings of leaves and flowers adorn the corners. From the information on the inscription, we do not know whether Mastrofrangoulis from Volisos and Petros are the artists of the carving or the craftsmen who restored the church.

2. **The *Ikonostasi*.** In the church, the *Ikonostasi* is made from walnut and features top-to-bottom carvings of scenes from the Old and New Testaments. Decorative carvings of plants, grapevines, pomegranates, pears, and quince surround these scenes. All of these depictions are overlaid with good-quality gold, making the entire structure impressive in its expression of religious living and also its artistic truth. This type of carved-wood Ikonostasi can also be found in the churches of Mesta, Armolia, and Nenita, and they seem to have been made at the same time with the same degree of skill, Baroque style, after the destruction of Chios.

The *Ikonostasi* we described is only in the area of the church that is reserved for men. It is 5.5 meters wide and 6 meters high. As you enter the Holy Side Door, to the right the year of construction is carved: *"1836 ΙΟΥΝΙΟΥ ΠΡΩΤΙ"* (1836, JUNE FIRST.) The entire area is laid out in five identical levels. The second one features painted icons of the saints in an arched pattern above, in recessed spaces, and this section rests on the second step above the floor. There is a wide section over the main Ikonostasi, and another level above that which has a series of smaller icons that depict the life of Jesus. The fifth level symbolizes Jesus at Golgotha and, then, crucified.

The following is a detailed description by Galanos, presenting the icons seen on the five levels of the Ikonostasi:

a. To the right of the *Oraia Pyli* (Royal Gate), the *Pantokratoras* is depicted, seated on a throne. In his left hand, he is holding a diptych, on which is written in capital letters:"ΕΓΩ ΕΙΜΙ ΤΟ ΦΩΣ ΤΟΥ ΚΟΣΜΟΥ ..." ("I AM THE LIGHT OF THE WORLD ...") In the lower section of the icon is the name of the iconographer, "χειρ Χ" αναγνώστου 1837" "By the hand of X" *anagnostou* 1837." Beneath the icon, in the area of the "apron," the sacrifice of Abraham is engraved.

b. The icon of *Ioannis Prodromos*. He is standing, and his face is ascetical. He is holding a white belt, upon which is written in capital letters: *"ΜΕΤΑΝΟΕΙΤΕ ΗΓΓΙΚΕ ΓΑΡ Η ΒΑΣΙΛΕΙΑ ΤΩΝ ΟΥΡΑΝΩΝ"* ("Repent Ye: For the Kingdom of Heaven is at hand.") On the same icon, above and to the right, is Jesus Christ with Angels to His left. The rectangle in the lower right area depicts the prison, the executioner, Salome with the head of Ioannis on a platter, and his headless body. Beneath these is *"έτος 1869 Ιουνίου 4"* ("year 1869, June 4.") Agios Georgios is carved within the apron of the Ikonostasi. It seems that this position was reserved for the large icon of Agios Georgios.

c. On the southern side of the Ikonostasi, the *Evangelismos tis Theotokou* (Annunciation of the *Theotokos*) appears, while on its lower level there is a corresponding carved depiction.

d. The icon of the *Theotokos,* with Christ in her left embrace, is at the left of the Royal Gate. It is a beautiful icon with vivid colors, and carved beneath it on the Ikonostasi, the disobedience and exile of Adam & Eve is shown.

e. The icon of Agios Georgios is silver plated. Our villagers paid to have this silver overlay done in Constantinople, thus the following is inscribed:

"ΣΥΝΔΡΟΜΗ ΤΩΝ ΕΥΡΙΣΚΟΜΕΝΩΝ ΕΝ ΚΩΝΣΤΑΝΤΙΝΟΥΠΩΛΗ ΧΙΟΝ ΧΩΡΙΟΝ ΑΓΙΟΝ ΓΕΩΡΓΙΟΝ ΣΥΚΟΥΣΗΣ 1866 ΑΠΡΙΛΙΟΥ 8"

("CONTRIBUTION OF THE VILLAGERS OF

Carved icon from the ikonostasis:
The exile of Adam & Eve

Carved icon from the ikonostasis:
Crucifixion, taking down from the Cross, Burial

　　　　　　　　　　　　　　Pantelis A. Mavrogiorgis

AGIOS GEORGIOS SIKOUSIS, CHIOS, LIVING IN CONSTANTINOPLE, 1866, APRIL 8").

The carving in the apron of the icon depicts the beheading of *Ioannis*. Sometime in the past, the icon of *Prodromos* was placed in this position.

f. The icon of *Zoodochos Pigi*, the Life-Giving Spring, is a customary presentation of the icon and bears the signature, "χειρ Χ" αναγνώστου 1836 Ιουνίου 27" "By the hand of X" *anagnostou 1836 June 27."* Under this icon, there is a relief that also depicts *Zoodochos Pigi*. Above these icons and the panels there a frieze with a plethora of carvings exists, including *Osia Maria, Abbas Zosimas, the baptism of Jesus, the Conception, Jesus before Pilate, the Crucifixion, and the Taking Down of Jesus from the Cross.* Then there is the carving of the messengers of Joshua of Navi to Canaan; and on the corner is a large Angel with a trumpet to his mouth.

The upper part of the Ikonostasi has fifteen small, older icons showing various events from the New Testament. High above, as mentioned previously, is the Crucifixion of Christ, with Mary and His beloved disciple Ioannis on either side.

Of the four icons on the large Ikonostasi in the women's section, only one oil painting of *Agios Georgios* is old and dated "1848 αυγούστου" ("1849, August.") Above the icons, midway up the ikonostasi, the following is written lengthwise with large, black, capital letters, but it bears no date:

"ΠΡΟΣΚΥΝΙΤΗΣ ΑΝΤΩΝΙΟΣ ΤΣΑΜΟΥΤΑΛΟΣ"

According to his will, he leaves 500 gold coins 'for the salvation of his soul' to the church of Agios Georgios.

The will of X" Antonios Tzamoutalos, in the year 1834, October 26, Monday, 3:00 p.m., and witnesses.

X" Antonios Tzamoutalos is present today, and by going to the Holy Tomb of our Lord wants – for the salvation of his soul – to leave forgiveness to the world and asks the same forgiveness for himself, and wants to also provide his movable possessions in proper order, and for his life to come to a good end. **First, I leave to the churches of Agios Georgios** *of our village 500 gold coins to be dispersed*

---

as they wish, and with my blessing . . . .".

3. **The Feast of the Saint** *(Panigyri)*. According to the will of Sofronios Sepsis,

> *"On the name day celebration, chanters must be invited – as many as needed – and anyone who happens to be at the celebration of the Saint should be offered hospitality at the expense of the Saint. Relatives of papa Sofronios should also be invited to the celebration as founders."*

Also, in that same will of 1740 we are informed that

> *"the abbot (Board Member) Konstantinos, son of Michalis Kaligou, is obligated to slaughter an ox at the feast of the Saint, to secure good chanters, to give what is proper, and to provide a meal on Christmas and Agios Nikolaos, according to our ancient customs . . . ."*

As we are told, during the feast of the Saint, April 23 (probably also on November 3 when Agios Georgios *"tou mesa krevatiou"* is celebrated), a meal – which required using large pots for its preparation – was held. To meet the needs of preparing this meal, in 1812 the Agiorgousoi who lived in Constantinople sent **a very large copper cauldron, which was 0.84 meters in diameter and 0.47 meters high.** This pot still exists today. All around its edges, the following is written:

> *"Dedicated to Agios Georgios Sikousis by the blessed roufetiou of the lemonadon and pachsevanidon, 1812, April 1."*

The word *"Roufetion"* is from the Arabic *"Roufet"* and refers to a business association that the Greeks call *"Syntechnia"* and the Turks call *"Sinafi"* or *"esnaf."*

During the massacres of 1822, a Turk took the cauldron and sent it to a city in Turkey. Papa Seremelis, who was known as "the altar boy of *Mersinidi*," bought it from another Turk and sent it to the Monastery of *Mersinidi*. In 1919, three Board Members – Antonios Lelas, Ioannis Monioukas, and Michalis Nikitas – sent a letter to the abbot of the *Mersinidi* Monastery requesting that the cauldron be returned to the village, and he granted that request.

Not only had our villagers from Constantinople originally given us the gift of that cauldron, we note that they also gave Agios Georgios other

The historic cauldron

items like a skillfully crafted silver *hexapteryga*, the tabernacle, a candle holder, trays, a rosewater sprinkler with goldleafed lanterns, four ecclesiastical flags – one which bears this inscription:

"TH ΣΥΝΔΡΟΜΗ ΤΩΝ ΕΝ ΚΩΝ/ΠΟΛΕΙ 32 ΣΥΝΕΚΧΩΡΙΩΝ ΑΓΙΟΥ ΓΕΩΡΓΙΟΥ" ("A Contribution of 32 Fellow Villagers of Agios Georgios in Constantinople").

Furthermore, I remember the very beautiful silver chalice, with a goldplated interior. At its base, I saw that the following names were inscribed in three lines all around it.

Ioannis thalassinos	Nikolas anamisis	antonis mpihlivanis
Georgios soukas	michail orfanoudis	diamantis Kostaris
michalis mpilis	antonios anamisis	kostantis Xenos
georgios rousios	filippas Karavanas	georgios Mpitis
michail mitsos	dimitris nikolakias	michail pehlivanis
konstantinos mpilis	michail nikitas	
Konstantinos Michlivanis	monios hahalis	

I am of the opinion that the Holy Chalice and the Salver came from Constantinople, because the skill and workmanship displayed on them was identical in technique to the prior items that were dedicated.

B. The Church of *Agios Panteleimonas*

In the July heat, the celebrations of all of the healing saints occurred. On the first of the month, *Agioi Anargyroi*; *Agia Paraskevi,* healer of the eyes, on the twenty-sixth; and *"o iamatikos Panteleimonas,"* who heals all sicknesses and all invalids through his grace, is celebrated on the twenty-seventh. There is a folk saying that is based on this faith:

> *"Wherever there is a lame person and wherever there is a blind person, they should go to Agio Panteleimona."*

Initially, this saint was called *Pantoleon,* but he was named *Panteleimonon (Panteleimonas)* in honor of his philanthropic activities. Believers prayed and made supplications to this saint asking for his grace on behalf of a sick relative. He is a beautiful, fine lad with a sweet face, and it appears that he holds in his hands a healing box to grant the medicine of consolation and hope to whomever comes before his icon. His church was built to the south of the village and is on the main road that leads to the p*iso choria: Vessa, Elata*, and others. The road is somewhat wider at that point, and there is a small square with cafes. Years ago, this square also was a stopping point for cars.

The church has a wide front yard, with alternating strips of cement and mosaic flooring. It is both taller and larger in all its dimensions than Agios Giorgios. It has a double nave, with the men's side larger and taller than the women's side next to it. An arched wall divides the two naves. The church is narrow and not very architecturally complicated or decorated. An icon of the Saint is carved by the small window above the center door. A marble slab in the wall contains the following inscription:

*"ΑΝΕΚΟΔΟΜΗΘΗ ΑΥΓΟΥΣΤΟΥ 20 1849
ΔΙΑΧΥΡΟΣ ΙΩΑΝΝΗΣ ΠΟΥΤΟΥΣ"*

("CONSTRUCTED AUGUST 20, 1849 BY THE HAND OF IOANNIS POUTOUS")

There is an older church in that same location, but we were not able to find out precisely when it was built. We do know, though, that it certainly existed prior to 1740, since there is a document dated November 1, 1740 which mentions that the abbot of Agios Georgios had to give *"two okades of wax to Agios Panteleimonas, too."*

We know little more about this church other than that the Turks destroyed it in 1822, and that the first cemetery of the village existed there, as well. While the above information from Georgios Zolotas, historian of Chios,

---

       Pantelis A. Mavrogiorgis

The imposing bell tower of Agios Panteleimonas

gives us some idea, the elderly also speak about the existence of bones. I, too, recall the repository behind the altar, in which there were bones from ancient times. It seems as though that cemetery was no longer used after 1864, when the church of Agios Nikolaos was built and where the cemetery exists today.

The *Oxogeitonousoi* attend the church of Agios Panteleimonas. The functioning of the parish is rather peculiar, as the Board Members there are under the jurisdiction of the Board of Agios Georgios, whose members are known as *"Panepitropoi"* ("Upper Board Members"). Also, in an 1879 document, we find that rather than Board Members, the church has renters. While the following quotation is undated, it refers to this situation:

> *"Georgios Psyllos, Antonios Vekios, Stefanos Kakaridis, and Panagiotis Pouleros rent Agios Panteleimonas in 1879 for two years at 1,000 gold coins per year, which will be received by the Board Members of the great church, who are obligated to oversee the regular functioning of the church of Agios Panteleimonas."*

While the renting of churches is somewhat odd, we nevertheless encountered a similar situation in Agios Giorgios, when the priest Manuil Pantevgenos was in debt for 60,000 *aspra* and rented *Agios Giorgis* for four years. Also, in 1740 Konstantinos Koligos was appointed abbot (Board Member) for two years, with certain obligations. In this case, it seems like a rental situation. I believe that this was a custom of the times, since I encountered it in the codexes of other villages, as well.

It is worth the trouble for us to discuss the bell tower of the church a bit further, since it imposingly dominates the entire village. It is built of marble stone, chiseled and cubed without much skill or care. It is about twenty meters high and is noteworthy for the way it was designed and the measurements calculated at a time when there were no civil engineers. It is architecturally distinguished by its height of five stories structured with a combination of horizontal bases, vertical pillars – which secure the small columns – all connected by arches. So these arches relieve the basic straight line of the construction.

The building of this tower is credited to the initiative of Dr. Georgios Dellas son of papa-Stamatios, who I believe to be the first Agiorgousis to have studied medicine, but who had the misfortune to be killed young. Initially, I heard, the bell was hung on a very tall holly tree at the left corner of the church. On the opposite side was a spruce tree, and there was a very tall eucalyptus in the front yard of the church. Today, however, not one single tree exists there.

In 1905, Dr. Dellas urged the parishioners of the village to build a bell tower. They eagerly offered farm produce, money, personal work, and their beasts of burden to transport materials. The project required 450 gold Turkish lira. A Building Committee was organized and included priest Demetrio s Barlis, Georgios Stefanos Kakaridis, Ioannis Georgios Vafeias, and Hatzi Kostanti s Bouras. The first craftsman to work with the plan was Ioannis Skolarikis, but when he died, Demosthenis Doulos completed the work.

Manolis Frazelas, who lived in Russia, and Manolis Kostaris, who lived in Egypt, donated the bells in 1905. The clock and the lightning rod in the bell tower were dedicated in 1953 by our villagers in America, Panagiotis and Lemonia Samaras, which is noted on a marble wall slab. In the last decades, the Board Members have cared very much for the church, as evidenced by the repeated repairs and painting they made Villagers from America – Giannis and Eleni Mountis, Manolis Frangakis, Giannis and Kostas Sakoulas, and Dr. Kostas Toulambis – also sent gifts that allowed the church to obtain the necessary consecrated vessels, whereas we initially borrowed *hexapteryga* and such items from Agios Giorgis. Now the church had both internal and external decorum.

C. The Church of *Agios Nikolaos*

Agios Nikolaos is honored throughout all of Chios as the protector of sailors, since the island is known for sailing. On December sixth, following the feast days of *Agia Varvara* and *Agios Savas*, the feast day of *Agios Nikolaos* is celebrated. Due to this close proximity of celebrations, the people refer to these days as *"ta Nikolovarvara."* As children, we would say,

> *"Agia Varvara gave birth, Agios Savas received it, and Agios Nikolaos heard about it and went to baptize it."*

I believe that these tidbits of village folklore spiritually enrich our religious celebrations.

The church is built to the east of the village, from where one can see the sea. The Saint represents a watchman for our village. It's possible that in ancient times a watchman would be stationed at the *"Vigla,"* which is down the road. Today's church is actually the reconstruction of an earlier one. The first church existed before 1740, as shown in a document dated November 7, 1740, from which we are informed – among other things – that the abbot (Board Member) of Agios Georgios *"is obligated to hold a meal on Christmas, according to the ancient customs, and also on the feast day of **Agios Nikolaos** . . . ."*

The first church met the same fate as the other churches in Chios: It was torched by the Turks in 1822 and reconstructed in 1864. There is a marble slab in the wall over the center entrance, which reads (in capital letters):

"This church of Agiou Patros Nikolaou, which you now see, was erected anew from its foundations at great expense through the generosity of the honorable, pious Chiotis Ioannis Georgios Kanouzis, who died on the island of Syros. His beloved wife, Irini, daughter of priest Michail Pisias, a famous priest and most venerable man from Chios, devoutly completed this work. So whichever pious person comes here to venerate, may he say, 'Eternal be the memory to those who faithfully erected this church and also to the municipality of Sykountion.' In the month of August 1864."

So the church, according to the inscription, was reconstructed at the expense of the pious Ioannis Kanouzis, and when he died, his wife Irini, the daughter of the priest Michail Pisias, had the construction completed. Irini Kanouzis, later on, voluntarily and inviolably grants property she inherited from her deceased spouse to the church of *Agios Nikolaos* in a written document, which was definitely created by an educated individual, as Panagiotis Pouleros, the village secretary, was not well educated.

"Today, on Monday, the 10th day of the month of October 1877, the following appeared before me in person: Panagiotis Pouleros, public secretary of the village of Agios Georgios Sykountos, and Irini, widow of Ioannis Kanouzis, who confessed before me, the secretary, and the Elders and Board Members of this village who, as trustworthy witnesses, personally signed below that she voluntarily and inviolably gives to Agios Nikolaos, the church of our village, the following property she inherited from her deceased spouse according to the dowry agreements, a copy of which was preserved in the archive of our village, under the following conditions.

From the amount which would be collected from the sale of all of these properties, one-third should be used to decorate the church of Agios Nikolaos, while the remainder should be kept by the church, with the obligation that the Board Members every year should hold a memorial service in memory of Agios Nikolaos, and the name of her deceased spouse should be commemorated.

Secondly, if other individuals ever appear and argue their rights to inherit any of these properties, Irini Kanouzis will not take responsibility, so the Board Members and Elders are obligated, in all such instances, to render the properties if such an inheritance right is proven to be true.

Pantelis A. Mavrogiorgis

If the Elders or Board Members breach any of these terms, this agreement becomes invalid."

The church does not have a noteworthy architectural plan. It was designed with a wide nave, is quite tall, and is covered by a gabled shingle roof, upon which the dome is positioned. I have in my hands an agreement I will copy exactly that the Board Members made with Kostantis Tsoflias regarding the covering of the church floor with slate.

"Based of the design of the floor of Agios Panteleimonas, Kostantis Soflias will cover the floor of Agios Nikoloaos, in agreement with the Board Members of the village for the sum of 300 gold coins. If this does not occur according to our agreement, he will not be paid.

February 26, 1866"

Behind the altar, within a walled area, is the cemetery of the village. Above its door, written on a small Thymianousian slab, the following is written:

"ΗΥΡΥΝΘΗ ΚΑΤΑ ΟΚΤΩΒΡΙΟΝ 1914" *(Widened in October 1914)*

The widening began at the northern side, from which stones were removed, and dirt was brought from other areas. This is one of the reasons why the land in this particular area remains too shallow for burials. Manolis Strovilas, the President of the community, had a new extension built in 1986.

D. The Chapels of the Village

1. *Agios Isidoros* or *Sideros.* I consider it purposeful to discuss what led to the martyrdom of this Saint, which took place on our island, following which *Agios Sideros* became the protector and patron saint of Chios. In 253 A.D., when Decius was Emperor of Rome, that was the year that Agios Sideros was martyred. He hailed from Egypt and served in the Roman Army, coming to Chios with a fleet under Admiral Noumerius.

   Isidoros embraced Christianity, and his idol-worshipping shipmates betrayed him to Noumerius. Due to Isidoros' faith and persistence, Noumerius ordered him to be tied onto boards and whipped. After that, he commanded that Isidoros be tied hand and foot to the tail of a raging horse, which then dragged him to *Nechori*, where he died from the wounds his body suffered on the rugged terrain of the road. This inhumane torture caused "rocks to break and trees to cry." According to tradition, the mastic produced by the mastic trees

Agios Sideros

Pantelis A. Mavrogiorgis

are tears for Agios Sideros. Agia Myropi buried him, but his holy relics were later stolen by the Venetians and ended up in St. Mark's Church in Venice. In 1966, the Venetians returned a portion of those relics, which are preserved in a sacred repository of the Metropolis of Chios.

Our own chapel is located to the west of the village, at a height that offers an extended view. It was built between *Afalotades* and *Achlantropi*, on the road to *Vessa*. The feast day of *Agios Sideros* is May 14, in a season when we are surrounded by blooming and fragrant trees and bushes.

Men, women, and children attend the vesper and, on the morning of the Saint's feast day, they come for the liturgy to honor "the pride of Chios." From when we were children and went into the church, our first job was to lift the slab on the floor that had the trap door beneath it that led to an area where human bones had been discovered in the past. There were also human bones outside the northern part of the church in a particular opening in the ground. I believe that those bones were either from the massacres that occurred in Chios in 1822 or from deaths due to the plague that devastated Chios, since huts, "lazaretta"– were discovered in that area – where those infected with infectious diseases were brought.

In 1934, a terrible storm occurred and lasted all night long. Unusually strong winds damaged the village mills, uprooted trees, and broke branches. Lightning struck during that fearsome night, hitting two very tall cypress trees near the door of the church and the chapel as well, resulting in a dangerous crack in the structure. Following this, "the brothers" renovated the church, constructing a porch outside with permanent built-in seats and tables, ideal for picnics. They also created a fountain and decorated the surrounding area, making it worthwhile for visitors to enjoy. In the old days, on the day of the feast, a celebration would take place in the village and include dancing and the playing of *"vielounia."* (violins).

2. *Agia Marina.* Passing *Vessa* and heading to *Lithi*, we encounter an isolated, countryside chapel, built by Agiorgousoi, within the mountains. This is from a narration by the late Giorgis Mylonas, called the "Blessed One," since he always used the expression, *"Evloïmene anthrope, evloïmenon mpaidi."*

> *"I have heard from the older people that one of the builders, a certain Vekios or someone else, had gone to Vessiana for*

wood. In a pile of wood, he discovered the icon of Agia Marina and brought it to the village. They had wanted to build the church at Makri, but the icon had left that area and went to the place where he found it. Because of that, they decided to build the church in that location. They constructed it and placed the icon inside but, once again, it disappeared and returned to the woodpile, which is where they ended up building the current church of Agia Marinas Further down the road the foundations of the first church they built are visible."

There is yet another related document that the brotherhood of Agia Marina has. It says:

"Before me, Panagiotis Pouleros, the secretary of the village of Agios Georgios Sykountos, appeared the 'brothers' of the holy church of Agia Marina that is in the location Petrodos in the village of Vetsan, Antonios Vekios, Ioannis papa-Vekios, and Dimitris Mylonas and me to compose this document to place the following 'brothers' in the aforementioned church: Mr. Antonios Pitsos, Stefanos Nychtas, Vasilis Mylonas, Hatzi Georgios Vekios, Ioannis Hatzivekios, Pantelio Mylonas, Kostantis Skouloudis, Ioannis G. Galanos, and Nikolaos Karavanas, all twelve of whom will be obligated to maintain the sacred church in all ways. Therefore, this document certifies and secures the fact that it was created in Agios Georgios on Sunday afternoon, August 3, 1875, and was read clearly and loudly and signed by all present, including myself."

3. **Agia Triada.** This parish is located to the south on the road to *Tholopotami*, at the border of the village. Its feast day is celebrated on the Monday following the Sunday of the Pentecost. Panagiotis Dellas, the son of *papa* Stamatis, was among the most affluent landowners of the village and built *Agia Triada* about twenty to twenty-five years ago. He was known as *"Vrakas"* and was easily distinguishable among others since he tended to wear good quality britches.

4. **Agios Kosmas o Aitolos.** On ground above *Agia Triada*, prior to ascending to *Tholopotami*, there is the newly built chapel of the venerable *martyr Kosmas o Aitolos*. It is located in the forest of the School, which is now called *"Dasaki Galanou,"* in honor of Alexandros Galanos. This chapel was consecrated on August 24, 1988, the

Pantelis A. Mavrogiorgis

Agia Triada

day of the anniversary of the death and the feast of the Saint. The priest Georgios Sakoulas assembled a "brotherhood" from the high school graduates of our village. These brothers shared the expense of the icon of the Saint, a work of art, and placed it into the chapel of *Agios Isidoros*, where villagers would gather from the evening before to honor the *"Aitolo,"* as they called him, on the morning of August 24. The children, who were registered with the brotherhood of the same name, were also called *"Aitoloi."* With money from the brothers and offerings from local Agiorgousoi and Agiorgousoi in the United States, the church was built with a Byzantine design, and thus the desires and purpose of "the brothers" were realized. The president of the Agios Georgios Sikousis association in New York, Argyris Monis, showed great interest in this project. The church was consecrated in the summer of 1988.

Kosmas, o Aitolos is the Saint of the enslaved Hellenes. He was from Nafpaktia, became a monk, and spent some years on *Agio Oros*, the Holy Mountain. During that period, when other monks were occupied with empty discussions around the topic of *kollyva* (memorials) and whether they should take place only on Saturday but not on Sunday, Kosmas left the ascetic life on *Agio Oros* and began his educationally enlightening activities around 1760. He went all over Greece, holding a staff and wearing a satchel on his shoulder, preaching the word of God and urging slaves to learn to read and build schools, since he believed that was the only way for the Greek nation to be liberated. All Greeks respect him, as do the Turks. This sacred preacher and national apostle was murdered by the order of Kurt Pasha on August 24, 1779. The Agiorgousoi in Chios were right to honor *Agios Kosmas* and from what I know were the first. Four years ago, one more church was built in *Sklavia* in the name of *Kosmas Aitolos*.

5. ***Christos - I Metamorfosi* (Transfiguration of Christ).** This church is dedicated to the religious event of the Transfiguration of the Lord on Mount Tabor. There Christ, filled with light, showed his disciples his power and glory. The depiction of that event is impressive. The icon presents a mountain with three peaks. Christ is in the middle, illuminated; Moses is to His right; and Elijah is to His left. At the foot of the icon Peter, James, and John have fallen, their heads are bowed and they are dazzled.

The chapel, is on the road halfway to *Tholopotami* and built in a forested area of pines, is in one of the most scenic locations of the village: *Makri*. Behind the altar and beneath a precipitous rock, flows a small amount of the best quality spring water in Chios. A reservoir has been built across from the fountain to provide water for the *mourki* (fields) further down. From the ruins of the tower, it appears that this area was Genoese. *Makri*, along with other land in *Sklavia*, belonged to the family of Fornetto Ioustiniani, known as *Tsekou*. I was not able to ascertain when or from whom the Board Members of the church of Agios Georgios bought this land.

While I am not certain how much this following document pertains to the sale of the specific estate referenced above, I will present it. However, I doubt that it bears any relation to that estate.

> *"In the name of the Lord, Amen. Before me, the Notary, and the undersigned witnesses Marou, widow of the deceased Giorgis Kapeliaros, a Tholopotamousian, and her sister, Despinou, wife of Michalis Kliamenakis have appeared. They have admitted that they are selling their personal lands, fields in Makrin, and all that they contain, with the*

Consecration of the chapel of Kosmas Aitolos summer 1988

*trees located next to the property of Panagiotis Sigounis
and the road. They are selling it to Agios Georgios Sikousis
in the person of the Board Members Antonios Kostaris and
Diakogiannis Papatsigroudis, for the complete price of sixty-
five aslania, which the above sellers received in total. Thus,
as both parties are satisfied with the payment, they render
to him the properties to use as he wishes – to sell or donate
them as a dowry free of obligations and unencumbered.
They promise to do a 'chotzetion'* (ownership title) *for the
owner. Thus they agree and admit on Thursday, June 27,
1815, at three o'clock, with witnesses*

*Nikolis
Giorgis Soukas, Witness
Papa Kostantis Tsikolis"*

The church sold this estate to Hatzi Giannis Pouleros around 1938,
and the money was earmarked for the reimbursement of the fields
bought to build the new school. Every year, on August 6, when the
church celebrates, the Agiorgousoi and the *Tholopotamousi* gather.
Many bring food and drink and get together in groups in the forest
area after the service. In the afternoon, the actual celebration takes
place in the village.

6. *Panagia* (Virgin Mary). Among the mountains of Tholopotami,
Armolia, and Agios Georgios is *Notso Kipos* (Inner Garden) where
the chapel of the *Panagia* was built. The feast day is celebrated on
August 15. This place has abundant water and trees. There are
three springs, one at the *Apano Notso Kipo* (Upper Inner Garden),
at an estate owned by *Tholopotamousians*, and two springs with
reservoirs and fields cultivated by Agiorgousoi. Right next to the
upper fountain, which is covered so that the women can do their
washes, is the old church of the Panagia. As the historian of Chios
Georgios Zolotas believes, this church probably belonged to the
Catholic Genoese, who were the owners of the estates in which
the crumbled towers still exist. The Board Members of the village
church of Agios Georgios bought the one estate, as the following
contract demonstrates.

*"In the name of our Lord, Amen. The brothers, Mr.
Giakoumidis and Ioannis, sons of the deceased Frantzesko
Markopoulo, are present. They sell to the church of Agios
Georgios Sikousis, through a complete and universal sale,
their paternal mansion called the Inner Garden, as it is,*

Pantelis A. Mavrogiorgis

The church of Christos at Makri
(Photographer: A. Sami Bey, 1937)

with its towers, garden, and fields with trees, cultivated and wild, together with the lower fountain and one-third of the upper fountain. The mansion, known as the property of Mprisi, which they own with Frangan, son of the departed Andrea Markopoulo, as well as two-thirds of the upper fountain will remain under the jurisdiction of the sellers. All of the other items contained within their paternal mansion consisting of land and gardens with trees, I say, that they sell to the church of Agios Georgios. The aforesaid mansion is next to Mr. Pipi Markopoulo, son of papa Ioannis Karagelos, from Tholopotami; next to Antonio Masouri, son of Frangas Markopoulo; and next to the street. The mansion sold for 60,000 sixty-thousand gold coins, which were counted out by the Board Members from the money of the church of Agios Georgios, and the sellers received it in its entirety. They hand over to the ownership of the church their paternal mansion, to be done with as they wish: to sell, donate, or anything else. The sellers promise to not hold the church responsible to pay nor to be obligated to do a chotzetion (ownership title) either. Therefore, the present agreement was written on Thursday, February 25, 1843, at seven o'clock.

Giacomo marcopoli (I affirm)
Battisto marcopoli (I affirm)
Michele di Sidoro, Witness
Michele Sperco, Witness
Michail Alitridis
Nikolaos Fiorentis, Recorder"

7. **Agios Giannis o Prodromos.** From old notary documents, both the location and the church were called *Agios Ioannis tou Lambardou*. In the village, the name of *papa* Nikolis of Lambarda appears in a sale document of 1622, and he is consequently referred to as the builder of the church. To the east of the village, beneath the mills, where the ground declines abruptly and stops at the foot of the mountain, is where the chapel of *Agios Giannis* is built, in remembrance of his dreadful beheading.

The story of the beheading is quite impressive, has inspired artists of all ages, and sparked the popular imagination. Those who were part of this dramatic event included King Herod, his wife Herodias – who wishes to have the head of Ioannis "on a platter" to satisfy

The Panagia at the Notso Kipos with the arch of the fountain
(Photographer: A. Sami Bey, 1937)

her erotic passion for him – and their daughter Salome, whose wild dancing causes her father to become so crazed that he decides to offer the head of the Saint to her and her mother as a gift. The drama culminates in the blood-drenched head of the Saint always shown in some corner of his icon; and in Byzantine iconography, he presented as a bent over, skeletally thin man imbued with otherworldly holiness.

The chapel of our village is well cared for, built in idyllic surroundings. In front of it stands a century-old spruce tree that spreads protectively over it. In the center of the yard, there is a deep well, and at the borders of the property are half-ruined farmhouses. These indicate to me that there must have been a garden there, and it is also possible that it served as a hermitage for monks. During my childhood, an ascetic nun lived there.

The common belief of the people is that Agios Ioannis was the doctor who could cure malaria. For this reason, sick people would tear off pieces of their clothing and tie them to the bars of the windows of the church. This was the way the people would bind their sicknesses to the church, as "they tied" to sorcery whatever they could not achieve through natural means. We all fasted on the day of the Saint, even forgoing oil.

They say that *Ai Giannis* was the doctor who could cure malaria, because his body went into spasm when they cut off his head. Others claim that Herod suffered spasms similar to those that occur with malaria but that they were pangs of guilt that seized him due to the death of *Agios Ioannis*. The church celebrates his feast day on August 29, and it is one of the best celebrations in the village. There is yet another celebration that occurs on June 24, but to a lesser degree.

8. *Agios Charlambis.* The small church of *Agios Charalambos* lies at the northwestern edge of the village on the road to *Lavidorki*, near the last of the houses. At the time, this very old chapel with two or three cypress trees in front, and its darkened walls overgrown with foliage, gave me the impression of melancholy abandonment. Liturgies are held a few times during the year: on February 10, which is the Saint's name day, and when someone has vowed to do a liturgy for the salvation of one's soul.

Fortunately, since then, the church has been repaired and is in very good condition. The Saint, according to popular belief, fights the plague, an illness that in the past killed both people and animals.

Pantelis A. Mavrogiorgis

Agios Ioannis o Prodromos
(Photographer: A. Sami Bey, 1937)

Agios Charalambos
(Photographer: N. Sakoulas)

Agios Konstantinos
(Photographer: N. Sakoulas)

Pantelis A. Mavrogiorgis

Agios Giannis o Theologos
Photographer: N. Sakoulas)

Iconographers depict *Agios Charalambos*, as a priest, trampling on a wild monster or on a wild woman from which smoke issues, thus symbolizing the plague.

9. *Agios Konstantinos.* This is a new church on the road to *Lavidorki*, a bit further down from Agios Charalambos. Kostas Zymnis, son of Stamatis, built it twenty to twenty-five years ago. As it is known, the celebration occurs on May 21.

10. *Agios Giannis o Theologos.* This very old church is northwest, about an hour's distance from the village, in a closed, airless location by the river near *"tou Nola to Pigadi"* - Nola's well. The historian of Chios, Georgios Zolotas, describes it as

> *"an old chapel to which the Turks, in vain, tried to set on fire in 1822."*

The church celebrates on May 8, and the "brothers" hold a liturgy.

11. *Agioi Viktores (Minas, Viktor, Vikentios).* This is a very small and isolated little church that sits in an imposing environment at the outer northern boundaries of the field area of Sikousis, beyond Agios

Agioi Viktores at Droposi
(Photographer: A. Sami Bey, 1937)

Pantelis A. Mavrogiorgis

Giannis Theologos. This location is known as *Droposi*, probably from the many waters in the area. The chapel was built on a stone mount with a running-water spring across, which is used to water the small estate alongside it. A spreading spruce tree provides shade and welcomes travelers. I remember, as elementary school students, that we would spend the first day of May there with our teachers.

From *Droposi*, an area planted with pine trees begins and leads to the monasterial lands, to *Platanos*, and to *Agioi Pateres*. The feast day of the church is celebrated on November 11, which is the same day Chios was liberated from the Turks.

12. **Agios Thomas.** This is an old church located at a height of about 600 meters in an area called *"Piso Nera"* in the northeast part of the village. From its height, the landscape spreads below in a giant radius and is quite impressive. There is a spring there and an old reservoir.

The church celebrates on the first Sunday after *Pascha*. In a document from 1757, in which the Board Members of the church of Agios Georgios were appointed, it is mentioned that these men will also preside over the parishes of Agios Panteleimonas and Agios Nikolas. It impresses me that these same people were also given jurisdiction over Agios Thomas. I have copied portions of this document from page 210 of the village Codex 1043.

> *"1757 November 7, today parishioners, Elders, and priests gathered to select Mastronikolas Giannakakis and Giannis Sfalakakis as Board Members of the Church to serve for (?) years, and at the end of their term will give an accounting to the parishioners. They will seek advice from Board Members Mise Manolis Petrokokkinos and Mise Manolis Skaramangas, and these four people together will also be in the churches of Agios Nikolas, Agios Panteleimonas, and Agios Thomas . . ."*

(Note: The Codex 1043 states on p. 192 that Mise Manolis Skaramangas and Mise Manolis Petrokokkinos had authority over the churches. It seems like they were overseers.)

13. **Profitis Ilias.** This Saint holds a peculiar place that touches upon the boundaries of myth and religious fantasy among the chorus of saints of the Church. Within this framework, it is believed that *Ilias o Thesvitis* did not die but instead ascended into Heaven in a fiery

The Chapel of Profitis Ilias

chariot and remains there as a foreteller of the "Second Coming" of Christ. There is speculation that during Christ's time on Earth there was a forerunner who some called Ioannis and others called Ilias (Elias). There is yet another belief that has this prophet living in the high areas of the plain and mountain peaks, from where he lifts the clouds and sends the rain. He is the Saint of Light and seems to be related to the Sun God Apollo and the Cloud Gatherer Zeus. The name Elias bears a similarity to the name *Helios* ("sun" in Greek). As Christians, the people turned from worshipping the sun – as they did on the mountain peaks with chapels in graphic splendor – to venerate Elias.

There is another tradition for the construction of churches on mountaintops: The Prophet Elijah was a sailor. Due to numerous hardships, he left the sea and settled in a place where people knew little of boats and the sea. To find the right place, he would walk around with an oar on his shoulder and ask people, "What is this thing I'm holding on my shoulder?" He would continue walking to higher and higher areas until he located people who had no idea what the oar was, and that is the place he chose to settle down. We

Pantelis A. Mavrogiorgis

read of a similar event hundreds of years earlier in Homer's *Odyssey* (Od. 30, 6. 120ff). The Soothsayer Teiresias urges Odysseus, once he reaches his palace and kills Penelope's suitors, to take "a well-built oar" and reach up to "men who do not know the sea." Odysseus meets a traveler who is "holding a garden rake on his shoulder," so he stakes the oar into the ground and builds a beautiful altar dedicated to King Poseidon.

Let's visit our own chapel, which is barely distinguishable upon one of the highest peaks of the cluster of mountains in central Chios, above Agios Thomas at a height of about 800 meters. From this wild peak, tamed only by the existence of the church, you are unable to see much of anything. The surrounding area, where the earth meets the sky, seems to reach right up to Heaven. The area of Kambos is spread below it, and beyond is the Aegean Sea and Asia Minor. This chapel was neglected for years. Today it has been reconstructed, and facilities have been installed for pilgrims' benefit. In past years, whoever managed to go up there on the eve of the Saint's feast, which occurs on July 20, had to stay up all night in order to attend the liturgy the following morning. Today, there is a road for cars to travel, so a large number of pilgrims attend to celebrate and honor the Saint on his feast day.

E. The List of Priests

We will close this lengthy chapter that refers to religious life with the enumeration of the names of village priests which can be found in the codexes and various notary documents of the village, where they have signed as witnesses for dowry agreements and wills. The year listed across from the name is taken from the chronology of the signature and that is how we can give an approximation of each one's life.

1. Priests

Papa – Nikolis of Lamparda	1622
Papa – Xenos Melissinos	1747
Papa – Kostantis Tornaris	1777
Papa – Nikolis Psaros	1777
Papa – Vasilis Chamalaki	1777
Papa – Giorgis Kalargyros	1777
Papa – Giorgis Vasilaki	1781
Papa – Nikolis Tornaris	1781
Papa – Giannis Kalargyros	1781
Papa – Stamatis Vekaki	1780
Papa – Giannis Eftaxiotis	1780

Papa – Stavrinos 1789
Papa – Giorgis Papavasilaki 1789
Papa – Panagiotis Manastros 1789
Papa – Dimitris Kalargyros 1791
Papa – Giorgis Promatakis 1793
Papa – Vasilis Krakas 1793
Papa – Stamatis Nikoloudis 1793
Papa – Michalis Michalaki 1796
Papa – Giorgis Sklavaki 1796
Papa – Vasilis Xenaki 1805
Papa – Vasilis Akraki 1805
Papa – Stamatis Giannakaki 1808
Papa – Giannis Papavasilakis 1808
Papa – Kostantis Tsikolis 1815
Papa – Vasilis Alikastos 1815
Papa – Diako-Giannis Papatsigroudis 1815
Papa – Antonios Fragkakis 1818
Papa – Dimitris Papachatzis 1818
Papa – Michalis Xas 1822
Papa – Giorgis Akrakis 1830
Papa – Giannis Soukas 1830
Ierodiakonos tou Giorgi Souka 1830
Papa – Stamatis Spanoudis 1835
Papa – Giorgis Toublis 1837
Papa – Chatzis Bekakis (or) Vekios 1843
Papa – Giorgis Foustanas 1837
Papa – Nikolis Soukas 1848
Papa – Vasilis Chatzi – Arakas 1857
Ierodiakonos Papa-Georgiou Toubli 1853
Papa – Kostantis Kostaris 1849
Papa – Nikolas Pilavas 1851
Papa – Giorgis Pnevmatikos 1851
Papa – Dimitrios Fountoulis or Fountoulakis 1866
Papa – Nikolaos Giannakakis 1866
Papa – Chatzis Ioannis Tsoflias 1883
Papa – Kostantis Toras 1868
Papa – Emmanouil Pappous 1872
Papa – Giorgis Kolivas 1877
Papa – Ioannis Koutelos 1870
Papa – Dimitris Kaïmenos 1876
Papa – Chatzis Stamatis Dellas 1875
(Sakellarios)

Pantelis A. Mavrogiorgis

Papa – Stamatis Fineskos 1885

2. **From the list of priests** of Chios, which was composed on **August 29, 1898** and which exists in Codex 1887 of the Metropolis of Chios, we copied the following:

   Papa – Diamantis Salagaras
   Papa – Dimitris Barlis or Choras
   Papa – Michalis Tsiknis
   Papa – Giannis Vizaniaris (or Tsotsos)
   Papa – Panagiotis Monis (I met him personally)
   Papa – Giannis Dellas or Ntellas, son of Michail

3. The following priests are known to me **personally**:

   Diako – Pilavas
   Papa – Stelianos Salagaras (the son of *Papa* – Diamanti)
   Papa – Antonios Mouzithras
   Papa – Panagiotis Dellas or Ntellas (brother of *Papa* – Gianni Della)
   Papa – Giannis Sakoulas, son of Nikolaos, who is still a priest today
   Papa – Giorgis Sakoulas, son of Nikolaos, who is still a priest today
   Papa – Giannis Salagaras, son of *Papa* – Stelianos, still a priest
       today in *Zyfia*
   Papa – Argyris Mylonas, ordained in April 1988 by Metropolitan
       Dionysios of Chios, and serves as a priest in *Vessa.*

PART THREE

HISTORY OF EDUCATION
&
LOCAL GOVERNMENT

Pantelis A. Mavrogiorgis

CHAPTER 22
Education in Chios

As an educator, I would really like to write the complete history of our schools. However, it is unfortunate that I do not have the necessary data at my disposal to give me the capability of creating such an account. Therefore, I will present a general framework to illustrate how the schools in Chios functioned during the Turkish occupation, among which is the elementary school of our village.

A. The First Schools

To discuss education, this can only happen for Chora from the 16th century, when the Genoese still occupied Chios. At that time, the first school was located near the church of *Agios Vasileios Petrokokkinon*, whose ruins can be found in the Public Garden of Chora. Later on, the school moved a little further out to the parish of *Agion Anargyron Egremou*, and other schools were also founded, such as that at the parish of *Agion Viktoron Aplotarias*.

In these schools, some of the teachers were medical doctors and clergymen, some of whom were noteworthy and others mediocre. There were also erudite Chians abroad, like Emmanuil Glyzounios, Leon Allatios, Adamantios Koraïs, who enriched the education of Greek letters in Chios, as well. The Great School of Chios was in operation from 1792. It is located across from the Metropolis of Chios and continues to this day as a *Gymnasio* and *Lykeio* (middle and high school).

Even though the movement in education was more prevalent in the capital of Chios, a general lack of education prevailed in the villages. The majority of people were illiterate. Some people learned from clergymen or notaries what was known as *"Kollyvogrammata,"* which allowed them to read without really understanding what they were reading.

Some exceptions were the schools that operated at the monasteries of Nea Moni and Agios Minas, where the *Ethnomartyras* Patriarch Grigorios the 5th also studied. Zolotas mentions the *"Didaskaleion"* of the Mastichochoria in 1759, which possibly was in the village of *Armoleia*, but he does not give us any additional information.

B. The Schools after 1822

After the massacres of 1822, and after the reconstruction, which began around 1830 in Chios, there was some official movement toward the founding of schools in villages. What was known as the *"Grammatodidaskaleia"* (elementary schools), were overseen by the Metropolitan of the area, who approved the hiring of teachers selected by the Elders, priests, and parishioners who undertook the payment of the teachers' salaries. We found the following document from the year 1887 in an envelope at the Metropolis of Chios. It provides one example of the hiring process for teachers at that time.

"The undersigned Elder advisors, Board Members, Trustees, and the rest of the parishioners of the village of Chalkeious agreed unanimously today to hire Mr. Panagiotis Giavilis as follows:

1. We hired the aforementioned Panagiotis as a teacher in our School to teach the approved lessons in the circular method. (This referred to a style of teaching where the best students taught other students, all under the supervision of the teacher.)

2. The appointment and salary are for a period of one year from today. His annual salary will be three-and-a-half thousand (3,500) grosia, which the Board Members of our village, who are serving at that time, will pay in timely installments every three months.

3. Simultaneously, all students in the School, without exception, are to pay the customary amount of Saturday tuition to the teacher.

For the validation of the above, we prepared two similar documents, to which we affixed the seal of our village.

Chios, Chalkeios village, September 1, 1889."

We continue with a sample showing the approval of the Metropolis related to the hiring of a teacher.

"The teacher, Spyridon Manes, from the village of Kallimasia, is approved to teach elementary education lessons at the elementary school of his village, according to the program approved by the Holy Metropolis.

The present document was published, based on the document of the village, dated September 5, 1896.

In the Holy Metropolis of Chios on September 18, 1896."

Pantelis A. Mavrogiorgis

The treasury of each church undertook the responsibility to provide the teachers' salaries from taxes or fund drives, *Tasa* or *Paroikada*, of the inhabitants; and from student tuition, which was not always money but often food – what was called "Saturday tuition" in the previous document. Tuition was usually used for the rental of private homes for teaching purposes.

The classes taught at each school depended upon the number of teachers. One teacher was able to teach up to three grades, while two teachers taught four, and three teachers had five grades, and another four teachers had six grades. The one with six grades was called the *"Astiki Scholi"* (City School).

In the document above from the Metropolis, mention is made about a program of instruction, however I do not know exactly what that means. In any case, Greek and Arithmetic were taught and, in the best case, Religion, History (of the Persian Wars), local Geography, and Singing (of ecclesiastical hymns).

C. Supervisor Pavlidis and the Schools

From a report written in 1911 to the Metropolitan of Chios, Ieronymos Gorgias, by Dimitrios Pavlidis – who studied education in Germany and was hired by the Metropolitan as Supervisor of Schools – we learn from his evaluation that there was no universal teaching program in the schools he visited nor were there common hours of operation. Generally, the school hours were 8:00 a.m. to 12:00 noon and 2:00 to 4:00 p.m. in the afternoon. Pavlidis writes that some schools started in the morning and finished in the evening. Generally the classes of older students were taught first, then the younger ones. If time remained, first graders were also given instruction. In one school which had many grade levels, Pavlidis says that the instruction was given to first graders for five-and-a-half hours a week; however, the children remained within the school building for about forty hours weekly!

The things we learned about the schools in Turkish-occupied Chios should not seem strange to us, if we keep in mind that in liberated Greece, legislation which promoted the opening of elementary schools with seven grades and a rich program was introduced in 1834. However, that type of school was never put into operation. The elementary schools continued to be *"Grammatodidaskaleia."*

As far as the required qualifications for personnel to be hired, they had to *"know reading and writing, the four arithmetic processes, and the initial elements of our sacred faith."*

The schools in Chios began functioning more systematically under Pavlidis, who obligated all the teachers to teach based on a specific time period program. He recommended that the schools be supplied with maps, abacuses, and other visual means for teaching. He also strove for the administrative organization of the schools and the keeping of official books, a list of students, report cards, a list of absences, and other innovations.

It is worth noting that, in the summer of 1913, Pavlidis created an educational conference for the continuing education of the teachers; this lasted for two weeks. At this conference, the teachers were taught Linguistics, Mathematics, Geography, and even Agronomy, bookbinding, songs, drawing, and Gymnastics. The teachers Alexandros Galanos, Lemonia Kambanis, and Anastasios Mavrogiorgis from Agios Georgios attended this conference.

D. Education in *Agios Georgios*

1. **The School for Boys.** From a Decision of the Metropolitan of Chios, written in our village's Codex 1045, the founding and operation of a school for boys can conclusively be traced prior to 1843. Sofronios of Chios gathered a committee of Agiorgousoi to organize and sell the last of the monastic estates, which were being held or arbitrarily claimed by those who were maintaining them. In the document, we read that,

   *". . . the money collected from similar sales **will be used for the teachers' salaries of the newly founded 'Koinou Scholeiou' . . . 1843—April 20."***

   From another manuscript book, located in the archives of our current school, I copied the following related information:

   "The Community School began operating from the year 1840. Initially it was located within the home of our fellow villager, Nikolaos Mizeros, and later on in the home of Nikolaos Hahalis. From 1864, it was relocated to the cells of the church of Agios Georgios."

2. **Past Teachers.** From the manuscript book mentioned above, notary documents of the village, and notes from the ever-memorable teacher, Alexandros Galanos, I discovered the following names of teachers who taught in the School for Boys during the Turkish Occupation up until 1912.

   a. *Papa* - **Petros Mavrogiannis**

   b. **Dimitrios Papadopoulos** or **Malliari** (1850). He was an educated man, exiled at the time of Othon; he knew medical topics and Byzantine music. Galanos notes that the following individuals learned music from him: *Papa* Diamantis Salagaras, Kostantis Koutelos, Stavris Mamas, and Giannis Vizaniaris or Tsotsos, who later became a priest.

He worked in the village for three years and then was dismissed. When they would ask him why he left Agios Georgis, he would answer, "Because the Agiorgousoi don't know silver from copper."

c. **Andreas Kyparissis** or **Psarianos**, 1864-1871. He taught in the old church of Agios Ioannis, across from Agios Giorgis, which he transformed into a school. He was well educated, which I ascertained from reading various notary documents he had written during 1866 and 1869.

d. *Papa* **Manolis Pappous** from Agios Giorgis, but he had little education.

e. **G. Tsimounis** from Nechori, who taught for two to three years.

f. **Georgios Koukadis** from Mesta, who was also an empirical medical doctor.

g. **Dimitrios Galanos,** the father of Alexandros Galanos from Agios Giorgis. He taught in 1875, 1876, and again from 1895 – 1900. Earlier on, he had taught at Olympoi.

h. **Stamatios Toras** from Agios Giorgis, 1881, 1882.

i. **Stylianos papa–Stamati Dellas.** He taught from 1885 – 1888. I happened to read his manuscripts, from which I formed the opinion that he was a very educated man.

j. **Georgios Hatzi–Stefanou Kakaridis,** 1888 – 1893. Mougeris, in his little book, *Topography of Chios*, writes that Kakaridis was a very good teacher.

k. **Charalambos Kefalas,** from Lithi, 1891 – 1892.

l. **Georgios Sotropas,** from Lithi, 1893 – 1895.

m. **Priest Nikolaos Skellas,** from Langada, 1900 – 1902.

n. **Stylianos Galatoulas,** from Agio Gala.

o. **Nikolaos Skandalis,** from Thymiana, 1902 – 1912.

p. **Alexandros Galanos,** from Agios Giorgis, 1902 – 1904, 1908 – 1916 and 1921 – 1933.

I will now present a document sent to the main priest of the village in 1904 by the Metropolis, showing that the notables were occasionally negligent and did not pay the teachers in a timely manner.

> *"To the Very Reverend protopriest and honorable Board Members of Agios Georgios Sykountos, Greetings in the Lord.*
>
> *The teacher of your village, who is in dire need of money, demands that you pay the salary that is due to him. Since the Elders of this current year did not undertake the obligation to pay such salary, the Church Treasury is now obligated to meet this responsibility. Therefore, we insist that you pay the salary from the Church Treasury.*
>
> *Do not forget that the churches and the Board Members strive for education.*
>
> *This is for your information.*
>
> *In the Metropolis of Chios, December 18, 1904."*

But this situation in our village is not the only case. I also encountered documents showing neglect for the payment of teachers in other villages.

3. **Number of Students and Grades.** The number of students who studied is a notable indication of the love and interest of the parents regarding their children's education. Codex 1887 of the Metropolis shows that there were only 30 students in the school in 1891. For the population of the village at that time, this was a small number. In that same year, Tholopotami had 30 students and Vessa had 20.

During the 1909 – 1910 school year, Kostantinos Amantos writes that Agios Giorgis Sikousis had five grades with 150 boys. We see how quickly the numbers increased over a period of twenty years. In the 1911 – 1912 school year, the supervisor Pavlidis writes that the school then had five grades with 157 boys and two teachers: Alexandros Galanos and Ierodiakonos Nikolaos Skandalis.

If some of the previous data gives the impression that the Agiorgousoi were not that interested in education, newer data illustrates that not only were they in favor of schooling for their boys but they also wanted their girls to learn to read, at least, under the difficult conditions of the times, during which many of the children went to school barefooted and poorly dressed. Here is a document written by Inspector Theodoros Stamatopoulos dated February 2, 1915, that gives us some significant information.

> "The Overseers of the Schools of Agios Georgios Sikousis demanded from the teachers of the Boys' School of the Community that a sixth grade be established for the first time this year, especially to include the twenty students who have been roaming the streets. This demand is not made by law, since the Schools are abiding by the regulations that were established in the past. Nevertheless, this demand is just. The teachers have also recognized the value of this request, however their objection is that there is no available space for this to occur.
>
> The Overseers understood this objection as an excuse and, lately, there have been sharp disputes and clashes between the Overseers and teachers.
>
> In order to develop a solution in this matter, I went to Agios Georgios Sikousis on December 21, 1914. I visited both of the Schools, the one which has two teachers and two classes of boys, and the one having one female teacher and one class of girls – housed in a common school building next to the Church (Agios Georgios).
>
> The teachers were right, because the school building truly has no room to allow a new grade to be housed there. In order to arrange this, it was decided to move the Girls' School to another house, thus the fifth and sixth grades can then be put into the newly empty room.
>
> This occurred with a more suitable venue found for the Girls' School, therefore the aforementioned matter ended in a way that was satisfactory for both the Overseers and the teachers of the Community of Agios Georgios."

Therefore, from 1915, the Boys' school operated with six grades, three teachers, and three classrooms. There were 182 students in two grades per classroom: 38 first graders, 38 second graders, 46 third graders, 25 fourth graders, 22 fifth graders, and 13 sixth graders.

4. **The Need to Build a School.** After inspecting the schools, Stamatopoulos, the supervisor, wrote a report in December 1915 that has important information encouraging the pursuit of education in our village.

> *"After completing the inspection of both of these schools, a meeting was held with the teachers and the members of the School Board, during which the various needs and deficiencies of the schools were discussed.*
>
> ***The need to build a new school for boys to replace the existing, very unhealthy, one was stressed. The Community has already recognized this.*** *Therefore, an appropriate document was immediately drafted and signed by both the Municipal Elders and the School Board members of the Community. That document was then given to me to act upon.* **Through this document, the Community promises to offer to the public the appropriate land, stones, sand, lime, personal work of the inhabitants and, additionally, more than 6,000 drachmas –** *expecting the public to undertake any additional expenses for the construction of a school building."*

As shown in the book *Praxeon (Deeds)*, the Community Council in 1927

> *"requests the expropriation of the plot of Stylianos Toublis* (an Agiorgousis who lived in Constantinople) *by the Plateia of Agios Georgios to be used as a gymnasium for children and for the erection of a* **Boys' School***. Later on, the Community Council makes another Decision that rescinds that first mandate and proposes to the Ministry that the land be expropriated instead for a Community Square."*

5. **Teachers after the Liberation.** On previous pages, we presented a chart of those who taught in the Boys' School until 1912, at which point Chios was liberated from the Turks. With the chart below, we complete the list with the names of teachers who subsequently taught, not as Community teachers, but as employees of the Greek Government.

     a. **Anastasios Mavrogeorgis** from Chora .... 1914 – 1950
     b. **Dimitrios Skandalis** from Thymiana ..... 1911 – 1915

c. **Georgios Dellas** from Agios Giorgis ...... 1915 – 1928
d. **Pavlos Grigoriadis** from Cyprus .... 1916 – 1917
e. **Nikolaos Patounas** from Agios Giorgis ... 1917 – 1918
f. **Georgios Madianos** from Volissos .... 1917 – 1919
g. **Michail Rimikis** from Leptopoda .... 1919 – 1923
h. **Ioannis Variadakis** from Vrontados ....
i. **Lambros Koufopantelis** from Vrontados . 1920 – 1922
j. **Klimentini Morfoutsikou** from Samos ... 1925 – 1926

6. **The Girls' School.** The schools that girls attended at that time were known as *"Parthenagogeia."* They came into being later than the boys' schools because the viewpoint that had prevailed for years was that girls did not need any formal education. Their lot in life was to remain at home, become familiar with household chores, and help their mothers, who tended to give birth almost every year.

In 1890, the *Parthenagogeio* began to operate in our village. The Metropolis of Chios had formulated a list of schools in operation in Chios in 1887 and mentioned that in Agios Giorgis, while a boys' school was functioning, there was no Parthenagogeio, whereas they did exist in other villages.

In Sikousis, the girls' school had four grades, and those children were taught by either one or two female teachers. In the 1909 – 1910 school year, Amantos writes that the school had four grades and 70 female students. In 1911 – 1912 there were 60 female students and one female teacher. Up until 1915, the girls also used one of the cells of the church of Agios Georgios. Afterwards, as mentioned in a prior section, the school was housed once again in a private home, which was initially Moulou's large house, still distinguishable from all the other houses in the village by its height. Then I remember the girls' school being in a two-story house owned by Gaginis near the olive press of Nikolis Sakoulas. That house had one room on the main floor and two on the upper floor that were reached by an internal staircase.

There was an article in the *Nea Chios* newspaper published on August 19, 1913 that credits the Agiorgousoi for the interest they showed in the *Parthenagogeio*.

"In our village, one of the most populated on the island of Chios, there was no Parthenagogeio in operation last year. We say this with deep sadness and attribute it to the bad administration of those in charge of the village, and to

the disregard by the Holy Metropolis and D. Pavlidis, the Overseer of the Schools. Now, once again, the new school year is approaching. Nevertheless we observe, in general, a lack of interest in our schools and teaching matters, and the unforgivable indifference of the authorities toward the future operation of the Parthenagogeio.

We do not want to believe that those handling the matters of our schools, as well as the Holy Metropolis and Mr. Overseer, will not seek to settle matters in a manner so as not to do injustice to our children – male and female – and not force us, especially in wintertime as occurred last year, to send them to foreign and faraway villages."

While we don't know if the school functioned during the 1913 – 1914 school year, we do know that it was in operation in 1915, as shown in the inspector's report. It had 74 female students and four grades. The inspector writes:

"Their numbers may increase considerably due to the implementation of the law of compulsory attendance which was deliberately not aimed at females, because of the lack of space on the one hand, and the lack of a suitable female teacher on the other hand."

The girls' school underperformed, in comparison to the boys' school where capable teachers taught, because – without us being critical – the female teachers at that time did not have the same qualifications as the male teachers, and they were also burdened by their family responsibilities.

The *Parthenagogeio* was in operation until 1928, at which time it was united with the boys' school. The following female teachers taught the girls until 1928.

a. **Maria Makaroni,** from Chora . . . . 1890 – 1894
b. **Angeliki Serafim,** from Chora . . . . 1895 – 1900
c. **Lemonia Kambani,** from Agios Giorgis . . . . 1901 – 1915
d. **Anna Chiotou,** from Kardamyla . . . . 1916 – 1920
e. **Kyriaki Tsamardinou,** from Chora . . . . 1916 – 1920
f. **Cassandra Prinou,** from Kallimasia . . . . 1920 – 1924
g. **Isabella Pipinia,** from Vrontados . . . . 1921 – 1923
h. **Maria Kampouri,** from Chios . . . . 1924 – 1928
i. **Cleopatra Vasileiadou,** from Chios. . . . . 1924 – 1928

Pantelis A. Mavrogiorgis

7. **The Coeducational Elementary School.** In 1929, the elementary school had both girls and boys together in classes. Alexandros Galanos was the principal, and Anastasios Mavrogiorgis, Giorgis Dellas, and the sisters Marianthi and Ekaterini Stavrinakis were the teachers. In order to accommodate the students, in addition to the three old rooms (cells) across from Agios Giorgis, a two-story house that had one room on the main floor and another on the upper floor was rented. This house was next to Stavros (the gate of the old Monastery), owned by Kostis Gelis or "Pashas". Thus five classrooms were provided, one for every grade; the fifth and sixth grades were taught in a single room.

The school building, by anyone's judgment, was completely unsuitable. Aside from the fact that the rooms did not get enough air or light, all of the male and female students in the private house, along with their teachers, were obligated to travel back and forth during every break to the courtyard of Agios Georgios, where the other students were, unless they chose to simply remain in the classrooms. Water and other necessary facilities were nonexistent. Therefore, the female students tended to go to neighboring houses, while the male students ran down to open fields with old and uninhabited houses. Fortunately, for breaks and Gymnastic lessons the churchyard was available; otherwise the children would have been in the streets. The school did have a very beautiful flower garden, though, with a seedbed of little trees, all the work of Alexandros Galanos.

There were other school activities besides Gymnastics. There were handicrafts, frequent school celebrations, required presentations by the children – which I sadly discovered no longer exist today, along with handicraft lessons, drawing, and calligraphy. In 1932, our school – under the initiative of Galanos and the active participation of the other teachers – planted the forest located at the "eyebrows" of the *Agriomelissa* mountain on the road to Tholopotami. The Community Council named this the "Forest of Alexandros Galanos," in his honor. It would be an omission and injustice to neglect to mention that Anastasios Mavrogiogis, the teacher, put forth exceptional effort toward the development of that forest once he undertook the directorship of the School in 1933. Galanos, once the first planting of little trees was accomplished, left the forest "in good hands."

Our school functioned excellently. Our teachers worked

enthusiastically *"na mas kanoun anthropous"* ("to make us human"), as they used to say in the village. The basic problem that existed, though, was the unsuitable school building, which eventually had to serve about 300 students every year. By the 1935-1936 school year, the student body numbered 327. Something had to be done about the construction of a new school building. We will present this issue in the following section.

8. **The Construction of a New School Building.** As we mentioned in a prior section, the problem of the school building itself was an issue that was first discussed in 1915. Years later, due to the interference of World War I, the destruction of Asia Minor; the division and internal political anomalies that followed in Greece, the topic of a new school building resurfaced for discussion around 1936.

a. **Officials Visit the Village for the Construction of a School Building.** The December 17, 1936 issue of the newspaper *Prodos* informs us that Bishop Ioakim Stroubis, Prefect Themistoklis Athanasiadis, and Dragotis, Superintendent of Public Schools, visited the village in order to promote this project.

> *"After Mr. Mavrogiorgis, the Director of our School spoke, the officials – accompanied by the Community Council and the School Board – examined various plots of land in order to select the most suitable one for the erection of the new school building. At noon, over a lunch offered by the progressive Community Council President Pantelis Patounas, all worked together to determine the amount necessary for the construction of the educational building. Truly, the appropriate amount was calculated and the work will begin soon."*

What a shame! After all of this, one would expect that the school would grow quicker than a mushroom! It seems, however, that this was one of those decisions made over a meal and called *"metaxi tyrou kai achladiou"* ("between cheese and pears"). Subsequently, we learn from *Proodos* (No. 2796) that on May 5, 1938 (a year and a half later), that those identical people returned to the village once again for exactly the same purpose. The Prefect Athanasiadis once again uttered *"big words"* that we have copied from the newspaper:

> *"I am looking forward to speaking with you publicly when I come, so that we can lay the foundation for the*

new school building in your village."

It is worth noting the praiseworthy verses recited by our village poetess, Kyriaki Kloutis, who was called *"I Gria Kori"* (the Elderly Maiden) by the villagers. She said the following to the Prefect:

"When your mother gave you birth,
and suffered labor pains,
she embrased the cypress tree
and made you a pillar (tall).

Sea, that you are across from us,
do not create such a current,
because two beautiful eyes
came to us from abroad.

You have the face of the lily,
the luster of the jasmine,
and if you go into the darkness,
the entire world shines."

b. **Expropriation of Land.** All of the above actions related to the building of a school actually had a positive result: the land chosen for the school was expropriated. In the May 10, 1940 issue of *Nea Chios*, we read the following notice:

> *"Through Royal Order, published in the Newspaper of the Government at the suggestion of the Ministers of Finance and of National Education, a forced expropriation for public benefit in order to build the Elementary School of Agios Georgios Sikousis, in the community of the same name, was proclaimed. This land which has an area of 3,282 square meters belongs to the Kollis brothers, Billis, Panagiotis Dellas, Kostantinos Galanos; and D. Platis and the inheritors of A. Kolyvas."*

c. **The Construction.** At the time that the construction of the school building was to begin, there were dramatic, historical events that occurred: the Greco-Italian war in Albania, the German Occupation, and the Civil War. For those reasons, construction did not commence until 1949, at the expense of the Association of Agiorgousoi of America and the exceptional personal work of the villagers, who worked eagerly, along with their beasts of burden, to transport building materials. They prepared lime, helped dig the foundation, and leveled the land.

The architectural plans were created by the Ministry of Education, and the execution of the work was undertaken by the very diligent builder, Georgios Fegaras from Nechori, under the oversight of the Committee appointed by fellow villagers in America, and comprised of Alexandros Galanos, Konstantinos Toulambis, and Pantelis Patounas, as well as the School Board members: Director Anastasios Mavrogiorgis, Antonios Toulambis, and Ioannis Bogiasklis.

The school building was imposing and beautiful, and it contained a spacious lobby – for students to use during break times, or when weather conditions were unfavorable – comfortable, well-lit classrooms, a personnel office, performance hall, help areas, a plumbing system, a large yard for recess and gymnastics classes, and a school garden.

d. **Inauguration of the School Building.** This event occurred with great ceremony in front of the leaders of the Prefecture and the leaders and inhabitants of the community. The Metropolitan of Chios performed the *agiasmo* (Holy Water service), and Alexandros Galanos gave a speech, followed by greetings from the Superintendent of Schools, and the Prefect of Chios. At the conclusion, a gathering was held in the new reception room for the officials and remaining guests.

We will select several excerpts from the speech made by Galanos, who was then retired as teacher and director, published in the November 21, 1951 edition of the newspaper *Proodos*.

> *"This bright creation, which is being inaugurated today, is an indisputable sign of the Chians' great love for education. It is a sacred altar of the muses and a workshop of Christian principles befitting Hellenes.*
>
> ***Neither time nor great distances were able to quench or lessen in the souls of our fellow villagers abroad, in the United States of America, the love for their birthplace, a wonderful virtue of the Hellene.***
>
> *Inspired by this, the Association vowed from afar to set the most important goal of founding a school and, to see it erected, they gathered and sent $25,000 up until today. The school building was built both through the*

The new school building with its auditorium

The Village Agios Georgios Sikousis

important personal work of the inhabitants, and the significant efforts of young students led by the teaching personnel."

On the front of the school building, there is a marble plaque inserted into the wall and inscribed thusly with gold letters:

"ERECTED AT THE EXPENSE
OF THE ASSOCIATION IN AMERICA
AGIOS GEORGIOS SIKOUSIS"

In this manner, the village was able to express its undying gratitude to its children abroad.

e. **New Additions.** The state endowed the new school building with eighty new desks and 50,000 drachmas, with which an expansion followed. It added a large handicraft room on the upper floor. This was done under the direction of the teacher Christos Vekios, who was also the creator of the school garden that totaled about six hundred square meters.

Later on, under Director Nestoras Tsikolis, restrooms with showers, a cafeteria, and a well-equipped playground were added.

At this point we need to refer to Nikolaos Kartalis, the director of the school, who strove for progress in every possible way, and the director today Georgios Mylonas, who works to maintain and preserve the good reputation of our school and who graciously provided me with any information I requested.

E. Teaching Personnel in Agios Georgios since 1929 - 1930

From 1915 until 1968, the school functioned with five teachers. Due to the continual lessening in the amount of students – which also occurred in all the other villages in Chios – from 1969 to 1972, the school had four teachers. From 1973 to 1986, there were three teachers. From 1987 until today, it operates with two teachers and forty-five students. A third teacher was added, since children from Vessa also attend our school.

In addition to Galanos, Mavrogiorgis, and Dellas, who taught earlier on at the boys' school, the male and female teachers who served at the coeducational elementary school are the following:

1. Marianthi Stavrinaki . . . . 1929 – 1938

2. Aikaterini Stavrinaki . . . . 1930 – 1937
3. Konstantinos Kostalas . . . . 1930 – 1933
3. Christos Vekios . . . . 1933 – 1935 and 1947 – 1961
5. Stavros Tsikolis . . . . 1935 – 1958
6. Antonios Dellas . . . . 1935 – 1947
7. Kimon Spentzakis . . . . 1935 – 1937
8. Maria Proïou . . . . 1937 – 1944
9. Aikaterini Perpinia . . . . 1937 – 1948
10. Ioulia Stroumbi . . . . 1938 – 1947
11. Maritsa Papadouli . . . . 1942 – 1944
12. Aikaterini Chondrogiorgaki . . . . 1943 – 1948
13. Angeliki Malfreda . . . . 1944 – 1945
14. Kanella Kalliteri . . . . 1952 – 1954
15. Angeliki Karakostanti . . . . 1954 – 1957
16. Kleopatra Siraki . . . . 1955 – 1959
17. Aikaterini Aikaterini . . . . 1958 – 1964
18. Antonios Vekios . . . . 1958 – 1960
19. Nestoras Tsikolis . . . . 1959 – 1971
20. Aglaïa Margariti . . . . 1960 – 1964
21. Georgios Tsikolis . . . . 1961 – 1962
22. Lambros Giannoulakis . . . . 1963 – 1970
23. Eleni Kokolaki . . . . 1964 – 1968
24. Leonidas Giasemis . . . . 1964 – 1965
25. Magdalini Papazoglou . . . . 1964 – 1965
26. Pagona Fragkou . . . . 1965 – 1970
27. Maria Rodaki . . . . 1965 – 1971
28. Georgios Karatzanos . . . . 1968 – 1969
29. Areti Galetsa . . . . 1968 – 1969
30. Antonios Amantos . . . . 1970 – 1973
31. Antonios Pitsos . . . . 1970 – 1971
32. Kalliopi Koutsouradi . . . . 1970 – 1976
33. Nikolaos Kartalis . . . . 1971 – 1976
34. Kleio Xydia . . . . 1971 – 1973
35. Evangelia Karavola . . . . 1973 – 1977
36. Dimitrios Tsagkatos . . . . 1976 – 1977
37. Aikaterini Valiadi . . . . 1977 – 1978 and 1979 – 1984
38. Theano Pagiavla . . . . 1978 – 1979
39. Ioannis Gialis . . . . 1978 – 1979
40. Maria Chila . . . . 1979 – 1980
41. Aikaterini Kostidou . . . . 1978 – 1983 (periodically)
42. Despina Melachrinoudi . . . . 1977 – 1982
43. Pantelis Toulambis . . . . 1977 – 1981
44. Kleopatra Zevgiou . . . . 1987 to present

45. Christos Varouktsis . . . .   1982 to present
46. Georgios Mylonas . . . .   1980 to present

F. Local Self-Administration

Administratively speaking, every city and every village belongs to an *Eparchia* (sub-Prefecture or County) or Prefecture. However, aside from this governmental structure, the city or village – as an autonomous societal unit – has its own local self-administration. During the years of the Turkish Occupation, as we know, the Elders ruled the villages. Two were selected annually and served a one-year term. We discussed their rights and duties in a prior section of the book. There were also the Board Members of the churches, who together with the Elders made up the Elders' Council, which included the priests and the Notaries (contract writers). It was noteworthy for that age that they would often invite the parishioners of the village to meetings when making certain decisions requiring village input.

From 1912, after the liberation, according to the laws "concerning *Demoi* (Municipalities) and *Koinotites* (Communities)," every city or village, in accordance with its population, was considered to be either a Community or a Municipality. The Municipal Councils and the Community Councils replaced the Elders' Councils, the Elders of the Municipality of Chios, and the Vekils of the Mastichochoria. These councils, elected by the citizens – initially only men, and later on women, as well – through a secret ballot every four years, were given quite a few responsibilities determined by the State. They oversaw many governmental functions – such as elections, military enlistment, and health – but their main responsibilities were to tend to local needs.

In order for the local needs to be handled, it was necessary not to limit the activity of a single Council to tasks such as office work and signing certificates for births, deaths, and so forth. For a village to maintain its culture while making progress, its initiatives, programs, and visions of the Council – most especially of its President – had to be realized. Therefore, party voting was not considered necessary in the elections of local rulers. It was determined that those who were to be elected be selfless in nature, have both the vision and power to perform the necessary tasks to realize their vision, and most especially that they have a love and a zeal for progress to be made in their village or city.

The Councils defined the basic local needs as cleanliness of a village and the creation of a healthy atmosphere through plumbing, lighting, roadways, finding and promoting financial resources, and seeing to the maintenance and elevation of the spiritual and cultural levels – in order to improve the quality of living. According to each case, the Council cooperated with the appropriate Public Service organization and more so with the Prefect, on whom the

Pantelis A. Mavrogiorgis

approval of certain decisions and granting of credit for work to be performed all depended. Financial support was obviously the moving force behind any project that might be proposed. Community resources came from government grants, property rentals, taxes from grazing lands, residents' taxes, personal work done, and donations of money or property.

From the Archives of the Community, I will present data showing the specific actions of the rulers of our village, including their duties and type of jurisdiction.

1. **The Rental of Grazing Lands.** These rentals provided the basic source of income for our village. The grazing lands rented were *Skafidi, Lakkoi, Skalia, Saliakomyti, Kaki Rachi, Profitis Ilias,* and *Kartera.* Those grazing lands were rented in the fall and used as *mandres* (enclosed winter quarters) for the flocks of sheep that grazed in north Chios during the summer months.

   From my childhood, I recall the graphic scene of the auctioning of mountains. One Sunday afternoon in the square of Agios Panteleimonas, which was where the auctions usually took place, the members of the Community Council, along with the Secretary, o sitting at a little table. The shepherds who were taking part in the auction were there, and the villagers were sitting on the steps all around, just passing the time. Giannis Beis, crier of the village, who added color to the entire procedure, would shout out the person's name and the price being offered. The entire event would end at sunset.

   Giannis Beis, in ending the proceedings would announce the name of the final bidder three times and the price offered in *drachmas,* then ask if there was any other interested bidder. After that, he would shout in a manner that no one could replicate:

   > *The time arrived* (instead of "arrived," he would say "approached"). *The sun has set and the mountains have become black. The last offer for Kartera* (for example) *is so and so* (a name), *with an offering of* (amount) *drachmas. Going once. Is there another offer? Going twice. Is there another offer? Going three times. Is there another offer? The auction is over. It goes to so and so, and the last bidder must pay the announcer's expenses.*

   Giannis Beis made a point to remind the person who had to pay him at the end of the auction.

After this parenthesis we will return to the documentation of data from the Archives of the Community.

2. **The Council.** Besides having the right to impose personal work for the reconstruction of facilities for the common benefit, the Council would, at times, impose various taxes, such as:

> **a.** Tax "upon the slaughtered animals."
> **b.** Tax "upon the lime furnaces." The tax levied depended on the number of kilos of lime produced.
> **c.** Tax on "the olive groves."

The Community Council also requested that the Ministries expropriate areas for the construction of public works. It appointed a Farm Committee, field guards to watch the fields, as well as the Supervisors and Board Members of the churches. The Supervisors and Board Members were appointed at Community meetings for a period of two years, and at the end of their terms of office the Board Members (Upper Board Members) would give a financial accounting of the revenues of the churches. The odd thing is that the Community Council also had jurisdiction over the behavior of the citizens, as is proven by a Decision from 1925, according to which:

> "(The Council) *forbids the playing of musical instruments on Sundays and the intoxication of the youth who walk the streets during the night singing and dancing, thus disturbing the citizens.*
>
> *The instruments are allowed on Meatfare, Friday, Saturday, and Sunday of Cheesefare. On Clean Monday and the Monday after Easter, the Sunday of Thomas, the day of the Annunciation, and the celebration days of the Saints Giorgios, Panteleimonos, Isidoros, the Transfiguration, and Agios Ioannis* (on August 29) *from 8:00 a.m. until 9:00 p.m."*

Subsequently, I will not refer to the activities of each Council of the village by name, because it would cause me to criticize some of them negatively, which I have no desire to do. Judging everything from my childhood years to the present, however, I can say that the Councils, together with the individual efforts of the parishioners, reformed the village and sent it in an upward direction. A lot of good things happened!

Work was begun in 1958 to pave all the roads with cement and install sewer systems, and this work continued until it was completed in

Pantelis A. Mavrogiorgis

the entire village. Daily availability of water for all houses since 1963; electric lighting on the roads, and by 1968 all of the houses had electricity. Rural roads throughout all fields and mountainous areas of the village were also built. It is worthwhile to mention these rural roads, because those of us who are older remember the goat paths and single-file pathways that we traveled to get to our fields. Rural roads were created and led from our village to: *Notso Kipo, Lakkous, Kostazou, Ponio, Skagia, Droposi, Platanos, Ereikani, Arodafni, Koumarous, Seladi, Argrelou, Piso Nera, Profitis Ilias, Patela, Agios Giannis, Neraki, Pigi, Kateleimmata, Neromylos, Michalarou, Malovrysidia, Xerokambos, Anifora, Kato Makri, Monachika, and Peristeras.* The farmers now use mechanized vehicles to go to all of these locations in the village. The beasts of burden have almost disappeared.

Finally (in 1984), telephones were installed in homes, whereas earlier the entire village was served by a community telephone. Due to the reconstruction of an old building, the village finally has its own Community Office. With the assistance of our fellow villagers in America, the cemetery was expanded, and the *Plateia* of the village was beautified, as was the school forest.

The Community Secretary, who works behind the scenes and does all of the writing, is the "right hand" of the Community President. In addition, the Secretary accommodates the villagers by assisting with any problems that pertain to the jurisdiction of the Community Office, and he is the closest colleague and advisor to the President. Therefore, there is good reason to commemorate those who participated in managing the affairs of the village. We will begin with the Elder Council Members, whose names appeared in the codexes and notary documents, and we will continue to mention the members of the Community Councils at various times.

3. *Gerontes* (Elders)

Nikolaos Giorgalos, Kostantinos Pouleros	1849
Stamatis Tsamoutalos, Giorgis Mountis	1853
Giorgis Nychtas, Diamantis Manolis	1854
X" Sarantis Askelis, Vasilis Papastamatis	1864
Apostolos Patounas, Kostantis Politis	1867
Panagiotis Kloutis, Antonios Pitsos	1868
Giorgis Kambanas, Panagiotis Pouleros	1872
Lambrinos Karazournias, Michalis Ntellas	1875
Michalis Papanikolas, Dimitris Barlis	1876
Ioannis Kallikas, Georgios Vafias	1877

Panagiotis Tsamoutalos, Vasilis Mylonas   1879
Spyridon Soukas, Konstantinos Flouras   1881
Kostantinos Kollis, Panagiotis Soukas   1882
Vasilis Vafeias, X" Nikolas Hahalis 1883, 1884
Antonis Hahalis, Nikolas Kalargyros   1888
Dimitris Frazelas, Ioannis Zymnis   1890
Dimitris Vekios, Ioannis Kakaridis   1891
Dimitris Monis, Georgios Papaemmanouil   1892
Kostis Sakoulas, Panagiotis Psyllos   1893
Nikolas Soukas, Panagiotis Patounas   1894
Stamatis Patounas, Georgios Xenias   1895
X" Lambrinos Pouleros, Michalis Kostaris   1896
Ioannis Sachlanis, Kostis Kostaris   1897
Panagiotis Patounas, Stavros Mamas   1898
Panagiotis Patounas, Kostis Kourgelis   1899
Ioannis Monis, Pantelis Patounas   1900
X" Nikolis Hahalis, Stamatis Bogiasklis   1901
Michalis Ntellas, Kostis Patounas   1902
Konstantinos Pries, Antonis Dellas   1903
Diamantis Patounas, Panagiotis Dellas   1904
Stamatis Patounas, Sarantis Psyllos   1905
Georgios Kostaris, Ioannis Barlis   1906
Georgios Vekios, Ioannis Torakis   1907
Eleftherios Koutelos, Nikolaos Mereos   1908
Diamantis Papanikolas, Georgios Xenias   1909
Panagiotis Dellas, Antonios Foustanas 1910, 1911
Stamatis Patounas, Kostis Kalargyros 1912, 1914

4. Community Councils

a. September 1914 – August 1916

President: Ioannis Xenias

Council Members: Michalis Kostaris, Ioannis Vafeas, Georgios Vekios, Eleftherios Koutelos, Nikolaos Kollis, Ioannis P. Varis

b. October 1916 – July 1917

President: Ioannis Vafeas

Council Members: Nikolaos Kollis, Georgios Vekios, Antonios P. Patounas, Eleftherios Koutelos, Michail Kostaris, Ioannis P. Varis

c. December 1917 – May 1921

President: Nikolaos Pouleros

Council Members: Ioannis Varis, Konstantinos Tsimaris,

Michail Kourgelis, Ilias Nychtas, Antonios Patounas, Ioannis Foustanas

d. August 1921 – August 1923
President: Athanasios Vafeas
Council Members: Ioannis Monioukas, Stamatis Bogiasklis, Diamantis Papanikolaou, Stamatis Zymnis, Nikolaos Sakoulas, Nikolaos Kollis, Nikolaos Flouras

e. January 1924 – October 1925
President: Nikolaos Patounas
Council Members: Panagiotis Dellas, Georgios Foustanas, Thomas Barlis, Konstantinos Mamas, Michail Tsoflias, Dimitris Politis, Panagiotis Mountis

f. October 1925 – October 1928
President: Nikolaos Patounas
Council Members: Ioannis Soukas, Ioannis Kalargyros, Ioannis Vafeas, Stylianos Tsoflias, Antonios Patounas, Nikolaos Pouleros

g. November 1928 – August 1929
President: Ioannis Kalargyros
Council Members: Ioannis Soukas, Nikolaos Patounas, Nikolaos Pouleros, Ioannis Vafeas, Stylianos Tsoflias

h. September 1929 – December 1929
President: Panagiotis Billis
Council Members: Nikolaos Patounas, Nikolaos Flouras, Diamantis Papanikolaou, Konstantinos Soukas, Ioannis Kostilis

i. January 1930 – June 1932
President: Nikolaos Patounas
Council Members: Ioannnis Kostilis, Konstantinos Soukas, Nikolaos Flouras, Antonios Monis, Diamantis Papanikolaou

j. February 1936 – June 1936
President: Georgios Thrapas
Council Members: Stefanos Nyktas, Panagiotis Mountis, Apostolos Hahalis, Antonios Patounas, Nikolaos Kollis

k. June 1936 – December 1944
President: Pantelis Patounas
Council Members: Nikolaos Billis, Stylianos Vafias, Nikolaos Mizeros, Apostolos Hahalis, Antonios Patounas

l. January 1945 – June 1947
President: Ioannis Papastamatis
Council Members: Panagiotis Varis, Georgios Kolyvas, Antonios Patounas, Savvas Tsoflias, Ioannis Soukas

m. July 1947 – January 1949
President: Pantelis Patounas
Council Members: Stylianos Vafias, Apostolos Hahalis, Nikolaos Mizeros, Antonios Patounas, Nikolaos Billis

n. January 1949 – May 1949
President: Panagiotis A. Patounas
Council Members: Adamantios Salagaras, Stylianos Koutelos, Alexandros Mountis, Ioannis Vafias, Konstantinos Mylonas

o. June 1949 – May 1951
President: Pantelis Styl. Patounas
Council Members: Ioannis Vafias, Alexandros Mountis, Stylianos Koutelos, Konstantinos Mylonas, Adamantios Salagaras, Panagiotis Varis

p. May 1951 – January 1955
President: Konstantinos Flouras
Council Members: Eleftherios Monis, Stefanos Billis, Georgios Mylonas, Xenofon Germanos, Ilias Salagaras

q. February 1955 – May 1959
President: Konstantinos Flouras
Council Members: Stylianos Koutelos, Vasileios Salagaras, Ioannis Vafias, Nikolaos G. Mylonas, Thomas Barlis, Stamatis Nyktas

r. May 1959 – August 1959
President: Ioannis Strovilas
Council Members: Spyros Tsoflias, Ioannis Mylonas, Nikolaos Kakaridis, Panagiotis Patounas, Evangelos Kostaris, Georgios Mylonas

s. September 1959 – February 1961
President: Panagiotis Patounas
Council Members: Spyros Tsoflias, Georgios Mylonas, Nikolaos Kakaridis, Evangelos Kostaris, Ioannis Strovilas, Ioannis Mylonas

t. February 1961 – August 1964

Pantelis A. Mavrogiorgis

President: Ioannis Mylonas
Council Members: Ioannis Strovilas, Georgios Mylonas, Spyros Tsoflias, Nikolaos Kakaridis, Panagiotis Patounas, Evangelos Kostaris

u. August 1964 – August 1967
President: Konstantinos Flouras
Council Members: Ioannis Strovilas, Ioannis Papastamatis, Panagiotis Papagiannakis, Georgios Kakaridis, Achilleas Patounas, Panagiotis Billis

v. September 1967 – September 1974
President: Panagiotis Patounas
Council Members: Panagiotis Billis, Georgios Kloutis, Vasileios Mizeros, Stylianos Soukas

w. October 1974 – May 1975
President: Nikolaos Kartalis (Director, Elementary School)
Council Members: Ioannnis Strovilas, Achilleas Patounas, Ioannis Papastamatis, Panagiotis Billis, Vasileios Mizeros, Michail Kalipetis

x. June 1975 – December 1978
President: Ioannis Strovilas
Council Members: Ioannis Papastamatis, Georgios Mylonas, Ioannis Lambrinoukas, Antonios Flouras, Panagiotis Nyktas, Konstantinos Xenias

y. January 1979 – December 1982
President: Dimitrios Koilis
Council Members: Georgios Kouniaris, Dimitrios Anamisis, Konstantinos Kloutis, Antonios Papagiannakis, Panagiotis Patounas, Georgios Mylonas

z. January 1983 – December 1986
President: Emmanouil Strovilas
Council Members: Nikolaos Vekios, Stamatis Ntoulos, Ioannis Lambrinoukas, Georgios Kouniaris, Dimitrios Koilis, Georgios Monioukas

January 1987 ---
President: Emmanuil Strovilas
Council Members: Nikolaos Vekios, Panagiotis Kikianis, Stamatios Ntoulos, Konstantinos Papastamatis, Dimitris Koilis, Konstantinos Xenias

---

The following individuals spent the greatest amount of years as Presidents of the village: Nikolaos Patounas or Kaikaki, Pantelis Patounas, Kostas Flouras, and the current President, Emmanuil Strovilas – who also showed interest in the publication of this book.

5. Secretaries of the Community

> a. Panagiotis Stamatiou Dellas, from 1914
> b. Alexandros Galanos, from 1916
> c. Georgios Monis, from 1918 to 1938
> Ioannis Patounas, served for a short period
> d. Ioannis Isid. Frangakis, from 1939 to 1964
> e. Pantelis Ioan. Frangakis, from 1965 to present

G.   *Mnimones* or Notaries

In ancient Greece, the secretaries who wrote and kept private deeds, such as contracts, applications, court deeds, and so forth were known as *"Mnimones."* They were also referred to as *Ieromnimones*, because their "Archives" were kept in the temples. This practice passed on to the Romans, who then instituted Notaries or Notars (Notarius comes from the Latin Nota: note). They were authorized to compose court deeds, precisely like the current Notaries.

The institution of notars was established in Chios by the Genoese. When the Turks came to Chios, they recognized all present and future deeds as valid, without the need for Turkish approval. Sometimes a seller, in order to assure a buyer, would say,

> *"Let's go to the Master Kadi for him to also make a Hotzeti"* (title of ownership).

The Elders of the municipality in Chora elected the Notaries. We must also accept that in the Mastichochoria, the public would elect the notaries. At Agios Giorgis, the Notaries during the past century were Georgios Mountis, who did not seem to be very well educated, then Hatzi–Panagiotis Pouleros, and lastly Nikolaos Pouleros until the year 1913. They documented the deeds in codexes, which are kept in the historic Archives of Chios today. I will illustrate some of this work, while preserving both the syntax and spelling within the documents.

> [**Ed. Note:** Due to the above statement of the author, who copied the following documents in their original form, for the sake of English speaking readers, the syntax and punctuation in these documents has been edited to make them easily comprehensible.]

A. DOWRY AGREEMENT

"In the name of the Father and of the Son and of the Holy Spirit, Amen. This is an agreement for the present marriage. Michalios Papaspanoudis and his wife, Despinou, have a daughter named Kyriaki, whom they wish to marry to Pantoleos, the son of Stamatios Vekios. According to the custom of our village, they first want to give him their blessing as the first dowry gift.

Houses in the middle of the village near the daughter of papa Georgios Toumblis. However, the same father-in-law is obligated to take care of them as he should. We will give fields we have in Arodafni to divide in two, so that our son-in-law may select the part he wants. There is another field in Ponio, near Hatzi Apostoli, which will also be divided in two; and he may select one – cultivated or wild. Another field is in Plagia, near Niamonitis Vizaniaris and the road. Another field in Poron is for them to eventually share with her sister. Another uncultivated field, located in Langada near Kalis Sapogiani and Antoniou Karazournia. Another field, located in apano Makri the lower three steps which are close to Diamantis Kostaris and his father. And 15 little copper jugs, each with the capacity of two okades. The value of these fields is 18 grosia.

Furthermore, the father-in-law also gives to this same daughter-in-law one patikion, the field in Makri, as a gift. But as he is to live close to his daughter, Kyriaki, and Stefanos Kostylis, he is also giving her one at Keramargia close to Diavatou and Panagiotis Poulerou worth 3 grosia.

In the year 1869, January 28. Georgios Mountis, Mnimonas of the village"

Observations:
1. **Farm locations:** *Arodafni, Ponio, Plagia, Patedes, Langadakia, Apano Makri*
2. ***Patikion:*** These are the gifts which the father-in-law or husband-to-be gives to the bride.
3. ***Dosimon:*** the tax
4. ***Vastagas* ?**
5. ***Pakirika:*** copper (kettles)

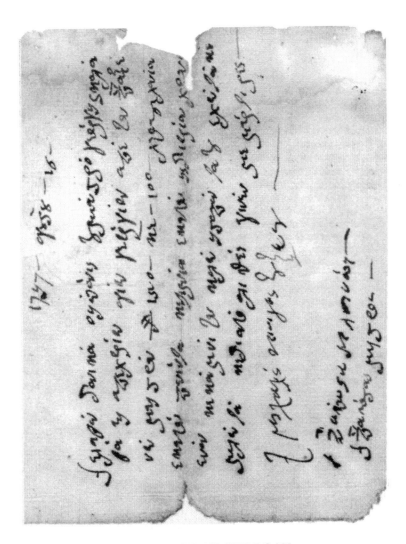

SAMPLE OF AN OLD LOAN

TRANSCRIPTION

"1747, August 16

Ioannis, son of Mastrogiorgi Sklavaki, from the village of Agios Georgios, received from papa Xenon Melisinon, aslania 150 – timinia 100. I say silver coins one hundred and fifty, and he pledges that he will honor this commitment now and in the future with everything he has. For the authenticity of this document, the following witnesses attest.

Michail Kinigos of Xenou   Papakostis Melisinos   Papaxenos Melisinos"

Pantelis A. Mavrogiorgis

SAMPLE OF AN OLD PAYMENT

TRANSCRIPTION

"Today, Antonis Mountis and Papa Hatzis Vekakis are present worked for the church for one full year and is giving a clear accounting to all of the priests and parishioners of the village, young and old, and he does not have to take from the church or mourkin (estate) nor give anything at all."

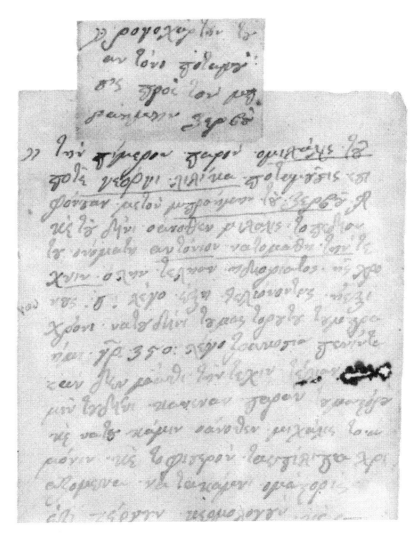

SAMPLE OF AN OLD AGREEMENT

TRANSCRIPTION

"Today, Michalis, son of the late Georgis Lilikas Potamousis, is present, and came to an agreement with Braïmin of Zerrvoudi and that Braïmin teach Antonios, son of the aforementioned Michali, the entire skill perfectly in six years. After a six-year apprenticeship, Michalis will give to Braïmin 350 grosia. If Antonios does not learn the skill perfectly, no compensation at all will be given to Braïmin. Michalis is to buy an anvil and bellows for the necessary furniture to be made by the crafts-man, who will dress his apprentice with the appropriate clothing and shoes. Thus they hasten and confess and make present in the year 1845, May 8.

Pantelis Kontos, Witness   Papageorgios Foustanas, I attest"

Pantelis A. Mavrogiorgis

B. WILL

"In the name of the Holy Trinity. Today I have been invited to the home of Mr. Nikolaos Orfanoudis during the year 1873, in the month of March the 11th, Saturday, 3:00 p.m.

Because I am ill, while I still have my sane mind, I am hastening to perform my last and Christian duties. First, I hand over my soul to my all good God and Creator, and I order that my body be buried with all of the priests of our village. I forgive everyone who ever made me sad or treated me unjustly.

Therefore, as an indication of my paternal loving care, I hand over to my child, Konstantinos, my belongings: all homes, fields, vineyards – tame and wild, which are movable and immobile from a nail to a needle, that he become the master of the house and owner of all my possessions.

Second, I leave to my daughter, Viola, wife of Stamatios Lithis, the 100 grosia that she received some time ago as her inheritance.

I leave to Agios Georgios 10 grosia, to Agios Nikolaos 10 grosia, to Agios Panteleimonas 10 grosia, 5 grosia to my spiritual father, papa–Stamatios Dellas.

However, the houses I left to our child will become his only after my death and the death of my wife, Argyris. And, once again, this same Konstantinos remains obligated to look after his father in everything he needs until his end, to take care of him in his old age as he ought to do. And at his death, according to the custom of our village, for the sake of my soul to hold memorials on the ninth day, the fortieth day, and after one year.

Therefore, an indication of my present will was made so that it could have the validity and the application at all times with the judgment of the honorable witnesses.

The Elders	*The Mnimonas*
Georgios Kambanas	*Georgios Mountis*
Panagiotis Pouleros "	

Observations:

This is characteristic of the religious spirit that is expressed with a request for forgiveness and with the gold coins, which are offered to churches for the "salvation of soul," as they used to say. In other wills we read, they would leave an amount of money to Agios Giorgis, known as *"Katathesimo,"* so that the

---

appropriate church services (*"mnimosina"*) could be held, when they did not have children.

Another ascertainment from the will is that the parent, when "he would write" his belongings to his sons, since the daughters had wedding dowries, the sons were obligated to take care of their parents in their old age. So we would often hear from elderly villagers,

"Tou 'grapsa ta kala mou gia na m'echei."

C. BUYING AND SELLING

"Today, Panteleos Hatzi–Varlas, son of the deceased Georgios, is present of his own free will and not forced to sell his house in the mesa chorio near Nikolis Korantis. He is also selling his fourno (oven), as it is, to Nikolis Fotis, son of the late Michail, and to Kalein, daughter of the late Nikolis and wife of Stefanis Bogiasklis, for the price of 345 grosia, the total of which the seller is pleased to have received from the buyers. As the seller is pleased, he transfers the property to the authority of the buyer without penalty to do as he wishes, to sell it or donate it. And thus they hastened and agreed on September 23, 1849, Monday, 3:00 p.m.

He notes: Nikolis receives the fourno and gives 230 grosia. Kali receives the outer, small house and gives 115 grosia, with witnesses:

Nikolas Georgalos, Elder
Kostantinos Pouleros, Elder
Lambrinos Tachas, Board Member
papa-Georgis Soukas, I attest"

D. LOAN NOTICE

"August 16, 1747

Ioanis, son of Mastrogeorgis Sklavakis, received from papa-Xeno Mizeron of the village of Agios Georgios 150 aslania – and 100 timinia for a period of one year. He pledges that he will honor this commitment now and in the future with everything he has. For the authenticity of this document, the following witnesses attest.

Michalis Kynigos of Xenos
papa-Kosti Melisinos"

Chapter 23
Village Residents of the Past

In the codexes and various notary documents, I happened to encounter names of former Agiorgousoi, some of which still exist today and some of which have disappeared. My preference is to list those whose names still exist today, as an indication of respect to our grandfathers and great-grandfathers. The date after each name indicates the year of the document in which that name was discovered. Many of the surnames have the diminutive ending "-aki." Regarding last names, there is a peculiar custom in which the actual name is changed this way: While one's official name in the nominative or subjective case is *o Vekakis* (masculine gender), it is the custom to put that name into the neuter gender, for example, *to Vekaki* ("the Vekaki").

There are also baptismal names in this list, which no longer exist today, like "Niamonitis" or "Monios," which parents gave their children at that time in honor of the monastery of Nea Moni. For example, there was "Monios Strovilas," the last individual to acquire a name from a monastery. I was also told of a female named "Monou," which was the name of *papa* Mouzithra's wife.

Nikolaos Psaros	1627	Antonios Kostaris	1815
Michalis Skouloudis	1632	Giorgis Soukas	1815
Georgios Kalargyros	1635	Vasilis Koutelos	1818
Niamonitis Samaras	1656	Michalis Alexantris	1818
Nikolas Papagas	1658	Giorgis Koumelas	1818
Monios Savlas	1665	Nikolas Soukaki	1820
Kostas Tzikolis	1673	Monios Kostatzos	1820
Nikolas Psaroudakis (Psaros)	1685	Lambrinos Tachaki	1826
Niamonitis Papagas	1688	Ioannis Fratzeladi (Frazelas)	1826
Konstantinos Glykas	1699	To Gelaki (Gelis)	1826
Konstantinos Mitsoudi (Mitsos)	1728	Sideris Likouridis (Likouris)	1830
Giorgis Toras	1743	Nikolas Monidi (Monis)	1830
Michalis Hahaloudis (Hahalis)	1743	Vasilis Milonadi	1831
Giorgis Mamas	1743	Papaspanoudi	1832
Giannis Papavasilaki	1808	Stefanos Dellas	1833
Kostantis Xadi (Xas)	1814	Ioannis Kakaridaki	1833

Kostantis Platidi (Platis)	1836	Kostantis Patras	1849
Antonios Tsamoutalos	1836	Papa Hatzis Vekaki	1851
Michalis Gianginis	1837	Konstantinos Bouras	1851
Isidoros Patounas	1837	Ioannis Psallos	1867
Antonis Mountaki	1838	Dimitris Glykokos	1869
Kostas Galanoudis (Galanos)	1839	Stamatis Antonaros	1870
Lambrinos Priedis (Pries)	1839	Michalis Bitis	1873
Giorgis Toulaki	1839		

Chapter 24
The Village After the Liberation

The goal in what we are writing at this point is not really to inform our readers about the wars that followed our liberation from the Turks in 1912. It is more to offer a general framework for the contributions and sacrifices made with the blood of our fine young boys from the village of Agios Georgios Sikousis on the battlefields for the freedom of our country.

A. The Balkan Wars

The liberation of Chios falls within the events of the First Balkan War (1912-1913), which was fought by the Balkan peoples – Serbs, Montenegrins, Bulgarians, and Greeks – who allied themselves against Turkey to stop the oppression of the enslaved Christians, as well as to secure their own national autonomy. Following the glorious battles that took place in *Sarantaporo* and *Elassona*, on October 27, 1912 *Katerini, Grevena, Kozani,* and *Thessaloniki* were liberated and *Giannena* won its freedom on February 21, 1913. Aside from the victorious battles on land, the Greek Navy liberated *Imvros, Limnos, Mytilini, Chios, Samos,* and *Ikaria.*

The war ended with the crushing of the Turkish Army on all fronts and the signing of the Treaty of London on May 17, 1913, after which the Allies each tried to define the borders of the areas they had taken. Bulgaria demanded to occupy Thrace and Eastern Macedonia, as well as *Thessaloniki* and *Monastiri.* The Greeks united with the Serbs against Bulgaria, with Romania eventually joining the Allies.

Thus, in 1913 the Second Balkan War began. After fierce battles in *Kilkis, Lachana,* and the *Doirani,* the Greek Army arrived in *Alexandroupoli* and took Eastern Macedonia and Western Thrace. Bulgaria was defeated in this war, which ended on July 20, 1913 with the Treaty of Bucharest.

B. World War I (1914-1918)

From the beginning of the 20th century, Europe had been divided into two opposing camps. On one side was the "Triple Alliance": Germany, Austria-Hungary, and Italy. On the other side, the "Triple Entente," which included France, England, and Russia.

In 1914, serious financial differences, along with political and national opposition faced the Great Powers, which opposed each other. The murder of Francis Ferdinand, heir to the throne of Austria, happened at Sarajevo, Serbia and caused the war. The war was fought on three distinct fronts. In the west, Germans faced the Anglo-French powers; in the east, the Russians faced the Germans and Austro-Hungarians; and in Serbia, the Serbs successfully struggled against Austria-Hungary.

With the passage of time, the Bulgarians and Turks entered the war on the side of Germany. When Japan, Portugal, Romania, China, and the United States also became involved, then the war was considered to be worldwide in nature. After the Greek Prime Minister, Eleftherios Venizelos, had a dispute with the Greek King Constantine – who was accused of being a Germanophile actually supported Greek neutrality – Venizelos left the government and formed a revolutionary government in *Thessaloniki* on September 26, 1916. Venizelos joined the Western Allies, England and France, with three army platoons – Serron, Crete, Archipelago.

On May 29, 1917, with the departure of Constantine, Greece united once again and officially proclaimed war. The Greek military took part in various battles and claims a special triumph in its victory at the Battle of Skra. This battle created a sort of national pride for the Greeks and forced the Allies to acknowledge the contributions of the Greek Army on the Macedonian front and the liberation of Thrace. The war officially ended on July 29, 1919 with the Treaty of Versailles in Paris.

Agiorgousoi Who Died in the Battle of Skra
1. Attonis, Antonios G.
2. Attonis, Konstantinos G.
3. Kalargyros, Antonios Nik.
4. Papanikolas, Panagiotis G.
5. Soukas, Nikolaos I.
6. Stroumbos, Ioannis Dim.
7. Tsikolis, Eleftherios M.

C. The Catastrophe in Asia Minor

The devastating destruction in Asia Minor, an event that influenced our contemporary history and changed the borders of our country, has all the characteristics of a tragedy, as created by the ancient Greek spirit in literature. Days of overwhelming glory and national pride evolved into days of misfortune and national humiliation. Hellenism was uprooted from the area of the very ancient Hellenic Ionia.

The Greeks of the East became grievous shipwrecks and were scattered by the waves of the Aegean, naked and devastated, to the shores of Mytilini, Chios, and wherever else; and they fought from there and established new homelands. I believe that whatever we suffered then was the result of an irrational operation and a burden too heavy for our shoulders to bear. It is likely that our prior victories had made us arrogant and cursed, phenomena for which we paid a heavy price historically.

Let us examine the events. When World War I ended, Greece, with wings of victory, asked that northern Epirus, Thrace, and the western portion of the Asia Minor Peninsula be ceded to her, as approximately 200,000 Hellenes inhabited the area. Satisfaction of that claim was not easily gotten. It happened that the Italians occupied Attalia and planned to overtake other areas in Asia Minor, as well. The Greek Prime Minister, Eleftherios Venizelos, found an opportunity to assert a claim and was told to take over the Vilaetion of Smyrna as an authorized agent of the Allies. The Venizelos government, in order to curry favor with the Allies and succeed in having its requests met, agreed to send a contingent of the Greek Army to Ukraine, as the Westerners had undertaken a campaign against the new Soviet state.

1. **The Takeover of Smyrna.** On May 2, 1919, Greek forces disembarked in Asia Minor and overtook Smyrna in a few days, without much resistance. While the Greeks living there rejoiced, the Turks reacted fanatically under the leadership of Turkish Army Colonel Kemal Ataturk, who nevertheless was a fierce opponent of the sultan's administration. Kemal reorganized the revolutionary army and, with the support of the Italians, began to attack Greek positions on the outskirts. Venizelos, with the approval of the Allies, sent military support to Asia Minor, but not for fighting purposes. It is apparent, at this point, that the Allies began to realize the power of Kemal.

2. **The Treaty of Sevres.** The second advance of the Greek Army reached Prusa. On August 10, 1928, under favorable conditions for the Greeks, the Treaty of Sevres is signed with the Allies, and Smyrna and the surrounding areas are granted to Greece. However, Kemal's revolutionary government does not recognize the agreement, so the war continues.

In the meantime, general elections take place in November 1920 in Greece, resulting in the Venizelos Government being voted out; and King Constantine returns, after a referendum. These events underscore, once again, the dissention and division among the Greek people: the Venizelists on one side, and the Royalists on the opposite side.

Using the return of Constantine as an excuse, the French turn to Kemal for political reasons. The English supported the Greek position, but they provided no economic or military aid. Venizelos' opponents had accused him of involving Greece in the Asia Minor misfortune, but the Gounaris government continued the campaign instead of negotiating with Turkey – out of fear that the Greek people would see it as a betrayal and abandonment of the vision of the *"Megali Idea"* ("Great Idea").

3. **Defeat at Sangario.** On June 27, 1921, the Greek Army attacked – with the goal of capturing Ankara, in order to quash Kemal. Kioutacheia, Afion Kara Kisar, Eski Sechir were taken, and the army approached the Sangario River. Kemal diverted the opposing Greeks, moving them far from their supply base in order to launch a surprise attack at the Sangario River. On August 13, 1921, they fought for ten days at a front spanning eighty kilometers. This was the beginning of a retreat that signaled the downfall of the Greek Army.

4. **Destruction of Smyrna.** On August 27, 1922, the "Tangalakia," Turks of the East, were enraged and set fire to Smyrna, slaughtering people, raping women and children, taking their caravans, capturing prisoners – all of this occurring before the dispassionate gaze of the Allied fleet anchored in Smyrna. The ethnomartyr Metropolitan of Smyrna, Chysostomos, was also one of the victims. We lost about 92,000 men in Asia Minor. The above information is hardly superfluous, since Agios Georgios Sikousis alone lost fifteen young men.

Agiorgousoi Who Died in These Battles
1. Anamisis, Nikolaos K.
2. Dinias, Stamatios D.
3. Zymnis, Dimitrios G.
4. Kolyvas, Stavros N.
5. Kolyvas, Sotirios N.
6. Kouniaris, Nikolaos D.
7. Mereos, Georgios N.
8. Mizithras, Ioannis A.
9. Patras, Georgios K.
10. Patounas, Ioannis D.
11. Pries, Stylianos A.
12. Skouloudis, Argyris I.
13. Skouloudis, Stylianos I.

Pantelis A. Mavrogiorgis

14. Tsaketas, Agisilaos P.
15. Psaros, Ioannis P.

Asia Minor Campaign Folk Song

We will close this section with a related folk song.

"You, the mountains of Ankara and of Asia Minor,
May you never blossom, May you never flower
for the evil which we suffered on the 13th of August.
The mountains filled with bodies and the fields with lads,
And other children are prisoners, and others are wounded.
And one child from our land says to the other children,
'I see, children, you're getting ready to go to our land.
Don't fire a rifle. Don't sing a song.
And if my mother and my father ask you,
tell them that I got married here in Turkey.
I took the slab as a mother-in-law, the black earth as a wife:
Two cypress trees embracing above my grave.'"

D. World War II: Greco-Italian War

The results of World War II still retain a wide scope and great importance and define, to this day – and probably for years to come – the journey and fate of humanity. When this war ended, the world was divided according to the victorious protagonists, Anglo-Americans and Russians. This created two spheres of influence, the American and the Russian, with two opposite social and economic systems: Capitalism and Communism.

During war, the English, French, Russians, and Americans were fighting against the Axis Powers: Hitler's Nazi Germany, Mussolini's Fascist Italy, and Japan. The war began on April 1, 1939 when the Germans attacked Poland, and ended on August 6, 1945 in an inhumane way; the atomic bomb attack on the Japanese cities of Hiroshima and Nagasaki.

Within the framework of World War II, after the Germans had taken Poland, Denmark, Norway, Belgium, Holland, and France, the Italians declared war against Greece. They had taken Albania already, and they invaded Greece from Epeiros on **October 28, 1940.**

1. **The War in Albania.** I remember, I was a high school student. Our lives changed drastically. On Sunday night, I was enjoying a movie. On the following morning, I heard the sounds of war sirens shrieking and freezing our hearts with dread. At night, the entire *Chora* was

---

wrapped in darkness, and so it remained every night until we were finally liberated.

Schools closed that next day, and all of us high school students got on the road and headed for the village. Everything around us scared us; melancholy and worry were in the air. In the village, the atmosphere was heavy. The men left their wives, children, and parents, and headed to the front.

Amazingly, the initial days of agony and uncertainty were followed by days of great enthusiasm and patriotic excitement, since messages kept arriving proclaiming the victories of our army in the snowy Albanian mountains. The Greek Army passed the Morava and overtook Erseka and Korytsa on the grounds of northern *Epeiros*. "Korytsa, on November 22, 1940 welcomed the victorious army, dressed in blue and white flags, and the Greek inhabitants are at their doors offering our infantrymen raki and sweets."

They continued on to *Moschopoli* on November 24; to Pogradets on November 30; Premeti, *Agious Saranta*, on December 6; to *Argyrokastro* on December 22, with its mostly Greek population celebrating its liberation. That same day, so close to Christmas, our army took Himara, and then Kleisoura on January 10, 1941.

It is hard to find comparable parallels with the impressions we made abroad, the enthusiasm we experienced at home, and the victory songs we created. Greece crushed the hordes of forty-three million.

I am of the opinion that the epic battles in Albania expressed the recent self-awareness of our Nation before the amazed eyes of humanity. "This struggle was an offering of souls and the resurrection of consciences." The women of *Pindou* carried ammunition over the rugged mountains during the battles. Women from all over Greece gave courage to their fighting men through the letters they wrote, the warm breath of their love, and their thoughts.

In Agios Georgis, the women lived with their minds and souls turned toward the front. They made wool pullovers, sweaters, and socks and sent them to the men. Morning prayers and night vigils were held, begging for the victorious return of their relatives. When the mailman arrived and delivered letters, there was a stir in the entire village, as people waited – with their hearts in their mouths – for news of their children.

At the time, there was only one radio in the village, so when there were news, everyone gathered around it. On the night of April 6, 1941, we heard news that tortured our souls.

> *"Thessaloniki, the city of Agios Dimitrios, in is in the hands of the enemy."*

The Germans had taken it. In the crushing silence that followed, the radio station signed off with the national anthem.

2. **The Germans Enter Greece.** On April 6, 1941, after taking over Yugoslavia, the Germans entered Greece. Our army was forced to capitulate to Hitler's ironclad troops. Our heroic fighters, embittered and exhausted, take the road home. For days, as they walked away from the front, they asked for bread and water as they passed various villages. Whoever did make it back home arrived as a grievous shipwreck. This was the fate of the "Little" before the military might of the "Big."

Agiorgousoi Killed:
1. Kalargyros, Eleftherios K.
2. Michaliadis Georgios P.
3. Varis, Nikolaos G.

In closing this section, I will quote verses from Giannis Ritsos.

> *"They descended with ripped uniforms, with old rifles,*
> *without bread in their knapsacks, without bullets.*
> *Only with bitter, angry rivers,*
> *they were closing the paths behind them.*
> *They had walked for months and months*
> *on unknown rocks.*
> *On the snow, one left up there*
> *one hand, one foot.*
> *Another left a large part of his soul.*
> *Everyone left one or more dead . . . ."*

E. The German Occupation

The Germans occupied parts of Greece beginning in May 1941 and ending in September 1944. Italians or Bulgarians occupied other parts of Greece. This period left me with an indelible impression, through experiences that were unknown to me earlier. I came to understand, in a tangible way – not from theory – the true meanings of the words "slavery" and "freedom." I also learned about the sweetness of life and the bitterness of death. I came to know

---

wretched people, inhumane individuals, insatiable crows who trampled upon the living corpses of fellow humans in order to get rich. These were years when one person stood across from another: *"Homo homni lupus"* ("Man is wolf to man.") as the Latins said. Although forty-five years have passed, my memories and recollections are so vivid as to make it seem like the events only took place yesterday.

1. **The Germans at Agios Giorgis.** It seems like yesterday when, on May 5, 1941, a Wednesday afternoon, two military cars filled with German soldiers drove into our village to occupy it. Our behavior was actually quite reckless when I think back on it. Quite a few of us gathered in the Plateia to have a first-hand look at the Germans who had come to Chios and occupied the Chora two days earlier. Fortunately, the Germans did not bother any of the men or women. "They said that they came as friends, not enemies...." Their presence in our village, though, gave us a different message, especially when they set out for Vessa and Lithi to set up military guard posts, as well. All of us returned home, silent and with frozen hearts.

   The very next day, the village was already breathing heavily under the burden of slavery. The cafes closed up. There was a piece of paper glued onto the door of Stavris Stroumbos' café. I approached it, and here is what I read:

   > *"a. The Greek soldiers will hand over all their weaponry.* ***In two days, anyone who still possesses steel weapons and munitions will be shot...***
   >
   > *b. No one is allowed to be on the streets after 9:00 p.m.*
   >
   > *c. Any disturbance of the peace is* **punishable by death**.
   >
   > *d. Lights must be put out at night.*
   >
   > *e. Stocks of olive oil, petrol, and foods must be reported with their specific amounts...*
   >
   > *Etc.*
   >
   > *-- in Chios, May 5, 1941"*

   When I saw the phrases, "will be shot" and "is punishable by death," I realized what awaited us in the future.

2. **The Behavior of the Germans.** The most characteristic events that define this period were the inhumane behaviors of the cultured and civilized Germans. These events spawned starvation, a black

Pantelis A. Mavrogiorgis

market, emigration to the Middle East, and a national resistance.

The Germans were taking our food. The villagers were starving, but the occupiers were pressuring the Community leaders to give over our eggs and fuel. They would go into our gardens for fruits and vegetables and into our pens for goats and lambs. If only it ended with these things!

Here are two examples that are characteristic of their barbarian behaviors: One day a starving little child was digging in a barrel of rubbish beneath one of the German houses to find something to eat. I watched a German soldier kick this little child, who ran like a hunted dog. Another time, an elderly villager from the northern villages was unaware that, in *Aplotaria*, we had to walk on the right side of the road. A German guard sent that villager to the other side of the street with two powerful kicks.

I realize that these examples are rather small in the face of the atrocities like the concentration camps and mass deaths. The beautiful shore of Kontari often resounded under the chilling thunder of weapons aimed at people, and the yellow sun was the first to face these dead bodies of those executed.

3. **Starvation and the Black Market.** It was not the Germans alone who caused death; starvation spread across the land like a plague. In the summer of 1941, we managed to survive, as there were fruits, vegetables, and a new harvest of wheat and beans. The problems began when the supplies ran out, because the merchants began to hide food and then sell it at higher prices. The farmers who had an excess of fruits and oil did even better. Thus, the *"Mavri Agora"* ("Black Market") was developed.

The black marketeers thrived, as villagers began exchanging household goods, dowries, and jewelry *"anti pinakiou koukion"* ("for a plate of beans"). Beans were actually the monetary unit of the time. You would pay for meat, fish, oil, and other supplies with beans. Wheat bread was a luxury. The bread on our table was made from seeds of broom stock or corn.

At that point, I came to understand the greatest corruption of one's conscience. In the village, some were dancing, while others were dying of starvation. At least sixty-five people died. Every ideal, every moral principle, every value, had been wiped out in the face of self-preservation. Each person was trying to live one more day, since the following day was blurry and uncertain. It is my opinion that from then on human values were shaken, and the age of modern man began, which is imbued with the spirit of "prosperity" and "hedonism."

4. **Assistance from the Red Cross.** From May 1942, during a dreadful period in our lives, the International Red Cross intermittently provided us with food, hope, and consolation. We would run to get the rations they allotted us, depending upon the size of our households. They would distribute flour, sugar, raisins, beans, and other items.

On February 7, 1944, our acclaimed Allies, the British, sent five airplanes to bomb the Swedish steamship, "Viril," which was anchored in the Port of Chios and loaded with foods from the Red Cross. This resulted in the deaths of eighteen Chians; the Swedish representative, Nilson; and the wounding of an additional sixty to seventy individuals. What is particularly odd is that these airplanes, as though intoxicated, were flying low and firing on those who had taken refuge anywhere from the wharf to the Public Garden.

5. **Heading to the Middle East.** From the spring of 1942, isolated individuals and families began fleeing to the Middle East. They would leave during the night on fishing boats from *Karfa, Agia Ermioni, Katarachti,* and *Mersinidi,* for the shores of Turkey. They were terrified of being caught by the German guards stationed along the shores. In order to make this journey possible, they often sold whatever possessions they still had to raise enough money to pay the fare. Once they reached the opposite shore, they would wait until morning and head for the closest Turkish guard post.

The Turkish guards, depending upon what orders they had received and who had given them those orders, would move the refugees from Tsesme by boat, where there was an Anglo-Greek contingent, to various Middle Eastern countries, Cyprus, Syria, Springs of Moses (Suez), even further into the depths of Africa to the Belgian Congo where housing encampments had been set up. Men of military service age made up the groups of Greek military bodies that belonged to the Allied Headquarters of the Middle East, with Cairo as the seat.

About two hundred and eighty people left our village and went to the Middle East. Of this number, the four who died were Stamatis Kounios, Thomas Andreadis, Eftychia Perivolaris, and Efstratios

Perivolaris. The five-member family of Antonis Michaliadis met a tragic death in a shipwreck, as did the five-member family of Nikolaos Toras, and Argyro Pantelogianni, Irini Karazournia, and Kyriaki Hahali. This terrible accident occurred on April 8, 1942 near the shores of *Neas Efesou* (Kousandasi), due to the captain running the motorboat aground on a reef.

6. **National Resistance.** Among the irresponsible phenomena of these dark days, fortunately Greek men with a conscience still existed. They formed resistance groups, the largest of which were the E.A.M. (National Liberation Front) and the E.D.E.S. (National Democratic Greek Army). In the village, almost all of us enlisted in the E.A.M. Our responsibilities were to spy on the Germans and those who were cooperating with them and to distribute secret flyers, since it was not possible to develop armed resistance on the island.

The Germans, fortunately, limited themselves to living in the southern part of the city, the "Triangle," and they were protected at night by barbed wire fences they installed on three of the roadways. The resistance started to become more substantial when small military units were sent from the headquarters of the Middle East.

7. **Iasonas Kalambokas in Chios.** On November 10, 1943, at Notso Kipos, which was actually a countryside location between Tholopotami and our village, three unknown men appeared and raised the suspicions of the field guard, who requested their identification cards. Instead of responding to him, they opened fire with automatic weapons they had hidden inside of their clothing. When the villagers heard about this, they began to worry about what these men really wanted.

The Germans reacted quickly and began ringing the bells nonstop to gather us and shove us all together in the courtyard of *Agios Panteleimonas*, where German soldiers, armed with machine guns, surrounded us. The one in charge asked for our help in annihilating the rebels. The President of the Community and the police station guard were put in charge of forming three guard posts, which were set up at the village mills, at the peak of Profitis Ilias, and at the *Voukrano* – the mountain near the Monastery of Agion Pateron. Two Agiorgousoi at a time would take shifts at each of the posts, with the goal of spotting those three unknown men who had killed the German guard.

That night, when the Germans left the village, they took Stylianos

Xenias, Antonis Patounas, and young Christoforos Salagaras as hostages. After some time, they exchanged them for other hostages. They also took hostages from other villages in Chios, holding them for about twenty days.

With the victory of the Russians at Stalingrad, the Germans began retreating from occupied territories including withdrawing from Greece. It was then that we learned the identity of those unknown men and found out that they were part of an official spy mission under the auspices of the Middle East Headquarters. One of our villagers, N. Karasoulis, who handled the wireless radio, was a link to the spy network, whose main individual was the officer Iasonas Kalambokas, who was disguised and systematically observed the movements of the Germans. This brave lad met an unfortunate end when the Germans surrounded him and killed him two days before they left the area. He was killed further up from *Aplotaria* on the road called *"Agiou Symeon,"* which has since been named "Kalamboka Street" in his honor. Later on, a bronze statue of Kalamboka was placed at the *Vounaki.*

Chios was liberated on Sunday, September 10, 1944. Doxologies and all-night celebrations followed during the first twenty-four hours of the liberation.

8. **Poem by Kyriaki Kalargyrou.** Here are several couplets from a rhyme written by Kyriaki Stavrou Kalargyrou, a fellow villager known as *"Giogiodina,"* pertaining to the German Occupation.

> *a. I want to tell you a story about the Black Marketeers, and all that we suffered from these thieves.*
> *b. The Germans brought Death to take us, and the Black Marketeers took notice of it.*
> *c. Black was the market that the wheat burned, and its price reached 500.*
> *d. They sold us the kum-dari corn for 600, and sold seed from broom stock for 500.*
> *e. They were not Christians, they were not baptized, they were only geared for profiteering.*
> *f. Eight months passed this way in Forty-one (1941), and Forty-two arrived with teary eyes.*
> *g. The feasts passed very miserably, and carnival was quite despairing.*
> *h. Everyone became green; most were bloated* (from starvation)*. They went around in the streets, and they become unrecognizable.*

Pantelis A. Mavrogiorgis

i. No one was moved, no one was saddened. Only the Red Cross became our savior.

j. Forty-two passed, Forty-three came, but we saw little difference, small consolation.

k. We toiled through Forty-three, too, and Forty-four came with this tyranny.

l. Thirty million for one oka of wheat. In exchange they sought walnuts and oil.

m. This great history will remain Unforgettable during the time the Germans came.

n. With the power of God, Christ, and the Virgin Mary, the bright day of freedom also came.

o. Unforgettable heroes, crowned with laurel, brought freedom to us and are always glorified.

p. The three countries (United States, Russia, England), the triumphant ones, like the Holy Trinity, once again raised the blue and white in Greece.

q. This day will be written in History, with all its gold letters: Holy Freedom.

F. The Civil War

During the time of the German occupation, the Greek Government had relocated to Cairo, where a noteworthy military and naval power had formed. It was comprised of officers who had abandoned Greek territory and men who had immigrated to the Middle East, as we explained earlier. Aside from the armed forces abroad, armed units were also formed by the resistance organizations in the interior. E.A.M., which was under the auspices of the Communist Party and had attracted the largest masses of the populace, as well as the armed forces of E.L.A.S. (the Greek Popular Liberation Army), were in charge of almost all of the rural areas of Greece.

Antagonism began to infiltrate the resistance groups of the interior, which indicated a movement toward national divisiveness; it appeared rather quickly and seemed somewhat unavoidable. This is the case, especially if we consider that the Greek Government – with the King in Cairo and the EAM -held areas of Greece – represented two extremely opposite socio-economic systems.

In May 1944, in order to bridge the gap, Prime Minister Georgios Papandreou, after meetings that took place in Lebanon, formed the Government of National Unity with ministers from the Greek exiles in Cairo and from members of EAM. On October 12 and 18, 1944, the Government of National Unity relocated to Athens. The composition of this government harbored the

---

seeds of civil war.

The first phase, the *"Dekembriana"* clashes, began on December 3 and lasted for about forty days. There were bloody confrontations between ELAS and the government, and Athens experienced savagery and ferocity like never before.

The war ended with the Treaty of *Varkiza* on February 12, 1945. Some units of ELAS refused to abide by the Treaty, and as a result of pressure and persecution from the official State they became active in the countryside once again, and the second phase of the Civil War began on March 30, 1946. The war spread throughout Greece, and there was destruction, pillaging, fires, executions, revenge, and counter-revenge, so the Greek grounds were drenched with the blood of brothers. Within a three-year period, and after creating ruination throughout the land, the war ended on August 30, 1949 with the battles in the mountainous areas of *Grammos* and *Vitsi*, where the "Democratic Army" of the resistance groups was defeated.

I don't believe that there is anything harsher and more savage than a civil war. It seems like a curse from God. The Roman orator and philosopher, Cicero, wrote,

> *"Omnia sunt misera in belis civilibus sed nihil miseries quam ipsa Victoria."*

In other words, "Everything is wretched in civil wars, but nothing is more wretched than that victory itself." Truly, who is the victor, and who is the defeated in such a war? It is an indisputable fact that the results of the Civil War were influencing the political and national choices of the people until recently.

Agiorgousoi Unjustly Killed in the Civil War

1. Volos, Ioannis Is.
2. Dellas, Nikolaos P.
3. Koumelas, Georgios N.
4. Papastamatis, Sotirios I.
5. Seferakis, Michalis I.
6. Sfyridis, Konstantinos N.
7. Tsamoutalos, Georgios K.
8. Tsikolis, Kyriakos N.
9. Fineskos, Theodoros A.
10. Kalargyros, Antonios A.
11. Mountis, Konstantinos G.
12. Kouleles, Apostolis

Pantelis A. Mavrogiorgis

Memorial of the Fallen

G. The Monument of Fallen Heroes.

In 1961, a marble monument was created and funded by the Agiorgousoi of America so that the Community could honor those who lost their lives during the various the wars. Viktoras Fineskos, a sculptor from the village, created that memorial. It was placed in the courtyard of the church of Agios Georgios, in the garden of the old elementary school.

Marble slabs form a wide fringe, and the square platform in the center has two steps. In the middle sits an orthogonal base with crossed flags on the north and south sides carved in relief and bound together with a soldier's helmet.

These words are carved into the *eastern* side of the monument:

"ERECTED AT THE EXPENSE OF THE ASSOCIATION OF AGIOS GEORGIOS SIKOUSIS IN AMERICA"

The carving on the *western* side reads:

"TO THE IMMORTAL HEROES OF AGIOS GEORGIOS SIKOUSIS, 1961"

A pillar with a sharp, triangular tip rises from the pedestal and is crowned by an eagle with spread wings. The names of all of the village heroes are inscribed in large script on the southern side of this pillar. We all gathered on a Sunday in 1962, following a memorial service, to witness the unveiling of this monument. It was preceded by a speech made by the Director of the School, N. Tsikolis, who then invited the Prefect of Chios to reveal the monument. A sacred hour followed, during which all the names of the fallen heroes were read, along with the battles in which they died. An Army contingent was present to render the appropriate honors with firearm volleys. From that point on, at every national holiday, a laurel wreath is placed at the monument, in gratitude for the sacrifices made by the heroes.

Pantelis A. Mavrogiorgis

Chapter 25
The Village Today

The appearance of the village is different today. Housing, financial development, social surroundings, and the cultural climate all contribute to the appearance of contemporary life. Many houses, which have undergone external and internal renovations to meet modern standards are occupied. New houses have also been built with architectural plans and suitable construction skills.

Inside the houses there is good-quality furniture, radios and televisions, refrigerators, heaters, and we've even reached the point where there are radiators and telephones in many of the homes. The old dirt roads that used to become muddy are now clean and cemented, and there is a sewage system in place. There are very few beasts of burden that remain, since many Agiorgousoi now have farm machines and are able to go to their fields along the farm roads that were created during the past few decades.

Aside from all of this, the village now has quite a few passenger cars and small trucks for private use. There are snack bars and clubs, so that people no longer have to wait for village celebrations in order to have fun. People from the surrounding areas and Chora also come to patronize these "*Kentra.*"

The clothing worn by the men and women of the village no longer bears the mark of local color and customs, which have all but disappeared at this point, unfortunately. The local dialect has also been altered, and the code of social behavior has noticeably changed. These days, since most children continue their education after elementary school and go on to high school, the traffic becomes heavy, trips are routine, and communication among people has become easier.

The most important factor, however, for the improvement of the lifestyle of Chians now is the elevation in financial status. Agios Giorgis went from being a poor village, filled with misery, to one of the most prosperous villages in Chios, thanks to the endless diligence of the Agiorgousoi. Many have opened their own trade stores in Chora. Others have filled public and government positions. There are quite a few who have academic jobs, while others have become sought-after craftsmen. Some have gone to sea, and a significant number have left with their families to live abroad.

Today, Agios Giorgis has 878 permanent residents. There is a Cooperative of Mastic Producers and an olive oil production partnership. There is also a pre-school, an elementary school, and a continuing education department for adults. The village has a Cultural Association that works toward elevating the spiritual quality of people's lives. The President Mr. Nikolaos Koilis and the Council, have been strong supporters of the publication of this book. There is also a Soccer-Athletic Association, a rural clinic, and a police station.

What we can say, in conclusion, is that today's village shows no evidence of the events that occurred in the past which I documented in previous pages. Yet, for me, those were unforgettable years.

As I end this work, I must admit that the old village dwells within my soul, along with the carefree life of my childhood years.

Pantelis A. Mavrogiorgis

The renewed village: evidenced by the new houses

Chapter 26
Immigration

During the initial years, only a few villagers had left Agios Giorgis for America, Australia, and France. Others traveled back and forth to work in Smyrna and Constantinople for periods of time but earned little. At that time, foreign lands were considered bitter and poisonous, as only the man would go, leaving his family for years at a time with only a letter sent to relatives every two months or so.

After the war, but more specifically between 1950 and 1960, there was a wave of emigration from the village and from all of Chios. At that time, entire families, not individuals alone, would leave for America, Canada, and Australia. Some individual workers would also go to Germany. There was much reshuffling of the population that occurred then, with many moving abroad and others to other areas of Greece. Many left for Chora, Athens, and other cities, as a result villages almost emptied out. The Agiorgousoi of Athens organized themselves into a very active association. What is noteworthy here is that those who did emigrate did not totally uproot themselves from their villages, they did not allow it to be abandoned and to wither.

When they did leave Greece, they took their families, their icons from their homes, their religion, their customs, songs, and dances to their new country in order to preserve them and teach them to their children. Thus Hellenism was not lost. In the countries where they settled, they progressed financially and socially. Whereas many had left as workers or employees, they have became businessmen, and quite a few became scholars.

These former villagers come back frequently and are a significant factor in the financial and cultural advancement of the village. Half of Agios Giorgis still lives in the village, while the other half resides in America and other areas. Additionally, the permanent residents often travel to visit their relatives abroad. There is not a single Agiorgousis who has not gone as a visitor either to America or Australia, which is evidence of a noteworthy upgrade of their lifestyle.

Immigration has become significant in the further development of the village, since those who emigrated financially assist their relatives here and wholeheartedly provide financial assistance for all projects that end up making village life better. While taking care not to be unjust to those who offer such assistance, I must single out the Agiorgousoi of America because they are so

---

Pantelis A. Mavrogiorgis

numerous and work through their organization as the "Agios Georgios Sikousis Society." This association was founded in 1920 and reorganized in 1967. I will copy several representative articles from its first Charter.

"FOUNDING OF THE ASSOCIATION

All Chians living in Trenton, N.J. hailing from Agios Giorgios Sikousis decided with one mind to establish an Association for the common benefit of our Community in which we first saw the light, were brought up and were educated.

Article 1

The goal of the Association shall be to raise capital for the sake of our Community through monthly contributions, gifts, or celebrations.

Article 2

Registration in the Association is only allowed to those who come from Agios Georgios Sikousis and reside in the United States.

Article 17

The income of the Association is allocated for the needs of our Community, most especially the urgent needs. What we refer to as 'urgent' concerns the water supply of the Community or the building of a School.

Article 20

In the end, we call upon the aid of all our fellow villagers for the continued success of our work.

March 1, 1920"

In order not to limit the scope of the Association by merely referring to its Charter, we will detail some of its socially beneficial works.

1. The construction of the elementary school.
2. The replacement of cement pipes with iron pipes for the water of *Platanos.*
3. The creation of a heroes' memorial to honor those killed in action.
4. The opening of a road to *Alonakia.*
5. The beautification of the *Plateia Mpou*, honorarily renamed *"Plateia Apodimon" (Emigrants Square).*
6. The maintenance and furnishing of the kindergarten, elementary school, and playground.

7. Support for the Greek Navy.
8. The beautification of the school's forest *"Alexandros Galanos."*
9. The creation of an athletic field.
10. The financial support of the Soccer Association, the Educational Association of Sikousis, and the University of the Aegean.
11. Major contributions toward the founding of the Community Office.
12. The erection of the church of *Agios Kosmas o Aitolos.*
13. Various philanthropic offerings.

Finally, the emigrants in America undertook the expenditure of the publication of this book about the history of the village. Their unanimous and wholeheartedly supportive decision to continue the sponsorship of mutually beneficial works allows us to pass on to the next generation information about the history of our village. More so, it will help future generations to understand how the Agiorgousoi won every benefit in their lives with hard work, honor, and conscientiousness, faith in God, and love for their homeland.

For all of that, we are truly grateful to them.

Pantelis A. Mavrogiorgis

DONORS FOR THE
CONSTRUCTION OF THE SCHOOL

In order to render honor and set a proper example, we will close this section with a chart of our fellow villagers in America who contributed money for the erection of our school and detail that contribution in U.S. dollars.

Str. Vafias	$ 1,393	Al. Vafias	$ 390
Em. Frangakis	1,334	Fil. Vafias	384
Christ. Mereos	822	Io. Xenias	380
Nik. Vekios	822	P. Xenias	380
St. Flouras	802	St. Zymnis	378
Ioan. Mountis	797	Vas. Thrappas	373
A. Vyzaniaris	712	A. Myrisis	354
Kon. Monis	560	Thom. Koutelos	338
Lemonia Moniouka	540	A. Hahalis	336
Geor. Samaras	497	I. N. Mountis	336
Geor. Patounas	485	S. Monioukas	336
Pant. Fotis	482	A. Koutelos	324
St. Vafias	481	N. Soukas	308
Chr. Thrappas	474	Sot. Tsoflias	300
Filip. Perivolaris	474	Ap. Kounios	298
Ioan. Agouridis	472	K. Monioukas	291
Pan. Paroikas	472	Panag. Samaras	285
Ioan. Vekios	442	N. Vafias	280
Ioan. Andreadis	442	D. Manolakis	279
Emman. Pappous	438	Stam. Mountis	260
A. Germanos	436	I. Perivolaris	260
Adam. Monioukas	421	Isid. Monioukas	238
Nik. Rousakis	427	D. N. Monioukas	236
S. Tsamoutalos	118	Vas. Manolakis	233
Ant. Frangakis	422	St. Hahalis	222
A. Sachlanis	422	K. Tsoflias	200
Nik. S. Sakoulas	420	El. Sakoulas	179
Spyr. Tsaketas	417	N. Patounas	177
Arg. Patras	415	Nik. I. Sakoulas	176
K. Patras	415	Leon. Papastamatis	158
S. Fineskos	410	P. Vekios	157
Adam. Vafias	403	Stam. Kalargyros	154
G. Andreadis	397	P. Patras	134

I. Flouras	$ 134	Ap. Vafias	$ 60
I. Zymnis	124	N. Toras	50
I. Parikas	121	A. Rousakis	50
S. Manolakis	103	Sar. Askelis	44
K. Mitsos	100	S. Toulos	38
S. Fotis	92	G. Hahalis	37
N. Mountis	90	I. Koumelas	20
N. Vyzaniaris	76	P. Salagaras	20
M. Bogiasklis	75	P. Soukas	20
A. Toulambis	70	P. Tsikolis	18
E. Zymnis	68	N. Monis	16
N. Myrisis	64	S. Galanos	13
N. Samaras	62		

The above names can be found carved into a marble slab
placed in the lobby of the school.

Pantelis A. Mavrogiorgis

ENDNOTES

1 G. Zolotas, *Istoria tis Chiou*, vol. A1, p. 274

2 S. I. Voutyra, *Lexiko Istorias kai Geografias*, 1889.

3 G. Zolotas, *Chiakon kai Erythraïkon Epigrafon Synagogi*, p. 167.

4 Ant. Stefanou, "I Latreia tis Artemidos eis tin Chion," *Zenon*, vol. 28, p. 153.

5 The names of those places which end with –ous -- like *Dafnous, Anthemous,* and *Elaious* came from adjectives ending in –oeis and indicate a multitude of similar things. For example, *Sykoeis* becomes *Sykous*. Feminine endings like –oussa or –ousa, are seen in *Oinoussa* and *Pityousa* (*Pityousa* is written with only one *sigma*, analogous to past continuous tense verbs like *zitousa* and *elthousa*.)

6 *Sykountios* comes from the genitive (possessive) case *Sykous* of *Sykountos,* with the ending –ios.

7 Trechakis, Archimandrite Kyrillos, *Chiaka Chronika*, vol. 2, p. 87.

8 G. Hatzidakis, M.N.E., vol. 2, p. 72. *Sykousis* derives from *Sykountios* to *Sykousios* to *Sykousis*. The ending –ousis refers to an inhabitant of an area and was widely used in Chios. Besides its use for –eis and –ous, it was also used with –ousis, as with *Kalamoti –ousis* and *Mesta –ousis*.

9 D. Rodokanakis, *Ioustinianai – Chios*, p. 23.

10 *Chrysobull* is a document of Byzantine Emperors, sealed with a golden seal. There is also the so-called silverbull.

11 G. Madias, "I Polichni: Agios Giorgis o Sykousis," *Proodos*, June 13, 1944.

12 A. Komnini, *Alexias*, Book 2, Chapter 12.

13 S. Kavvadas, *Oi Kodikes tis Chiou*, p. 8.

14 K. Amantos, "Kodix Agios Georgios Sikousis," *Chiaka Chronika*, vol. 1, pp. 126-128.

15 G. Zolotas, *Istoria tis Chiou*, vol. 2, p. 211.

16 A. Zolotas, "Vracheiai Epanorthoseis kai Diorthoseis," *Athena*, vol. 20.

17 Krousio, *Tourkograikia*, p. 306.

18 G. Zolotsa, "Synagogi Chiakon Epigrafon," *Athena*, vol. 20; K. Amantos, "Ekklesiastiki Istoria tis Chiou," *Ellinika*, vol. 4.

19 S. Nikiforou and G. Foteinos, *Istoria tis Orthodoxou Ekklisias*, p. 228.

20 Archimandrite J. Andreadis, *Neamonisia*, 1865, p. 13.

21 K. Amantos, *Istoria tou Vyzantinou Kratous*, vol. 2, p. 147.

22 Leonis Diakoni, *Istoriai VII*, p. 126.

23 K. Sgouros, *I Istoria tis Chiou*, Athens, 1930, p. 115.

24 K. Sgouros, *I Istoria tis Chiou*, Athens, 1930, p. 256.

25 From the Byzantine family names who had lands near the village of *Dafnonas* came the names of the following locations: *Kanavoutsato, Vestarchato,* and *Stratigato*.

26 K. Amantos, *Symvoli eis tin Mesaioniki Istoria tis Chiou.*

---

27 G. Zolotas, *Istoria tis Chiou*, vol. 2, p. 258.
28 G. Soteriou, "Archaiologiko Deltion, Parartima," 1916.
29 G. Zolotas, *Istoria tis Chiou*, vol. 2, p. 312.
30 There were six emperors in the Comninon Dynasty: Isaakios, Alexios, Ioannis, Manuil, Alexios II, and Andronikos. They were in power from 1057-1185.
31 High school principal K. Sarakakis presented a document in the church of Krinas, with a chronology claiming that it was founded on June 29, 1287.
32 G. Foteinos, *Neamonisia*, p. 228.
33 G. Zolotas, *Istoria tis Chiou,* vol. A1, p. 584.
34 G. Zolotas, *Istoria tis Chiou*, vol. 3, part 2, p. 329.
35 J. Thevenot, *Relation d' un vogage fait au Levand: Report on a Trip to the East.*
36 D. Rodokanakis, *Chios: Ioustinianai.*
37 A "Dependency" is a monastic estate, well outside the area of the monastery. Many times, the Dependency will have a church where one or more monks reside. It is dependent on the monastery to which it also has financial obligations. (Du Cange writes in his *Glossary*, "Cella monastic a majori monasterio dependens": a monastic place of residence, which depends upon a large monastery.
38 H. Bouras, *Chios*, Athens, 1974, pp. 53-54.
39 *Palaiokodikas Agiou Georgiou*, p. 65.
40 Measurements: one *orgia* has 324 square meters and is subdivided into 100 rings.
41 I. Andreadis, *Istoria tis en Chio Orthodoxou Ekklisias*, p. 229.
42 *Aspro*: a Byzantine coin and, later, a Turkish coin of little value. 3 *aspra* =1 *para*; 2.5 *parades* = 1 *moni*, 5 *nones* = 1 *metalliki*, 4 *metallikia* = 1 *grosi*. *Kefali*: (Lit., head) the capital; *Proventi*: interest (from the Italian word, *provento*, which means income or profit).
43 F. Argenti, S. Kyriakidis, *I Chios Para tois Geografois kai Periigitais.*
44 G. Zolotas, *Istoria tis Chiou*, vol. 1, p. 118.
45 K. Kanellakis, *Topografia tis Nisou Chiou*, p. 28.
46 S. Vios, *I Synchronos Chios kai i Palaia*, p. 94.
47 K. Kanellakis, *Chiaka Analekta*, pp. 391-92.
48 K. Kanellakis, *Chiaka Analekta*, pp. 391-92.
49 G. Veniadis, *I Nea Moni tis Chiou*, p. 38.
50 C. Amantos, *Arthra kai Logoi*, p. 59.
51 G. Zolotas, *Istoria tis Chiou*, vol. 1, p. 584.
52 S. Vios, *I Synchronos Chios kai i Palaia*, p. 98.
53 K. Amantos, "Ta Mesaionika Choria tis Chiou," *Arthra kai Logoi*, pp. 64-65.
54 T. Sarikakis, *I Chios*, p. 47.
55 K. Hopf, *Giustiniani: Dynastes de Chios.*
56 E. Alexandridou, "Ekklisiastiki Katastasis tis Chiou," *Chiaka Chronika*, vol. 1

[57] A. Karavas, *Topografia tis Nisou Chiou.*

[58] Aim. Sarou, *Chiaka en Athenais.*

[59] G. Zolotas, "Ta Sklavia," *Chios: Ioustinianai*, p. 734.

[60] D. Rodokanakis, *Chios: Ioustinianai*, p. 23.

[61] M. Katla, *Chios ipo tous Genouinsious.*

[62] M. Justiniani, *La Scio Sacra*, p. 5

[63] D. Rodokanakis, *Chios: Ioustinianai*, p. 22 (footnote).

[64] G. Zolotas, *Istoria tis Chiou*, vol. 3, p. 19.

[65] M. Grusius, *Turcograecia*, p. 511.

[66] K. Amantos, *Chiaka Chronika*, vol. 4, pp. 59-78.

[67] N. Foteinos, *Neamonisia*, p. 103.

[68] The inscription is on a stone slab in the wall on the left side of the temple in the fort. According to the translation made by Chris Mavropoulos, it says the following: *"There is no God except God and His Prophet, Mohammed. This church was built in 993 A.D. The peace of God be upon him. While on the 17th of April 1566 . . . Piali Pasha, the Admiral of the fleet of the Ottoman Emperor, Sultan Suleiman, came with one hundred and twenty slaves and conquered Chios. The aforesaid church became a mosque, a place for prayer. 'Doxa to Theo to Kyrio tou Kosmou,'" Periodiko Chiaka Chronika*, vol. 2.

[69] *Aktiname*: the name the Turks gave to the privileges granted to the inhabitants of an area.

[70] There were three categories of *"kefalikou forou"*: the rich paid 12 *(grosia)* gold coins, the middle class paid 6 gold coins, and the poor paid only 3.

[71] K. Theotokas, "Meleti peri ton Pronomion kai tis Dioikiseos tis Chiou," *Chiaka Chronika*, v. 17.

[72] T. Sarikakis, *I Chios*, p. 58.

[73] A. Vlastos, *Chiaka.*

[74] F. de Coulanges, *The Island Chios*, p. 207, (as translated by K. Choreanthi).

[75] *Bastias:* Batis, Ypatios; *Bolobos:* Bouloubasis, Police Commander; *Koskinistis:* the sifter of the mastic; *Konaxes:* head guard of the Administration Building; *Kaniski:* gift; *head mastic:* top-quality mastic.

[76] *Alikounta:* I prevent, delay; *Paidevgetai:* be punished; *Gerontiliki:* Council of Elders; *Aslania:* a type of coin.

[77] S. Kavvadas, *Oi Kodikes tis Chiou*, P. 46.

[78] *Panchiaïki* newspaper, May 16, 1927.

[79] K. Koumas, *Istoria Anthropinon Praxeon*, Vol. 12, pp. 550-551.

[80] N. Perris, *I Chios stin Ethnegersia*, p. 31.

[81] Ekdotiki Athinon, *Istoria tou Ellinikou Ethnous*, vol. 12, p. 110.

[82] A. Mamoukas, *Chiakon Archeion*, vol. 1.

[83] I. Filimonos, *Dokimion peri tis Ellinikis Epanastaseos*, vol. 4, p. 179.

[84] D. Kokkinos, *I Elliniki Epanastasi*, vol. 3, p. 218.

[85] V. Sfyroeras, "I Epanastasis tis Chiou," in *Istoria tis Ekdotikis Athinon*, vol. 12,

p. 244.

[86] I. Vlachogiannis, *Chiakon Archeion*, vol. 1, p. 323.

[87] V. Pasa, *Apomnimonevmata*, Chiakon Archeion, vol. 1, p. 269.

[88] N. Sotirakis, *I Matomeni Chios*, pp. 47, 49.

[89] L. Logothetis, *Apologia*, Chiakon Archeion, vol. 1, p. 381.

[90] V. Pasa, *Apomnimonevmata*, Chiakon Archeion, vol. 1, p. 288.

[91] G. Foteinos, *Apomnimonevmata*, Chiakon Archeion, vol. 1, p. 343.

[92] A. Argenti, "Epistoli," *Periodiko Athena*, vol. 34, pp. 117-124.

[93] V. Koukouridis, "I Iera Eikon tis Mammis mou," *Efimeris Nea Chios*, Jan.1, 1914.

[94] *Lepro (Leper)* is the name of a mountain between *Lithi* and *Sikousis*. It received its name because there was once a hospital for lepers there. What the narrator calls *askitari* probably refers to the ruins of that hospital.

[95] This refers to the 1827 campaign of Fabvier, the goal of which was the liberation of Chios.

[96] G. Zacharias, "Afigisi," *Efimerida Panchiaïki*, Dec. 1, 1912; A. Galanos, "Agios Georgios Dialexis," 1958.

[97] The Kalargyroudes were truly among the old inhabitants of the village. In the old codex, on pp. 66 and 67, as abbot of the Monastery, Ioannis Kalargyros signs as a witness on sales agreements during the years 1665-1669. On page 51 of the same codex, he does likewise. In yet another document, however, he uses the surname Kokkinokolos, a name retained by the narrator of this excerpt, an elder whom I actually met in the village.

[98] This is a location on the mountain *Fa*, which belongs to the community of *Lithi*.

[99] K. Kalargyros, "Afigisi," A. Galanou, Dialexis, 1958.

[100] A. Prokesh, in Argenti & Kyriakidis, *I Chios para tois Geografois*, vol 2, p. 1081.

[101] "I Katastrofi tis Chiou," *Periodiko Laografia*, vol. 8, p. 98.

[102] A. Pachnos, "Chios," from Drandraki, *Megali Elliniki Engyklopaideia*.

[103] K. Papamichalopoulos, *Ek ton Ereipion tis Chiou 1831*, p. 26.

[104] A. Polemidis, *Symvoli eis tin Istorian tis Chiou*, p. 153.

[105] S. Panagelis, *Odoiporikai Simeioseis*, pp. 16-22.

[106] P. Karakassonis, *Istoria tis Apeleftheroseos tis Chiou*.

[107] H. Pernot, *En pay Turc. L'ile de Chio*, translation by K. Choreanthi, pp. 114, 117, 130, 137.

[108] A. Smith, *The Architecture of Chios*, p. 62.

[109] H. Ludwig, "Im Paradies der Volksdichtung," translation by Xanthaki, from *Chiaki Epitheorisi*, vol. 25, pp. 18-19.

[110] Aid. Koukoules, *Vyzantinon Vios*, vol. 4.

[111] A. Stefanou, *Deigmata Neoellinikis Technis*, p. 80.

[112] From *pyr* for "fire" and *estia* for "home."

[113] A. Kyriakidou Nestoros, *I Dodeka Mines*, p. 126.

[114] K. Romaios, *Konta stis Rizes*, pp. 331-335.

[115] G. Mega, *Ellinikai Eortai*, p. 234.

[116] Isiodos, *Erga kai Imerai*, Verses 462-465, 446-448.

[117] D. Loukatos, *Ta Kalokairina*, pp. 102-103.

[118] D. Petropoulos, "Agrotika," in the *Periodiko Laografia,* vol. 18.

[119] Theokritos, *Eidyllio 7*, verses 155-156.

[120] "Ta Sika sto Sikousi," *Sikousis Magazine*, New York, 1987.

[121] D. Spanos, *O Egrigoros tis Chiou*, p. 57 and *Periodiko Laografia*, vol. 19, p. 311.

[122] J. Pernot, *Etudes de linugistique Neo-Hellenique*, vol. 3.

[123] Syngramma, *Periodiko Laografia*, vol. 16, p. 492.

[124] D. Vasileiadis, *Periodiko Laografia*, vol. 16, p. 496.

[125] G. Zolotas, *Istoria tis Chiou*, vol. 3, p. 82.

[126] A. Galanos, "Viotechnika Ag. Georgiou Sykousi," in *Argentis* magazine, vol. 1-2.

[127] Syngramma, *Periodiko Laografia*, vol. 14.

[128] G. Madias, "I Tyrokomia tis Chiou," *Aigaion Magazine*, vol. 1, p. 389.

[129] *Odysseia*, a – 355 -356.

[130] Drandraki, *"Argaleios," Megali Elliniki Engyklopaideia*, vol. 5.

[131] G. Madias, "I Polichni Agios Georgis o Sykousis," *Proodos*, vol. 4211, June 22, 1944.

[132] K. Romaios, *Konta stis Rizes*, p. 79.

[133] K. Romaios, *Konta stis Rizes*, p. 79.

[134] *Kodikas Agiou Georgiou*, No. 1045, Korais Library.

[135] H. Bouras, *I Chios,* Athena, 1974, pp. 53-54.

[136] A. Stefanou, *Deigmata Neoellinikis Technis,* p. 87.

[137] A. Galanos, "Dialexis," 1957, pp. 33ff.

[138] G. Zolotas, *Istoria tis Chiou*, Vol. 1, p. 584.

[139] A. Galanos, handwritten note.

[140] A. Galanos, handwritten note.

[141] G. Zolotas, "Ta Sklavia," in D. Rodokanaki, *Chios: Ioustinianai*, p. 734.

[142] *Kodikas Agiou Georgiou*, No. 17, p. 154

[143] G. Zolotas, *Istoria tis Chiou*, vol. 1, p. 585.

[144] K. Amantos, *Ta Grammata sti Chio kata tin Tourkokratia*, pp. 6-8.

[145] L. Kalvokoresis, *I Ekpaidefsi sti Chio meta to 1822*, p. 74.

[146] The Kerkyraian scholar, Nikolaos Sofianos, used the term "*Kollyvogrammata*" to refer to people who were able to read without really understanding what they were reading. Many illiterate priests would "read" the prayers during memorial services hence "*kolyva*."

[147] K. Amantos, *Ta Grammata sti Chio . . .* , p. 16.

[148] Herder, "Grammatodidaskaleion," *Paidagogiki Engyklopaideia*, vol. 3.

149 The schools were called *"Koina"* to refer to the elementary schools and distinguish them from middle education schools and because they belonged to the "Community."

150 K. Amantos, *Chiaka Chronika*, vol. 1, p. 145.

151 S. Stafyleras, *Prosfora Timis S'Ekinous pou Ipiretisan ti Chio*, p. 43.

152 *Polemiki Istoria ton Ellinon*, vol. 2.

153 V. Skoulatos, Dimopoulos, Kondi, *Istoria Neoteri kai Synchroni*, vol. 3.

154 V. Skoulatos, Dimopoulos, Kondi, *Istoria Neoteri kai Synchroni*, vol. 3, p. 98.

155 V. Skoulatos, Dimopoulos, Kondi, *Istoria Neoteri kai Synchroni*, vol. 3, p. 98.

156 L. Kalvokoresis, *Chronikon Katochis tis Chiou para ton Germanon, 1941-1944.*

SOURCES AND AIDS

Alexandridis, Ilias, "Tina peri tis ekklisiastikes katastaseos tis Chiou apo ton archaiotaton mexri tis 16s ekatontaetiridos" *Chiaka Chronika,* vol. 1, 1911.

Amantos, Konstantinos, a) *Ta Grammata eis tin Chion kata tin Tourkokratian 1566 – 1822,* Athens, 1976.
b) Chiaka zitimata
c) "Ta mesaionika horia tis Chiou" *Arthra kai Logoi,* Athens 1953
d) *Chiaka Chronika, vol. 5*
e) *Istoria tou Vyzantinou Kratous* vol. 2, Athens 1953 & 1957
f) "I Alosis tis Chiou ypo ton Tourkon," *Chiaka Chronika,* vol. 4

Andreades, Ioannis, *Istoria tis en Chio Orthodoxou Ekklisias,* Athens, 1948.

Axiotakis, Andreas, *I Nea Moni tis Chiou,* Chios, 1980.

Argenti - Kyriakidis, *I Chios para tois Geografois kai Periigitais,* Athens, 1946.

Vios, Stylianos, *I Synchronos Chios kai i Palaia,* Chios, 1937.

Vlastos, Alexandros, *Chiaka Ermoupolis,* 1840.

Vlachogiannis, Ioannis, *Chiakon Archeion,* vol. 5, Athens, 1910 – 1924.

Ekdotiki Athinon, *Istoria tou Ellinikou Ethnous,* vol. 15.

Zolotas, Georgios, a) *Istoria tis Chiou,* vol. 3, Athens, 1921 –1928.
b) *Chiakon kai Erythraïkon Epigrafon Synagogi,* vol. k. Athens, 1908.

Theotokas, Konstantinos, *Meleti peri ton Pronomion kai Dioikiseos tis Chiou,* Chios, 1913.

Kavadas, Stefanos, *Oi Kodikes tis Chiou,* Chios, 1950.

Kolvokoresi, Leon., a) *I Ekpaidefsi sti Chio meta to 1822.*
b) *Chroniko Katochis tis Chiou para ton Germanon.*

Kanellakis, Konstantinos, *Chiaka Analekta,* Athens, 1890.

Karavas, Konstantinos, *Topografia tis Chiou,* Chios, 1866.

Karakassonis, P., *Istoria tis Apeleftheroseos tis Chiou,* Athens, 1928.

Korais, Adamandios, *Atakta,* vol. 3 (Material on Chian Archaelogy), Paris, 1832.

Mavropoulos, Christos, *Tourkika Engrafa Aforonta eis tin Istorian tis Chiou,* Athens, 1920.

Bouras, Charalambos, *Chios: Odigoi tis Ellados,* Athens, 1974.

Nikiforos-Foteinos, Grig., *Neamonisia,* Chios, 1865.

Orlandos, Anastasios, *Byzantina Mnimeia tis Chiou,* Athens, 1930.

Paganelis Spyridon,	"Seismoi tis Chiou" *Odoiporikai Simeioseis,* vol. 1.
Pachnos, Alexandros,	*Chios,* in *Megali Elliniki Engyklopaideia Drandraki.*
Perris Nikolaos,	*I Chios stin Ethnegersia,* Chios, 1974.
Polemidis, Andreas,	*Symvoli eis tin istorian tis Chiou,* Athens, 1974.
Ekdotiki Ellados,	*Ekthesis Polemikis Istorias ton Ellinon,* vol. 2, Athens, 1968.
Rodokanakis, Dimitrios,	*Ioustinianai: Chios,* Syros, 1900.
Sarikakis, Theodoros,	*I Chios,* New York, 1950.
Sgouros, Konstantinos,	*Istoria tis Nisou Chiou,* Athens, 1937.
Spanos, Dimitrios,	*O Egrigoros tis Chiou,* Athens, 1980.
Stefanou, Antonios,	*Deigmata Neoellinikis Technis,* Chios, 1972.
Sotirakis, Nikolaos,	*I Matomeni Chios tou Eikosiena,* Chios, 1952.
Sotiriou, Georgios,	"Ta Christianika Mnimeia tis Chiou," *Archaiologikon Deltion, Parartima,* 1912.
Filimonas, Ioannis,	*Dokimion peri tis Ellinikis Epanastaseos,* Athens, 1860.
Charokopou, Antonios,	*O Vrontados kai I Istoria tou,* Chios, 1955. *PeriodikoTou en Chio Syllogou Argenti.*

FOREIGN SOURCES

Miklosich-Müller,	*Acta et Diplomatica Graeca,* 1860.
Krusius, Mart.,	*Turcograecia,* 1584.
Coulanges, Fustel,	*Memoire sur I Ile de Chio* (Translation by: K. Choreanthis)
Pernot, Hubert,	*L'ile de Chio* (Translation by: K. Choreanthis)
Smith, Arnold,	*The Architecture of Chios,* London, 1962.
Giustiniani, Michele,	*Scio Sacra. Avellino,* 1606.
Hopf, Karl,	*Giustiniani: Dynastes de Chio.*

SPECIAL SOURCES

Codecs of the Village of Agios Georgios Sikousis
Codecs of the Holy Metropolis of Chios
Minutes of the Community Board of Agios Georgios Sikousis
Archives of the Primary School of Agios Georgios Sikousis
Articles published in the newspapers *Panchiaki, Nea Chios, Proodos*
Galanos, Alex., *Agios Georgios o Sykousis,* two lectures 1957, 1958

PHOTOGRAPHS

TABLE OF CONTENTS

PART ONE: HISTORY

PART TWO: VILLAGE LIFE AND FOLKLORE

PART THREE: HISTORY OF EDUCATION & LOCAL GOVERNMENT

President
John N. Pilavas

Vice President
Nikolaos K. Papagiannakis

Secretary
John S. Bougiamas

Treasurer
George Bougiamas

Board Members
Kalliope Barlis
Panagiotis Billis
George Kakarides
Lambros Karazournias
Stefanos Nyktas
Demetrios Pilavas

Past Presidents
Nikos Psarros
George Pappous
John G Nictas
Argiris Monis
Antonios Doulos
Nikolaos K. Papagiannakis
Stefanos Doulos
Panagiotis Billis
John N. Pilavas